THE ANGLER IN NORTHERN INDIA

THE ANGLER IN NORTHERN INDIA

With list of Fishing Localities in India, from the Nerbudda Northwards, including Burma and Baluchistan

SKENE DHU

GYAN

Published by

Gyan Publishing House
5, Ansari Road
Daryaganj, New Delhi-110002
Phone: 011-47034999, 9811692060
E-mail: books@gyanbooks.com

Distribution Network
gyanbooks.com
India, USA, Canada, UK, Australia

ISBN: 978-93-6780-241-0 (HB)

First Published, 1910

2nd Impression 2024

Printed at: Gyan Press, Delhi.

THE ANGLER IN NORTHERN INDIA
Author: SKENE DHU

THE

ANGLER IN NORTHERN INDIA.

With list of Fishing Localities in India, from the Nerbudda northwards, including Burma and Baluchistan.

BY

SKENE DHU,

Author of "The Mighty Mahseer," "In an Indian Jungle," "Overheard."

PRINTED AT THE PIONEER PRESS
ALLAHABAD

1910

DEDICATION.

TO ALL BROTHER ANGLERS.

"A fisherman's education ends only with his life."

1

From the Hills the Bhagirati ; to the Ganges of the Plains
Till 'mid Hooghly's turbid waters, your current flows and wanes ;
Tho' your spirit is the same,
Forget your ancient name
And the pines and deodars and the mountains whence you came

2

Forget your crystal shallows, and your pools so clear and deep,
And forget your tossing rapids where the waters never sleep.
Past the mosques that look so white
'Neath the moonbeam's silvery light
As you surge your tireless way through the slumbering Indian night.

3

From the mountains, from the vallies, from your rivulets and streams,
Flow on O Mother Ganga, to the ocean of your dreams,
Through the parched and burnt up plains
That are crying for the rains
Past the holiest of cities, with their temples and their fanes.

4

Flow on O mighty river, till thy muddy current merges
With the cyclone's foam tipped billows, mid ocean's tossing surges
'Neath the monsoon's leaden sky
Till you ebb away to die
And the passing of your spirit is the storm-wind's mournful cry.

S. D

CONTENTS.

ERRATA.

Concerning the river at Jani-ki-Sang, this in error was called the Chiblat. The head waters of this river however run north of Kala Sarai, it being the upper waters of the Bahoodra river, that run below the Jani-ki-Sang bungalow. This stream joins the Hurroo some way below the Chiblat, and holds fish of 3 and 4 lbs. in places.

The *a* in Chiblat is pronounced *ar*.

Note that wherever in context the words "this year" occur, 1909 should be understood.

LIST OF MAPS.

PREFACE.

Apologies are futile, and criticism but too easy, therefore would I ask brother anglers to pass on to the Prologue.

PROLOGUE.

In launching this book upon an Indian public, it is but right to start with a clear explanation of its aims and limitations.

Firstly, it is by no means intended as a rival for that most excellent publication, "The Angler's Handbook," but is issued with a view of compiling a further list of localities, and bringing many of those already entered more up-to-date.

Also, it is published in the hopes that it may be considered as a continuation of "The Mighty Mahseer" as tho' supplementing the Chapter on Barbus Tor himself; practically none of the information concerning other fish, tackle, Useful Hints, etc., is again reprinted, nor are any of the plates of fish reproduced, though most of the fish are described in detail. Then, although the title Northern India might lead one to suppose only the Punjab and United Provinces were intended, the term Northern is meant, in a general sense, to take in the whole upper half of India, say north of the Nerbudda river, including however that river and its tributaries.

And I would humbly solicit that the maps be not judged from too high a standpoint, they are merely rough sketches to help out the letterpress. And I would ask also that criticism may be lenient from those who judge that the localities section might be fuller or more comprehensive. No one, till they have tackled the matter, can have any idea of the difficulty and amount of correspondence entailed trying to get the notes up-to-date. The delays that occur would matter little, were it practicable to spend a year or two on preparing it, but the very fact that sporting localities are so liable to change, makes it advisable that a book of this type should be published within as few months as possible of its conception. And I would be very grateful to those who would offer advice, and send notes, to ensure that a second edition should be a fuller and more comprehensive guide to Northern India.

My most cordial thanks are due to those brother anglers who have helped me with notes and information, and especially are they due to the following whose names do not appear in the text:—Lieut.-Colonel E. B. Lang (both for advice given and for so kindly designing me the cover), Lieut.-Colonel F. C. Rynd, H. R. Blunt, Esq., J. Phelps, Esq., Major R. Burton, Major E. R. Boileau, Captain H. Christie, Captain G. S. Palmer, H. H. Caffyn, Esq., G. C. Howell, Esq., and those others whose kindly advice and encouragement have helped me not a little. And here I would add one thing. Only three out of all the men that I have corresponded with have in any way been averse to the publication of localities. Now, while quite entering into their feelings, for I myself felt rather loathe to give away one or two places, yet I cannot but think, and I know many far more experienced anglers than myself in this country agree with me, that one can hardly disseminate fishing information too freely, for it must all tell in the long run and help in the preservation of Indian fishing. And in these days of transfer from Mandalay to Peshawar, and Quetta to Lucknow, most men will obtain more than they disburse in the way of knowledge of localities. Lastly, as anglers first coming to this country are always anxious to ascertain what literature there is bearing on the subject to which they may turn, I will here enumerate the few books there are.

First and foremost comes Mr. Thomas' "Rod in India," a book destined always to remain a classic to the Indian Angler. Though referring mostly to Southern India, and out-of-date as regards localities, its charm of diction and wealth of information on Indian fish and their capture make it a book that should be in the library of every angler out here. 3rd Edition, Rs. 11.

Second, the same author's "Tank Angling," Rs. 4-8, is indispensable to all who may have opportunities in that direction.

Third, "The Angler's Hand-book," 4th Edition, Rs. 8, is without doubt one of the best books ever compiled on angling in any country. If for nothing else, it would be worth possessing for the late Mr. Lacy's contributions on mahseer and tackle. That the localities section is falling out-of-date is only natural in any book on such a subject, especially in the East, where changes once inaugurated continue to progress at a rate not conceivable in the staider lands of the West.

Fourth, comes Dr. Walker's "Lakes of Kumaon," Rs. 4-8, but this book, published 20 years ago, must I fear be looked on as practically out-of-date, though pleasantly written by one, who was evidently, as skilful as he was enthusiastic, an angler.

Fifth, comes the "Indian Field Shikar Book," editied by Mr. Burke, 4th Edition, Rs. 5, to which a small portion is devoted to fishing. A most useful book for all shikaris.

Sixth, is "The Sportman's Manual," edited by Aflalo, but the scope of this book is so large (and as naturally follows the price is in proportion) that the portion on angling cannot be expected to do justice to the subject.

Seventh, is an excellent booklet by Major Rivett Carnac, published by the Pioneer Press at Rs. 1-8, entitled "Mahseer Tackle" which may well repay persual by experts as well as tyros.

Lastly, comes "The Mighty Mahseer," published by Higginbotham, Madras, 2nd Edition, Rs. 4-8, to which this book is intended to be a sequel. In it are plates of almost all the fish herein mentioned, also diagrams of mounts, scales of hooks, etc., and practically none of the information in it is reproduced in this book. It also touches on Trout Fishing in Kashmir, Ceylon and the Nilgiris, and fishing in the Andaman Islands.

This I think exhausts all the literature, at least all known to me, on the subject in India. It does not include of course Club booklets, such as the Giri, Pindi, Dehra Dun, etc.

I hear, however, that the close of this year may see a further contribution to Angling literature in this country, in the shape of a book by H. S. Dunsford, Esq., entitled "River, Lake and Tank Fishing in India," and the fact that this well-known sportsman is to give us the benefit of his many years of experience, should be good news to all brother anglers, and I myself for one shall look forward with great pleasure to possessing a copy of the work.

S. D.

CHAPTER I.

LIST OF FISHES MOST COMMONLY MET WITH IN INDIA.

Before commencing my list, I may as well repeat from "The Mighty Mahseer" the definition of remarks as used in the description of fish.

Fishes are in possession of five fins or pairs of fins, *i.e.*, dorsal fin (on back), caudal (or tail fin), pectoral fins (on breast) and ventral and anal (nearest the tail) underneath.

N.B.—It should be here noted that the tail of a fish is understood to be that part of the body between the anal and caudal fins, it being a mistake to call the latter fin itself the tail.

Then most fishes have a lateral line running from the gills to the tail on each side of their bodies; in some fish, especially scaleless ones, this line is much more clearly defined than in others.

L. l. signifies lateral line, and L. l. 24—26 means that there are 24 to 26 scales intersected by the lateral line.

D. signifies dorsal fin, and D. 3/9 means that the fin is composed of two different kinds of rays, *i.e.*, the first three are probably spines, the remaining nine being branched rays. A horizontal line signifies variation in number, an oblique line distinction into two different kinds of rays and a vertical line implies that there are two distinct dorsal fins.

Thus D. 7-8 | 1/10-12 means that there are two dorsal fins, the first consisting of 7 or 8 rays all of one kind, the second of one ray, probably

B

a spine, followed by 10 or 12 probably branched rays. D. may be replaced by V. A. P., or C. denoting the other fins.

2½ scales signify that there are 2½ rows of scales between the L. l. and the ventral fin.

Then barbels: these may be variously placed. If belonging to the nostril, they are termed nasal. If at end of snout, rostral; under chin, mandibular; and at corners of upper jaw, maxillary.

The Mahseer.—Barbus Tor. Family Cyprinidæ, Genus barbus. Found throughout India and Burma, runs to 200 lbs. in weight. Hindustani name Mahasir. The probable derivation of this word is from Matsya, the Sanskrit word for fish used in the Vedas, and as the mahseer is undoubtedly the sacred fish of India, it is more than likely that mahseer is simply a corruption of Matsya. Maha Sir, big head, is an alternative derivation L. l. 25—27, D. 3/9, 2½ scales. Description: head large, ditto scales, 4 barbels, lips thick. As to colour there are at least three distinct types—(*i*) The Punjab mahseer, silvery with scales becoming golden below the L. l. and fins reddish. (*ii*) The mahseer of the Nerbudda (in which river No. 1 is also to be caught) pale blue; and No. (*iii*) the jet black mahseer, an exceedingly handsome fish. No. 3 I have caught at their best south in the Kalinadi river, though I have seen them caught in the Punjab, but the ones caught north were not nearly so handsome or jet black in colour as those caught in the Kalinadi. The largest mahseer caught to date, fairly on rod and line, was caught within the last two years by Mr. Murray Aynsley, a well-known sportsman in the south of India. Caught in the Hutter river, a tributary of the Cauvery, and weighed, if I remember right, 104 lbs.

Barbus Carnaticus.—The Carnatic carp; same family and genus as the mahseer. This fish I have never seen or caught north of the Nerbudda, but as Day says it occurs in Northern India, I enter it here. Hind. Gid Kaoli; runs to 25 lbs. in weight. L. l. 30—32, D. 4/8, 3½ scales, 4 barbels. Colour greenish, with pale golden scales and gray fins. Mouth and scale much smaller than the mahseer's. Will take a small fly-spoon, also fly.

The Olive Carp.—Barbus Sarana. Same family as above. Northern India, generally; runs to 18 inches in length. L. l. 32—34, D. 3/8, A. 3/5. Colour golden to silvery white, fins light grey; sometimes rather a washed out looking fish, not so handsome as B. Chrysopoma the Olive Carp of Southern India. Occasionally takes fly, rises to gram on the Nerbudda (this however is B. Chrysopoma), and bites freely at worm, paste, or small dead bait.

Genus Labeo, comprises some 25 species all having nose under snout. The two best known are L. Rohita, the Rohu and L. Calbasu, the Labeo of Southern and Kalabanse of Northern India.

The Rohu.—L. l. 40—42 D. 15—16. Two small barbels. Colour blue-green above and white below, sometimes with red spots on scales. Fins are usually reddish, though sometimes almost black. Run big to 50 or 60 lbs. Will occasionally take spoon, but are essentially bottom feeders and are not often caught in rivers because of this. Bait, paste or worm.

Do not go off with the rush of a mahseer, but put up a good dogged fight. When on the feed, they send up at intervals three or four large bubbles.

The Kalabanse.—L. l. 40—44, D. 16—18; four barbels. Two distinct varieties, one blackish, the other dark green with red spots. Essentially bottom feeders. Bait, paste or worms.

The Barils.—Of this genus, some 14 different species in India, most of them only running to about 6 inches in length. The most important is Barilius Bola, commonly called the Indian trout, both because of his likeness to that fish in his spots, and because of his leaping out of water when being played. Found, Northern and Central India. Runs to 5 lbs., has large mouth, no barbels, small silvery scales, with two rows of spots generally bluish, though sometimes greenish. Tail orange, with black edge, though this is not always the case. Takes fly-spoon and fly; fights most gamely. Several other barils are to be found in the streams of Northern India, known usually by their small scales and coloured spots or blotches.

Megalops Cyprinoides belongs to the family Clupeidæ. Runs to 2 feet and more in length. Personally I have never caught this fish out of the Madras Presidency, but he is to be found in Bombay harbour, and Day says "throughout India," so I put him in here, more especially as, from a sporting point of view, he is second to no fish in India. Though an estuary fish, he becomes acclimatised to fresh water and thrives in tanks, especially those that are a trifle brackish. L. l. 37—42, D. 17—20. Large black eyes, dark green back, scales silver verging to pale blue below lateral line, large mouth, excessively bony and giving very bad hook-hold. First cousin to the tarpon. Takes a fly when small; best lure, a small live fish about 2 feet below surface. When hooked they go off with a grand rush, springing repeatedly feet into the air. They are for their size exceedingly powerful, even a 3-pounder in a big tank will run out 30 to 40 yards of line without a check.

The Murral.—Family Ophiocephelidæ, literally snake-headed fishes. Hind., Maral or Sowl. Nine species in India. Two most commonly met with up north are O. Striatus L. l. 51—57. D. 37—40. V. 6. and O. Marulius L. l. 59—64. D. 49—55, V. 6. Both run large to between 3 and 4 feet in length. The former is greenish black in colour, with light and dark bands on sides. The latter rather a handsome fish, dark silvery green with greenish blotches above L. l. and red below. Small white spot on each scale. Both have reddish eyes, with large flat heads and mouths full of formidable teeth. Almost all species of adult murral have an eye-like spot on caudal fin. Murral can travel short distances overland and have the power of aestivating in the mud of sun-dried tanks. In Burma it is no uncommon thing for a native, when he wishes to make you a handsome present, to bring you a lump of mud, which on washing proves to be a comatose murral. Needless to say, if eaten at once his taste is muddy, otherwise murral are one of the best fresh-water fish from an edible point of view in India. Sometimes take a small spoon. Live bait and live frogs are both good ways of fishing for them, and they will take a worm greedily. Found both in rivers and tanks, prefer muddy bottoms to shingley runs in former case. They always feed near surface and are very fond of basking on top of water. Small ones are sometimes called Dhok. Unlike most other fish, murral exhibit a certain amount of parental affection for their young.

Family Siluridæ.—This is one of the largest families known (including over 100 genera), and embraces all the fish that usually go by the name of fresh-water sharks in India. They are scaleless fish and have fleshy feelers attached to their mouths. These barbels are often numerous and frequently of great length. The commonest is that fish of many names.

Wallago Attu.—Called up north Bawalli, Laki, Lansi, Mulley and Paran, the three last names being if anything the most common. Often called by Europeans, especially down south, by his scientific name only. D. 1/4, V. 8—10, A. 86—98 ; four barbels. He runs very big to 100 lbs. in weight and over 6 feet in length. His head is enormous and absurdly disproportionate in weight to his body. Mouth full of rows of teeth. Anal fin running whole length of body, just stopping short, however, of ventral and caudal fins, and not joining with these. Small paran usually have dark blotches just behind gills. Takes fly, spoon and spinning bait sometimes in rivers, also occasionally rises to fly in tanks, greedy as regards live bait. Fights fairly well and is not bad eating.

The Goonch.—Bagarius Yarelli. An extraordinarily ugly looking monster. A. 15, eight barbels and six fins on belly, dirty grey green to brown in colour, with brownish marks, filaments on fins, with back and breast thorns. Runs to over 200 lbs. and 6 feet long. Takes spoon and spinning bait, also live bait, when big, sulks on being hooked. Often lies in the heaviest white water and takes bait almost before it touches water. The biggest known to have been landed on rod and line was 164 lbs. caught at Okhla.

The Silund.—Silundia Gangetica. Two small barbels, A.40-46, six fins on belly, back and breast thorns, colour light blue above, merging into silver, fins greyish. Not nearly so common as the two foregoing. Takes the same baits.

Genus Macrones.—Eighteen species, some of which attain to great size, 6 feet in length. They are usually called cat fishes, because of their long feelers. The two best known are M. Singhala, A. 11. D. 1/7/0, silvery in colour with back and breast thorns, and M. Tengara, A. 10, D. 1/7/0, four dark bands alongside. Both have eight barbels, long adipose fin and forked tails. They fight well when hooked, take spinning, live bait and worm. Singhala is one of the most common fish caught trolling in the lakes at Oodeypore Mind the thorns, especially the one in the dorsal fin. They often give vent to a curious squawk when being handled.

The Pufta.—Genus Callichrous. Called butter fish, not very common in North India. Runs to 6 lbs in weight. Long anal fin; four barbels, thorn on pectoral fin, but not on dorsal. Caught with worm and paste, also said to take a fly. Good eating.

The Butchwa.—Genus Pseudeutropius or Entropiichthys. There are some seven species of Butchwa in India, P. Garua being probably the best known. Runs to 2 feet in length, and up to 5 lbs.; eight barbels, A. 27—55, six belly fins, thorns on dorsal and pectoral fins. Formidable teeth. Colour silvery, with beautiful greenish sheen on back, when fresh caught, though this dulls and darkens very quickly. Takes small natural bait, fly-spoon, fly and worm freely, also cannot resist clotted blood. A most sporting little fish and very excellent eating. Mind his dorsal thorn when handling.

Genus Rita.—Four species, the best known being the Kuggah, a most evil and weird-looking little fish. Yellow-green in colour; six barbels, A. 12, V. 7-8. Both pectoral and dorsal fins have thorns, which are formidable and inclined to be poisonous. Run to a couple of lbs. in weight; when landed very lively and quacks like a duck. Are to be caught in the Jumna and Jhelum, and probably most other rivers.

The Indian Gudgeon.—Gobius Giuris, belongs to family Gobiidæ, most of his relations live in the sea. An ugly little fish, commonly called mudfish. Bait, worms. Hind. Gulu; scales lengthways, 26-34, D. 6 | 1/9, V. 4/4. Yellowish in colour, semi-transparent, flat head and mouth full of teeth. Runs up to 3 lbs. A peculiarity is that he possesses no lateral line.

The Chilwa.—Genus Chela. There are some ten species of this fish distributed throughout India. Generally known as Chilwa, and may be recognised by long flat silvery bodies, up-turned mouths and no barbels. Rise freely to fly, and have a habit of continually throwing themselves into the air on calm still evenings. They have a beautiful pale greenish tinge when first caught, but this quickly fades. None of the species run to more than a few ounces.

Family Notopteridæ.—Only one genus in which there are two species, *i.e.*, Notopterus Chitala and N. Kapirat. The former is the Seetul or Mohi, L. l. 180, D. 8—10, A. 110—125. Runs to 4 feet in length and 40 lbs. in weight, has minute scales and L. l. very distinct Back very bowed; colour silvery with purple cross bands, no barbels. Fish of over 14 lbs. seem often to have several black dots on tail. Grand sporting fish and very powerful, springing frequently out of water when being played. Spin with dead bait, small, as mouth is small for size of fish. Also sometimes takes worm. Narora and Okhla seem to be the places where this fish is chiefly met with. Though a bottom feeder, has a habit of rolling on top like Wallago Attu, but if both fish are present, the difference is easily told, by tapering tail fin and purplish colour of mohi, paran being more silvery and the gap between anal and caudal fins being conspicuous as they turn. Mohi are bony, except just belly which is considered a delicacy, but is too oily to be nice.

N. Kapirat.—Is a smaller edition of the Seetul. L. l. 225, D. 7—9, A. 100—110, is said to run to 20 lbs. but as a rule one never catches one over 2 lbs. Fish with worm, bait on bottom, and strike when float bobs vigorously. Rather a pretty fish when first taken from water; colour silvery grey, with golden head.

The Catla—Genus Buchanani—is a carp-like fish generally found in tanks, runs big, 100 lbs. and 6 feet in length. Head very large; colour, grey merging to silver, dark fins.

Entirely a bottom feeder ; bait, worm or paste. Coarse eating. Sends up at intervals one or two large bubbles.

The Mirga or Mirgil.—Cirrhina Mrigala, L. l. 40—45, D. 15—16 ; two barbels, runs to 20 lbs.; scales bright silver or golden, fins with black stains. Caught usually in tanks ; bait, paste or worms. Not bad to eat but bony. Fights well. Sends up at intervals a collection of small bubbles.

Cirrhina Cirrhosa.—The white carp. L. l. 42—44. D. 17—19 ; four barbels, runs to 1½ feet and over 2 lbs. weight ; a handsome silvery fish, with sometimes red spots on scales, but not always. Fins, silvery white, snout depressed with fairly broad mouth. To be caught on paste, bottom fishing, bites like a rohu or labeo, but is a bolder fish. Found in North, Central and Southern India.

Etroplus Suratensis.—L. l. 45, D. 18-19/14, V. 1/5. A pretty flat-sided fish with greenish transverse bands and little white spots. Mouth, small with prominent teeth. Runs to 2 lbs. Feeds on weeds, though will take worms and is generally a bold biter. Fight well for their size. Do not fish too deep for them, one to three feet. Is said to be found in Central India, but though I have caught many in South India, I have never come across one north of the Nerbudda.

Genus Mastacembelus.—M. Armatus, the Indian thorny-backed eel or bahm. There are other genus and species, but this is the commonest met with. Grows about 2 feet long ; colour brown. Likes muddy tanks or slow streams Bait, worm or dead fish resting on bottom. Great fry and spawn eaters so should always be destroyed. Not bad eating.

Family Clupeidæ.—(Under which also comes the Megalops) Clupea Ilisha. The Hilsa or Sable fish, Shad of Ganges, and Palla of Indus. An excellent fish for the table, said sometimes to take a white fly. Colour silvery, shot purple and gold. Spawns in streams.

Mugil Corsula.—The fresh-water mullet. Hind. Amvari. A small fish with minute scales. Swims in shoals and may be known by protruberant eyes that appear on surface of water Excellent eating, but will take no bait of any sort.

The Chirroo. –Sometimes called Charri Gad, also Kashmir trout, is a barbel, and has a large mouth placed like that of a dog fish. No teeth. In shape he is very heavy and thick at the shoulder, and tapers quickly to about the vent, after which his size is uniform to the tail. Scaleless, and is covered with thick greasy slime like an eel. Colour, dark grey above with small black spots, and belly silvery white. Runs to over 20 lbs. Flesh white, and when caught in rocky streams is fair eating, though bony. Fished for in Kashmir in May, June and July. Early in season worm is best bait, but later will take fly; not very particular as to pattern, Black Doctor, Jock Scott and Teal and Green are all good. Also takes frogs, mulberries, minnows and spoons.

The Choosh—Is a barbel, and has much the same habits as the Chirroo, but is a slower fish. In colouring also is much alike, save no spots and belly is yellow. Runs to over 20 lbs. The best localities in Kashmir for this fish are probably the Verhan, Liddar and Sind rivers as in these streams the fish seem more sporting, and are better eating than those caught in the main river. However, neither Chirroo nor Choosh can be called really sporting fish, and though they run large, they are seldom caught more than a few pounds in weight. Both of these fish are sometimes called "Gaurd" which is the Kashmiri word for fish.

The Snow-trout.—Also yclept the Himalayan and mountain barbel, belongs to the family Cyprinidæ, Genus Barbus, and are related to the mahseer and English barbel. They are bottom feeders, are scaleless and run to 4 and 5 lbs. Colour varies; some fish are a uniform darkish grey, while others are mottled on the back and sides. It is the speckled appearance of these latter fish that have earned them the name of snow-trout, in contra-distinction to Himalayan barbel. One peculiarity of these fish should be noted, which by the way is shared to a lesser extent by the mahseer, namely, that their roe is poisonous, though not fatally so. If partaken of at all freely, it is apt to cause vomiting and diarrhœa.

The following estuary fish are included in this chapter, since they may be said to reside in the Ganges and Indus, living as they do in the deltas of those rivers.

The Bamin.—Polymenus tetradactylus. L. l. 75-85, D. 8 | 1/13--15, V. 1/5. Runs to over 200lbs. and 6 feet in length; colour silver, greenish above and yellow below. To be caught spinning; a very sporting and exceedingly powerful fish, taking the bait with a rush like a mahseer, springing frequently out of water when hooked. Good eating.

The Nair.—Lates Calcarifer, the Begti of the Hooghly. L. l. 52, D. 7-8 | 1/11—12, V. 1—5. Sometimes also called the Cock-up. Colour, silvery grey, shot with green above. Runs to over 200lbs. To be caught, etc., same as Bamin, the only difference is that the Nair takes the bait gently. Good eating.

The Red (Rock) Perch.—Lutianus Roseus. Runs to 5 lbs. and over. Colour, a dull cherry red. A most sporting fish and powerful when hooked, always boring down among the rocks. To be caught spinning, also with live bait, his special predilection being for a prawn.

The Seer.—Cybium Guttatum. Five species, an allied fish to the mackerel. Runs big to 6 feet or more in length. Colour, silver with blue back. A splendid fighter like the bamin and nair, but essentially a sea fish. Caught by spinning. Very good eating.

CHAPTER II.

THE HIMALAYAN MAHSEER.

Though all that is written in "The Mighty Mahseer" may be taken as applying, to some extent, to the hero of this chapter, yet there is no doubt that the fishing in the big rivers of Southern India differs greatly from that to be obtained in the Hill streams of the north. On the other hand, the methods adopted in the Himalayan rivers might well be employed with success in the smaller streams of the south, especially those that issue from the Western Ghauts and brawl their short and restless course to the Indian Ocean. Therefore, the few notes strung together below are intended to be merely supplementary to the hints given in "The Mighty Mahseer," and the information on tackle, spinners, traces, etc., is not repeated. Nor to anyone in possession of the "Angler's Handbook" would it be possible to offer more comprehensive details about such subjects, than are contained in that most excellent publication.

The pages that follow must be taken, too, more in the light of hints to beginners, or at any rate to those, who though no novices in the gentle art, are yet scraping their first acquaintance with our friend the mahseer. And in what glorious scenery we find him, certainly that is one of the greatest charms of a fishing trip in the Himalayas. Brawling, tossing rapids, crystal clear pools, pine clad slopes and sheer rocky bluffs that tower into the blue above one; even if one's trip fails from a fishing point of view, surely all the above are some recompense, and no trip can be written down an absolute failure from which one returns braced up in mind and body. And what magnificent views one can get, especially if a passing storm has cleared the air. For there is no finer sight in the world than to stand some clear day on a hill top in the Himalayas as the sun sinks to rest, and gaze on the scene before one. Far below one glimmers a tiny silver thread, where some mountain stream murmurs its way to join the distant river. Tier upon tier above it rise the paddy fields, all glorious with their bladed carpets of richest emerald green, till colours blending harmoniously they merge in the deeper shades of ilex and rhododendrons. Then to the horizon stretch the mighty Himalayas, range upon range of pine clad peaks and grassy slopes, bluer and softer grow the distant ranges, till sentinels of the world, tower the eternal snows. And something sublime is there in those immense peaks, silent, cold, unchanging, they seem part of another world, a world of utter desolation, colourless, pitiless, lifeless. And so the dusk falls and the feeling of awe dies away, as the world contracts, and one turns to the cheering lights and humming life of the camp below. But I know that there are many prosaic souls who say they would a thundering sight sooner go on catching fish, and miss the scenery; and this being human nature, or rather the nature of the Britisher, I fear that I must plead guilty to a certain sympathy with that sentiment. Still, if the fish are off the feed, it is nice to have something to admire, so let it go at that.

Now, more and more is fishing becoming reduced to two schools, those who pin their faith in natural bait, and those who use the fly-spoon right through a trip. Of course, I need hardly repeat, that this is only referring to the hill streams, of which one may take the Giri as a fair example. In these rivers the fish usually run up to 20 lbs. with an occasional 30 or 40 pounder if one is very lucky, or the gods extra good to one. But the usual run of fish is something under 10 lbs. And personally, I must own myself an advocate of the latter school, not that I hold that one's basket will be the heavier, but that the pleasure is infinitely greater. And in matter of weight, I do not think that there is likely to be nearly that difference that some admirers of natural bait would have one believe. Let two men, equally good fishermen, take ten days' leave and fish down some Himalayan river. One uses natural bait and the other a fly-spoon. At the end I fancy the actual weight caught would work out very much the same. Probably, No. 1's individual fish would average slightly heavier, but then No. 2's bag would excel in numbers. And, allowing perhaps the three biggest fish to natural bait, the next six largest fish of each would probably be very much of a muchness. However, I am aware that this is hardly a possible test, as in very clear and low water the natural bait loses much of its advantage, whereas in coloured water the fly-spoon is practically useless. Of course there is that middle course which can be steered, and though one sometimes does it, like all middle courses, it is never really satisfactory. I refer to the use of two rods, one mounted with natural bait and the other with cast and fly-spoon, so as to use each alternately as the water suits.

But somehow, one is never really happy this way; the gut cast dries up, the cooly with the fancied rod has hung behind, the lurking feeling about that last fish that came short, 'if only I'd been using the other lure I would have had him,' all these trifles help to unsettle one's mind, and take away from the perfect pleasure of a fine day, on a pretty river, when fish are taking well. Now, although the natural bait can search out holes and heavy runs where the small spoon is lost, the latter can cover a lot more water and will lure fish from many a fairly shallow rapid, wherein the spinner would hardly care to trust his lure, unless he be a more than usual cunning hand. And if the fish are on the feed, I do not believe it is really necessary to fish so deep for the bigger ones, as so many people make out. Although in the deeper pools to you the water is opaque, and you cannot see down more than some six feet, remember the fish at the bottom, looking up through crystal clear water to the open sky, can see practically anything which passes within their range of vision. And how often, fishing from some height above the stream, does one see a big fish shoot up from hidden depths to inspect one's spoon. And here is another point, which so greatly enhances the pleasure of fishing, and which, therefore, is in my opinion one of the strongest arguments in favour of the fly-spoon. And that is the fact of seeing so much of what takes place. Standing behind some fair-sized boulder, and getting one's cast well out into a crystal clear pool, it is fascinating to watch the small dramas that repeat themselves so frequently. Time and again will a whole shoal of small fish follow one's spoon, to scatter in all directions as it leaves the water for another cast, then rallying again to the splash, one of the boldest among them will dash at the spoon and tug it violently, escaping the hooks in that marvellous fashion that fish are such provoking adepts at. And then how one's heart beats as a dark shadow seems to detach itself from a rock, resolving itself into a nice fish of 5 or 6 lbs. and slowly follows one's lure.

Then the happy moment when there is no hesitation, but almost as the bait touches the water, comes a flash of silver as a gleaming flank rolls in the current, and for a second one is uncertain if he has taken you or not, till the scream of the reel reassures you that all is well. And if using a fly-spoon, do not use too big a one, something between ¾ of an inch and 1 inch, and have it light so that it spins almost immediately on touching the water. If you mount your own, get the spoons made of thin brass so that you can just bend them with your fingers, the electroplating will bring them up to the required thickness. For remember the spoon need not be strong, its only function is to lure the fish to meet the steel. It is the hook, fastened to the swivel, that is going to do all the hard work. As regards shape, opinions differ, half hogged are good; and then colour, whether all gold, gold and silver, or all silver (the two latter are the best) and between them there seems to be very little difference when the fish are taking. And what a lot those last five words mean. If fish were always on the take, I firmly believe that one could wipe out at least three-fourth of the lures that man has devised. If fish are off, and you catch one on a silver spoon, then wild horses will not induce you to mount any other sort, and if by chance you lose your only one, the whole keenness goes out of your fishing, and the unfortunate cooly keeps as far from you as he possibly can. But let the fish be on the take, and no matter what lure you mount, every other cast seems to produce a fish eager to commit suicide. And use fairly strong gut, salmon, as even a one pound mahseer in the broken waters of a Himalayan stream can plunge and tug in a way that makes it seem a marvel that any gut can hold him. And then there is no telling but that at any minute you may get into a 15 or 20-pounder. And let not all the above concerning fly-spoon lead the beginner to assume that natural bait is not a good lure. In coloured water, heavy runs and at junctions try it by all means, but for the mounts, methods of using, etc., I would refer the novice to the "The Angler's Handbook" or "The Mighty Mahseer." Now, to fish a mountain stream with fly-spoon the simplest procedure is to fish down. Of course if one is marching up a river, one can fish up each rapid, but it is not so easy, and one misses a certain amount of water, especially in the shallower runs that cannot all be fished up without disturbing the fish as one moves. And do not miss the head of the rapid, because it seems too heavy, many a small back-water lies behind the rocks up in the white water, and if you can drop your lure in at the right angle, it may be accepted. There are two ways of fishing down an ordinary rapid ; which you adopt must depend on circumstances, such as volume of water and conformation of banks. If the run is not too heavy, wade in well above the pool and work slowly down, dropping your spoon in the slack water on one side, bringing it round through the current and up backwater on opposite side. Vary this procedure by occasionally paying out line and letting your spoon be carried down by the stream, then swinging rod top to one side, reel up through the slack water just clear of the current. You will find that hardly ever will you be taken when paying out line, it is only, with very few exceptions, when moving up stream that fish will take your bait. If you cannot work down stream by wading, approach the rapid about level with the head of pool and, keeping well back, drop your fly-spoon across under the opposite bank as near up to the shore as possible, then by raising your rod top let the bait swing with the current and bring it round up your own bank opposite to where it struck the water. And gradually work down the pool, till the current fails to spin your lure. Most of the fish you will find lie right up near the head of the run, though often the bigger fish seem to lie in the almost still water, especially where there are any big rocks in a pool, and it is almost always worth trying a cast behind these even though there be no appreciable current round them. And then the long shallow rapids that vary from one to three feet in depth. These are worth trying, especially in an afternoon. Wade down the centre and get out as long a line as possible, using your rod top to make your spoon travel across like a swinging bridge, occasionally reeling in so that it spins up the centre of the rapid. And in the Giri, particularly, if you are having no sport, it is worth trying these runs with fly, a lake trout size Blackamoor or Alexandra will often give some very pretty sport with the smaller mahseer. Now a word as to mounting fly-spoons. Personally, I am a great believer in a single mount, and that a single hook. One seems to lose far less fish that touch the spoon with a single hook than one does with a treble. Why this should be so it's hard to say, as theoretically with the latter one's chances ought to be better, except that the single hook has a bigger and freer sweep. And then the single hook is lighter and interferes less with the spinning of the spoon. It is very necessary though to frequently examine one's hook, as getting out a long cast in a rocky riverbed, it is astonishing how many hooks one can break at the barb. And one other advantage a single hook has, it is so infinitely easier to remove from the fish's mouth, especially when he is struggling violently. And do not, under any circumstances, use split rings, at least such is my advice. If you make up your own spoons, have wire rings made, that you can close with a pair of pliers. Though I have lost spoons, and mounts too, through these working open, when not watched, I have never had a fish escape through pulling one apart Use fairly small swivels, No. 6 or 7, but this is really for lightness sake, as a silver swivel is half a lure in itself. Now, as regards seasons for fishing: March, April, May, and part of June. Then middle of September till about 15th November, though of course, the latter period depends a lot upon when rains finish. April is perhaps th. best month of all. The time of day to fish depends a great deal on the height above sea-level of the river, and also a lot upon the weather. Middle of March to middle of April on the Kosi and Ramganga, one seemed to catch all one's fish between 10 A.M. and 3-30 P.M. On the Giri, in April when the weather was warm and clear, morning and evening seemed the best time. But on a hill stream really the pleasantest way is to shift camp most days, say about 6 miles. Then to start off, about 8 o'clock after a big chota-hazri, taking an extra cooly to carry the tiffin basket and to fish one's way steadily to next camp, stopping, say for an hour or two, between 12 and 2, and so arriving for a late tea. This plan has the advantage that one fishes practically all day long, has always fresh water before one, and soon learns the hours when fish are most on the take. As to rod, a 14 foot fly rod is hard to beat as an all-round weapon. If steel centred so much the better. This allows of a small natural bait being used on occasions, and also allows of getting out a decent line against the raging wind that so often sweeps down a Himalayan valley. I have heard men say that as a river was so low and clear, they confined themselves to a 10 or 11-foot trout rod. But this argument, though on first thoughts it seems all right, is hardly a sound one. For fine fishing with fly, or gram fishing on the Nerbudda, where one can let one's lure rove down with the current, this works well enough, but for casting a fly-spoon, its very lightness defeats its own object in fishing fine. For in a crystal clear hill stream, where the mahseer are not too well educated to man and his lures, it is not so much fineness of tackle as invisibility of self that is the important matter, so the longer the line you can get out the better. And curiously enough once you get a certain height, say 10 feet or so above fish, they do not seem to evince nearly the same shyness, whether it is that their limit of vision is restricted, or the refraction of the water distorts their sight, I cannot say. And another small matter is the lightness with which your lure falls. This I think is not a matter of very much moment. It is curious to stand well above a pool, and watch the results of a few casts. If the fish are not on the feed, or for any reason are inclined to be shy, the splash of your spoon sends any within range, scurrying for shelter. But on the other hand should they be hungry, the bigger the splash the more fish come rushing to investigate the cause. Some men have a great objectoin to using a very bright spoon in clear water. A scheme to obviate this, that was once shown me, was to hold the spoon in the flame of a wax match, as it then became covered with a thin film of wax which did not wash off in a hurry. I have tried this occasionally, but I cannot honestly say that I detected any improvement as regarded the fish taking, since with a small fly-spoon, except when fishing in the most crystal clear water, I do not think that it can be very much too bright, when one sees the silver flash that a small fish makes as it turns in clear water. And as a matter of fact it is my firm belief that fish very seldom do take a fly-spoon under the impression that it is a small fish; they do of course sometimes, when they are hunting about after small fry and your spoon splashes in near them, but generally it is pure curiosity on their part, and a fish having no hands grabs the spoon in his mouth to investigate the matter. For with a fish greed and curiosity are very much on a par. As regards wearing apparel nothing is so comfortable as shorts, made full and long. Also wear stockings, however hardened you may flatter yourself your skin is, if you wear socks the continuous wading and hot sun of the hills will blister you most painfully after a time. Wear good strong boots, and take two or three pairs, as the boulders of a Himalayan stream are exceeding hard on footwear; and boots that would last a season's snipe shooting or a year's fishing at home will go to pieces after a fortnight's wading in a hill stream. And if wading much, one's boots always seem to be getting full of gravel, and the feet of your stockings will wear out at a rate that may well cause adverse comment from your better half. And as stockings are none too cheap an item, the hint given in Chapter III on the subject may be found an economical expedient. A very useful article in hill streams is a good alpenstock, it allows one to wade and climb in places where one could hardly maintain one's foothold otherwise; they are to be bought in any of the hill stations for a few annas.

For those new to this country making their first trip into the Himalayas a few words of advice may not be out of place. Generally when leaving the beaten tracks, all kit has to be carried by coolies, and in making up loads they should not exceed 50 lbs. as a rule. It is not a good thing to overload one's coolies, especially if much climbing will have to be done. Heavy loads mean slow marching, and then, no matter how well you have worked out your weights, etc., all sorts of things will be produced by your servants at the last minute to be shoved on to the back of the cooly who protests least volubly. To carry your stores in, nothing can be better than the kiltas or baskets used by the hillmen, while a tin box is a good thing for your own most valued possessions. Also your bedding should be in a waterproof roll, as the heavy storms one gets sometimes in the hills have a way of saturating everything through in the minimum of time. And remember it is not advisable to travel too light in the way of bedding. Starting from Meerut or Ambala, say, in the month of May, it is hard to realize that inside a week you may be shivering some night at the top of a pass 7,000 feet high, or even a day or two's rain can produce quite chilly nights at an altitude of 4,000 feet and less. An eiderdown is one of the nicest things one can have for a trip of this sort, as it is both very light and very warm.

And before closing this chapter I would like to make a plea on behalf of the fish you catch. When possible, kill each fish after landing it. At home a priest is a common article in a fisherman's equipment, so why not out here. One can easily be made from any hard wood, simply a handle with a knob at one end, and the cooly can carry it. If using a flight of hooks, killing simplifies their extraction, more especially should your capture be one of the Siluroids. I know few men ever think of thus killing their fish, and I must plead my own guilt in the matter. One generally hands over the capture at once to the waiting cooly, so does not have the facts thrust on one's notice. But it is not a pleasant sight to see the painful gasps with which a mahseer dies, and if one has cause to sit down and watch a fish die, the matter is brought home to one rather forcibly. And a mahseer is very easily killed with a smart blow on the head.

And once again finally, let me add that all the remarks about fly-spoon refer to the smaller Himalayan rivers. Of course the man who uses in these streams natural bait, or a big spoon fishing deep, will have sport and perhaps return well satisfied with his trip. My only contention is that with the fly-spoon one has prettier sport with much less worry, and that the conditions more nearly assimilate to fly fishing on a Highland stream, with one great merit—to outweigh any disadvantages there may be—that at any minute you may be playing a 20-pounder. To fish, say the Ganges, from Rikkikesh to Hardwar, using nothing but a fly-spoon, would be a sheer waste of time. Fish you would probably catch, but the chances in such heavy water of your getting any of the monsters with which the river abounds, would be infinitesimal. Here if anywhere you must fish deep, and the same may generally be said concerning any canal falls.

CHAPTER III.

USEFUL HINTS.

The following few hints were not included in "The Mighty Mahseer" so are given a short chapter to themselves in this book, in the hopes that one or more of them may be new to brother anglers, and be found useful.

HINTS, FISHING AND TACKLE.

Preserving Deadbait.—Concerning one of the solutions which I gave for this purpose in "The Mighty Mahseer" and which I repeat herewith.

Formalin 1 oz.; glycerine 5 oz.; rectified spirit 5 oz.; distilled water 9 oz. I would now add that this being a fairly expensive prescription, if made at half the strength it amply suffices for the purpose. The formalin alone works out at a 5 per cent solution, and 2 per cent is all that is really needful. So that you can either have the prescription made up as it stands, and then add an equal quantity of water, or else halve the quantities of first three items and leave the fourth as it is.

And for those who wish further information on this subject, I append the two following which appeared in the "Answers" column of the *Pioneer*.

Fishing Bait.—In answer to "H. F. C." *re* Formalin as a bait preservative. There is no necessity to use glycerine; it may take away the smell, however, and does no harm to the preserving powers of a formalin solution. Get Schering's 40 per cent obtainable at any chemist. Use a 1 per cent (1 part of formalin to 39 of water) solution, if keeping the fish for any length of time. If bait is only wanted for the day, soak for a few minutes in a solution of 2 per cent. Wring out a linen cloth in the solution and carry the fish wrapped up in it. If preserving a number of baits for a long fishing trip, clean and wash; then soak first in a 2 per cent solution for 10 minutes, and then transfer to a 1 per cent solution. After the baits have been some time in the formalin they can be transferred to bottles or tins in which a few drops of the concentrated (40 per cent) solution have been sprinkled, and this method does away with the necessity for carrying a number of bottles of fluid. Formalin has a deleterious action on the finger nails causing them to split in a very curious manner, otherwise it is harmless.—R. E. N. N.

Fishing Bait and Formalin.—If minnows are required for spinning they can be preserved and also given a permanent bend, which will cause them to spin of themselves, by the use of formalin in the following way. Select the minnows required and kill them by flicking them on the back of the head with the finger nail and pin them with the curl required to a flat board One half of the tails should be curled one way and the other half in the opposite direction. Then if used alternately they will do each other a good turn by taking out the "kink" in the line.

"Formalin Solution," as bought at the chemist, contains 40 per cent of formalin, and mixtures made from this with water are usually referred to as containing so much per cent of "Formalin" not "Formalin solution." I shall give the strengths by measure, referring to the "Formalin solution" only. When the minnows are thus arranged they should be painted lightly over with a camel hair brush with a strong solution of formalin (three tea-spoonsful of formalin solution to two table-spoonsful of water). In a very short space of time they may be taken from the board and will look as if they had had curly tails all their lives, and should then be put into a solution for two days of the following strength: Five table spoonsful of formalin solution to a pint of water, *i.e.*, twenty fluid ounces—a whisky bottle may be taken to equal, roughly, 20 fluid ounces. Finally, the minnows should be taken out well washed in pure water, and then placed in a solution of the following strength: Two tablespoonsful of formalin solution to a pint of water. The following is important: The night before going fishing, as many minnows as are required should be taken out, washed in clean water, and then dropped into a small wide mouth bottle containing a very strong solution of salt. This will improve the shiny appearance and remove all taint of formalin. The above directions appeared in the *Fishing Gazette* last year, under the head of "Spinning the Minnow" by "Baz."—W. A. S.

When using fly-spoon or flies, some men carry a small file in their pockets. This is useful to sharpen up hooks occasionally. Personally, I have generally managed to break my hooks either against a rock or in a fish before this stage arrives.

Also, beginners should remember if using a fly-spoon it is absolutely necessary to have a suitable line, if you wish to fish with any happiness.

It is not a satisfactory scheme just changing your trace and spinning bait to put on a cast and spoon. Neither line is suitable for the other job, though if you do only have one line, use the heavier, as you can spin with this better than you can cast with the finer line. There is nothing so heart-breaking as trying to make a long cast with a fly-spoon and thin spinning line, and if there is any wind it is almost impossible to put your lure where you wish. The heavy line may appear coarse tackle, but this is more than compensated for by the facility with which you can drop your spoon exactly where you want, and the longer casts you can make. The King-fisher lines of Malloch, Perth, are about the best that I've yet struck for this country, for fly-spoon the size you require is No. 5, and for spinning No. 4. Or if Hardy's catalogue is by you, sizes 26C and 22E, of his parallel line types. Of course this applies to bigger rods, for small trout rods use stout trout lines.

Sticky Lines.—If a line becomes sticky it can often be cured in the earlier stages by stretching it, and rubbing in hard, red deer's fat or dubbin. The more friction used the better. And as tacky lines are a serious consideration in this country, I append the following cutting from the *Field*, which perhaps some would like to try for themselves.

Tacky air pumped lines.—Some few years ago I was given an undressed tapered salmon line made of plaited white silk, and an enthusiastic friend undertook to dress it by the air pump process, as he had set up a gas oven in which lines so dressed could be dried. The result was simply perfect, and the gillies on the Tay admitted that they had never seen such a beautifully dressed line. After the fishing season I was in the habit of detaching the forty-five yards of dressed line, and, having wound it on a pliable covered book would slip it off and put it away in a drawer till the next season; but two years ago I neglected to do this, and, talking to a brother of the angle one day, I said I would show him a perfect salmon line. On pulling some lengths off the reel I found, to my horror, that instead of the former smooth, enamel-like feeling, it was quite tacky, so I immediately put it on a winder and hung it out in the air, thinking that this would restore it to its pristine beauty. But no; if anything, the stickiness increased. Then there was a correspondence in the *Field* as to what should be done to cure tacky air pumped lines, and the consensus of opinion seemed to point to only one remedy—*viz.*, cremation!

Remembering what the line was when in health, I could not bring myself to throw it at the back of the fire without first trying some remedy; so I covered my hands with a thick lather of Lifebuoy soap, and passed the line through them into a basin of thick soapsuds, where I left it for an hour. I then passed it through house flannel, and was gratified to find that the sticky oil came off on the flannel; but it was a nasty job, as after pulling ten or twelve yards through the flannel I had to stop and wash the sticky filth from my hands. By this process quite two-thirds of the decomposed oil was removed, and after hanging the line up for a fortnight I removed the remaining third by pulling the line through house flannel saturated with terebene. When it had dried all tackiness had disappeared, and apparently the line was as good as ever, though, of course, the beautifull enamel-like smoothness of its first state was gone. I had a tapered air pumped trout line, which had also become tacky through being left on the reel, and it was quite evident that after the season these lines should be removed from the reel, or sooner or later the oil will heat and decompose, and so render the line tacky. I subjected this line to the same process, and cured it so effectually that I have been fishing with it this season.—T. M. W.

Remember that in speaking of right or left banks of a river, the observer stands facing the mouth with his back to the current.

A correspondent has suggested the insertion of the following hint on Etiquette, and as I am entirely at one with him in the matter, I quote his exact words: "I believe that it would be a good thing to point out, that if a man catches a fish in a pool, his pal should not at once come and cast into the same pool. It is such a usual and such a rotten game."

Now, quite a good scheme that I discovered in tank fishing was the following. When ground-baiting, and just before you begin to fish, throw in one or more small muslin bags, filled full of the paste or bait you are using on your hooks, tying the mouths of the bags up tight. Also if you are fishing a swim, it is not a bad plan to throw in a very thin envelope full of bran, which will dissolve as it floats down stream.

Concerning the dyeing, etc., of gut, Mr. Wells in his book "Fly Rods and Fly Tackle" makes a most interesting remark, and one that I fancy will strike a new note to most anglers out here. He lays great stress on the necessity for "dulling the glitter" of gut, when using it in clear water. This, however, seems to be no easy matter. The Editor of the *Field* states that rubbing it with crushed up dock leaves effects this. Mr. Wells has also made exhaustive tests in the visibility of different coloured gut, and found that in clear water, such as Indian streams usually are, ink-stained gut was perhaps the least visible, followed closely by pale green and unstained gut. He also states that dyeing gut reduces its strength from 15 to 40 per cent, but adds, that soaking in ink does not appear to be injurious to it. This is probably from the fact of the latter being cold, and the gut not being subjected to heat as if soaked in tea, or water in which green baize has been boiled.

Split cane rods.—Now that these are coming more and more into use, the care of one's rods becomes a still greater consideration, and at least once a year, when putting them away, they should receive a thorough coating of varnish. Manton of Calcutta sells a good fisherman's varnish, Rs. 1-4 a small bottle I think it is. If one's rods have to remain in the plains during the hot weather and rains, one cannot do better than hang them, tied loosely in their cases on a wall.

And while on the subject I quote an extract from Hardy Bros.' catalogue, both on how to put these rods together, and also concerning their care and preservation. "To put a rod together: Fix the top joint first, then the middle, and lastly the butt. In so doing, all joints should be gripped by the *metal* parts only. Avoid twisting the cane or wood. Any stuck joint, from wet or other cause, should be gently heated over a candle and allowed to cool, when it will generally come asunder. This will never occur if a little lubricant be rubbed on the joint before putting together."

NOTE.—"All rods, after use, should be taken to pieces and carefully wiped with a damp cloth or sponge, then lightly rubbed with a soft cloth or chamois, and any bent piece carefully straightened, placed in their bag loosely tied and hung up in a dry place......Rod tops should not be put into the covers joint first, as it is liable to bend the fine ends when tied against the handle of butt."

Snow water.—Now, the following short explanation may appear too obvious to be worth inserting, at least to those who have served more than a year or two in North India. But the matter is by no means obvious to the new-comer to this country, and I have met many men whose service has all been spent south of the Nerbudda, whose ideas of snow water were of the vaguest. For between the great rivers of the south and those of the north, there is a vast difference. July and August are common to both, in that the heavy rains that fall practically over the whole of India during these two months, affect the waters of every river in the Peninsula. September sees the big rivers of the north beginning to clear, and also those smaller streams of the south that flow into the Indian Ocean, taking their rise all down the Western Ghauts.

But the east flowing rivers, such as the Cauvery, Godavery and Kistna do not clear till much later, the N.-E. monsoon sweeping across India, till the heavy rain-clouds are caught and hurled back by the Western Ghauts, keeps their waters coloured and at a high level, till sometimes more than half way through the cold weather. But it is as the hot season progresses that the greatest difference becomes apparent. In May, for instance, when the vast Cauvery is running crystal clear, with its dwindling waters useless for purposes of irrigation, then the great rivers of the north, the Jhelum and the Sutlej, the Ganges and the Jumna, are sweeping down in mighty flood, filling canals and cuts, and spreading the precious fluid all over the sun-parched plains of the Punjab and U. P. For at a height of anything over ten to twelve thousand feet, in the Himalayas, the snow lies thick in the winter, and towards the end of March the sun, gradually attaining a heat sufficient to melt the accumulations, starts to do so, slowly at first, but more rapidly day by day, till the white waters filling every rocky tributary pour down to swell the big river with their opaque and turbid floods. And this would mean the end of all fishing in the north, were it not for the innumerable smaller streams, such as the Giri, Ramganga, Sohan, and such like, which take their rise in the lower ranges under 10,000 feet and whose waters are, therefore, not affected by melting snows. Also it is a curious thing that while in such big rivers as the Sutlej, Beas, Chenab and Ganges, as soon as the snow water has fairly started to come down, fishing is absolutely at an end ; in smaller rivers such as the Poonch and Siran, fishing may still be got in April and May. With these big rivers that flow 'neath the most mighty peaks in the Himalayas, the melting snows are a constant factor, but with such a river as the Poonch the accumulations of snow up above the head-waters are not vast, and often a bleak day or two, with cold wind, may check all melting for a short period. And then at nights with the temperature down to 30° Fahrenheit, the same occurs, and for a few hours next day the time depending on the distance of the angler from the hills, the river may be almost clear.

A fisherman, about whose skill there is no question, gives me the following notes :—

"To fish a still deep pool, in which one can see the fish, or which one knows by experience to hold them. Mount a spoon of about 1½ to 2 inches. This spoon should not be too bright, and should be made of very thin metal and semi-hogged. About 2 feet above it, put on such leads as may be required seeing the depth of water. Sling in your bait, and letting the leads sink almost to the bottom work your rod top round. The spoon being much lighter than the leads will sink much slower, and then the weight of the latter being dragged along the bottom, will cause the spoon to spin almost as well as if it was in a rapid. The two secrets are—to have sufficient weight to fish deep, and to have the spoon thin enough to ensure its spinning. To this end the mounts must be small and light. There is no doubt as to the success of this plan on occasions, but one must be prepared to lose a certain amount of tackle through the leads getting hung up."

"A tip for catching murral which I adopted with extraordinary success in the Bhatta river, a tributary of the Jumna. Fish in the deepest pools with a small natural bait, and leads, so that your lure sinks right to the bottom. Spin slowly."

The above is rather wonderful, and against all one's ordinary theories as regards the murral, who is so essentially a surface feeder as a rule.

HINTS, MEDICAL.

First Aids.—Now, the following few hints on this subject, I feel, call for but little apology for their insertion. On a fishing trip, especially in the Himalayas, one is often several marches from civilisation, and though accidents luckily are not of common occurrence, still they do occur. And it has been the author's misfortune to be present on three occasions (two of which ended fatally) on which a little medical skill or information would have been most welcome; therefore it is useful to have some knowledge, however small, to guide one on such occasions.

Snake-bites.—Immediately put tight ligature (see under Hæmorrhage), round limb above wound. Then cut out the bitten part with a sharp knife. Squeeze, and rub in well permanganate of potash. Give stimulants, not enough to inebriate, and allow patient to rest. It may be as well to remark here that while there is no objection to suction being applied to such a wound, if mouth is well washed out with antiseptics after, suction should never on any account be applied to wounds caused by bite of rabid animals. In latter case the poison is live, and no washing of mouth can make you safe, whereas the poison of snakes is what is known as dead poison.

Hæmorrhage.—Bleeding from small cuts is usually easily stopped by washing with cold water, and tying a pad over the place. If, however, a vein or artery is cut, the case is not so simple. Arterial blood is a bright red pulsating jet ; venous, a steady stream of darker colour. First lay sufferer on ground and raise limb in air to check circulation. Then try fastening a pad on wound, very often the blood tubes contract and the blood clotting ceases of itself to flow. This failing, apply a tourniquet above the wound. Take a handkerchief, fold up and tie loosely round limb ; insert a stick and twist till bleeding stops. Avoid stimulants. If wound in hand or lower forearm, it is useful to remember that a pad in fold of elbow, then forearm bent and tied by bandage, will generally stop flow of blood.

Fractures.—Nothing can be done with these except to bind the injured limb as loosely and comfortably as possible, and then get the sufferer to the nearest doctor as quickly as can be. The greatest care should be taken to avoid moving the limb more than necessary, as in this case a simple fracture may easily be converted into a compound one.

Concussion or head injuries.—Lay patient on back with head a trifle raised, and loosen clothing. Do not attempt to raise patient while unconscious.

Sunstroke.—Remove into shade and lay flat, loosen clothing and pour cold water on head and body. This, however, should not be continued too long.

Apoplexy.—Place in recumbent position, head slightly raised and loosen clothing. If head hot apply cold, but if extremities cold apply warmth. Keep patient still.

Dislocations.—Do not attempt to rectify these, best make patient as comfortable as possible and take straight to the nearest doctor.

If a single hook gets buried in the skin do not attempt to pull it out. Better not cut, but if possible push point through and cut off barb with pliers.

Drowning.—The treatment of the apparently drowned consists in the persistent use of artificial respiration, so long as any life remains. Before commencing movements mouth and nostrils should be freed from froth and water by holding head somewhat low, face downwards for a few seconds. Artificial respiration should then be immediately proceeded with. At the same time remove clothes and wrap up body as warmly as possible, use hot bottles or bricks if available to induce warmth. Also apply continued friction to extremities. Two points to note, do not press on stomach at all, and tongue must be kept out of mouth (if alone it might be necessary to pin it to chin, or bind it with string, so important is this). When patient can breathe, administer stimulants in moderation. To induce artificial respiration, place patient on back with a pillow under shoulders and by grasping the arms above elbow pull them upwards firmly and steadily till they meet above head (this is to draw breath into body). Keep in position 2 seconds. Then turn down arms and press them gently and firmly for 2 seconds against sides of chest (this to press air out from lungs). Pressure on breast will aid this. Repeat these measures alternately, deliberately, about fifteen times a minute, until a spontaneous effort to respire is perceived, upon which immediately stop, and proceed to produce warmth and induce circulation. Later, give stimulants in moderation and encourage sleep.

Since writing above, my attention has been drawn to the treatment mentioned below, which it seems is the latest method of restoring apparently drowned.

TREATMENT OF THE APPARENTLY DROWNED.

The two methods which, up to the present time, have been mostly used for performing artificial respiration on the apparently drowned, or on those suffering from the effects of suffocation by any noxious gases, have been those known as the Marshall Hall and the Sylvester methods, and through their use very many lives have been saved. The disadvantage in the case of both of them has been the labour involved. In the Sylvester method, with the patient in the supine position, the muscles would be relaxed, and the tongue very apt to fall back and block the entrance to the pharynx, while if any water had got into the air passages it would be less likely to escape, and would interfere with the proper entrance of the air. The same objection to the supine position obtains in a third method, the Howard, to a certain extent. The supine position is not maintained all through the treatment, however, in the Marshall Hall method, but the labour involved is very considerable, and a certain amount of room is required, which is not always available.

The method advocated by Professor Schafer, and now officially recognised by the police authorities, has two very great advantages. In the first place, the patient is laid in the prone position, thus obviating the danger of the tongue falling back and blocking up the pharynx, and at the same time helping in the escape of any water remaining in the lungs; and, secondly, far less labour is necessary. The whole procedure is exceedingly easy, and there is no risk of any injury to any of the internal organs, and it has this further advantage that no time need be lost after recovering the patient from the water while removing clothing.

The patient should be at once placed face downwards on the ground, with a folded coat, or rug, if obtainable, under the lower part of the chest, the arms extended in front, and the face slightly on one side, so as to keep the mouth clear. The operator should place himself athwart or on one side of the patient's body in a kneeling position, and facing his head; his hands should be placed flat over the lowest part of the back (on the lowest ribs), one on

FIRST POSITION OF THE OPERATOR.

each side, and the weight of the operator's body should be gradually thrown forward on to the hands, so as to produce firm pressure—which must not be violent—upon the patient's chest. In this way the air (and water if there is any) is driven out of the patient's lungs.

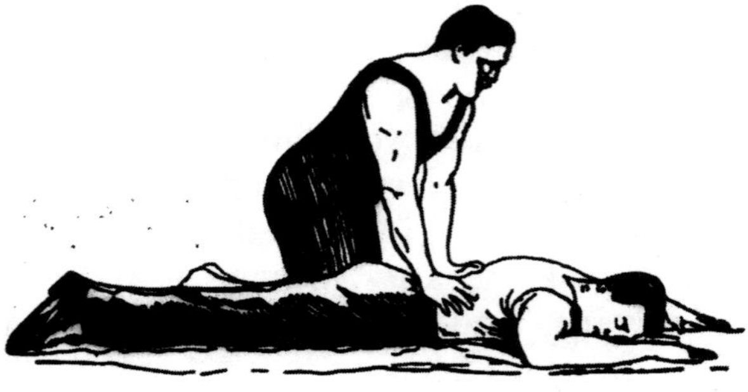

SECOND POSITION OF THE OPERATOR.

Immediately afterwards the operator's body is raised slowly, so as to remove the pressure, the hands being kept in the same position. This forward and backward movement (pressure and relaxation of pressure) has to be repeated every four seconds, fifteen times a minute, so as to approximate to the natural process of breathing.

These movements should be continued, according to Dr. Schafer's instructions, for at least half an hour, or until the natural respirations are resumed.

Among the advantages of this method of artificial respiration are that it can be carried out by one person, and that if any assistants are obtainable they can devote their time to the preparation of warm blankets and aids to the restoration of the circulation after respiration has been established. Professor *Schafer's method is, as already intimated, to be adopted by the* Metropolitan Police *in preference to the older methods now in use* and *also by the Royal Life Saving Society.*

Ammonia is an excellent remedy for bites, and stings, of scorpions, wasps, etc. Scrubbs' solution will do. Also a little rubbed on to mosquito bites allays the irritation at once.

For keeping off flies and mosquitoes, oil of lemon grass (or citronella) is good, also it has a pleasant smell. Another good solution is as follows :—Sweet oil 4½ oz., Oil Tar ½ oz. ; Oil Peppermint ½ oz., Kerosene oil ½ oz.

HINTS, VARIOUS.

Kerosene Oil.—It may be useful knowledge that one gallon of this should amply suffice for a Lord's lantern for over three weeks, burning it on an average three hours per night. As these lanterns use as much oil as perhaps any lamp that would be taken into camp, this would give any one a rough idea of how much oil to take on a trip. Your servants should say beforehand how much is required for their lantern, and this should be given them separately, otherwise they use yours *ad lib*, pouring it over their fire wood when latter is damp.

Flour.--About 1 lb. per head per day should be taken on a trip, this allows for a certain amount of waste. One small tin of baking powder per 7 lbs. of flour.

Sugar.—Depends so much on how fond of it your domestics are, most of them have a passion for it. If you carry 4 lbs. per week, assuming you take it in your tea, there will not be a very big surplus on your return.

Eggs.—Ten or 12 dozen can easily be carried packed in a box with bran and will see out a three weeks' trip, and longer, without going bad.

Muddy Water.—To clear, put in a pinch of powdered alum and leave for a short time, or stir for one minute with a lump of alum, then take out, and leave water to settle.

***Re* Tent Ropes.**—A hint to new-comers to this country. If it looks like rain see that the ropes are not too tight. If rain is heavy, they will tauten, and either the pegs will pull out, or the canvas tear.

A good idea is to have a shallow trench dug round the tent just under the eaves, this keeps the inside from getting flooded.

If you rise early and wish to lie down in the middle of the day, often the glare prevents one getting a sleep. It is a good tip to put a bit of black silk, a silk sock would do, over the eyes. It has a wonderfully restful effect.

Stockings.—Now, these if you are a patron of shorts and stockings, and do much wading in them, are liable to wear out very quickly, especially the feet portion. So possibly the following tip may be found of use, it is certainly economical. Cut off the top halves of each pair of stockings of which the feet are past darning, and having bought some ordinary Tommies' grey socks get these tacked on to the half stockings. Then whenever you wear out a pair of these, simply cut the tacking and have another pair fastened on. These socks are very cheap and wear well, their only fault is that they shrink tremendously after much wading, but the fact that the heel arrives in the middle of your instep, does not appear to produce any discomfort, curiously enough.

If you shoot a mugger or a gharial, the following is a good concoction if you want to keep the skin soft. I would add though that a saurian's skin does not go bad quickly like the skin of a tiger or deer. This is but natural. Wheatmeal—2 lbs.; Alum—1 lb.; Wood ashes—2 lbs.; Skimmed milk—4 quarts; Water—4 quarts. Make above into a paste and rub in morning and evening. The only skin worth removing is the underside, at least for making up into dressing cases, etc. I have seen quite a handsome rug however made of a mugger's skin.

Soldering.—There may be some who would like to solder their own mounts, rings, etc., but are deterred by the trouble of using a soldering iron. But there is a very good soldering paste now on the market by the name of Tinol. All that is necessary is to clean the parts to be soldered, then spread on some of the flux, and when heated a good joint is obtained. To heat use a small blow lamp. At home these can be bought very cheap, for one or two shillings one can be got quite good enough for this work.

N.B.—Tinol can be procured from G. Adams, High Holborn, London, from whom also a blow lamp suitable for use can be got for 1*s*. 3*d*.

For those who like to play about with tackle, chemicals, etc., I give the three following hints :—

Silverplating.—Without a battery. This may be useful to those who would like to try plating spoons, Devons, etc., and who are not great believers in Argentine cream and the like. Make a concentrated solution of chloride of zinc, dilute with equal volume of water. Place in plating vessel (copper or porcelain will do) and heat to boiling point. Now add sulphate of nickel till solution is green ; also a few fragments of zinc and a teaspoonful of powdered zinc. Boil articles to be plated in this for 20 minutes. Then burnish in usual manner.

To remove rust.—The following hint may be useful to shikaris of any genus, and also to such as are motorists. Make a solution of one part sulphuric acid to ten parts water. Hold rusted article in this for a short time. Then remove and dip into a bath of hot lime water, holding them there till they become so heated that they will dry immediately on being taken out. Then rub with some dry bran and rust should have completely disappeared.

To blue steel.—If the above treatment has removed the colour, or if as a preventive of rust it is desired to blue any steel article, the following hint will be useful. Immerse in the following liquid and then let dry: One part water to 20 parts hypo-sulphide of soda. Action is almost immediate.

And before closing this chapter, I should like to repeat what I wrote in "The Mighty Mahseer" anent the marking of fish, for there is no doubt that if a few keen anglers would do it, especially at such places as Tangrot, many interesting facts might come to light, and our knowledge of the mahseer be increased considerably.

"And a few words as to marking fish: this is much done at home, and if only a few more sportsmen would try it out here some interesting data might eventually be obtained about mahseer and other Indian fish, which would add very materially to the general knowledge on the subject. Of course out here the enormous size and length of rivers, the few English anglers, and the great number of Aryan brothers who fish by fair means and foul, are all considerations, and would probably mean that not 1 in 500 (and that is taking a sanguine view of the case) would ever be re-caught, by any intelligent observer. Still one here and there might be so caught, and every little helps in the way of information on such a subject. Anyhow, this might well be tried in tanks, especially where they are more or less private and preserved from netting by natives, and here data might fairly easily be collected concerning rohu, labeo, murral, wallago attu, megalops, and other such fish. By the courtesy of the Angling Editor of *The Field*, and the Secretary to the Fishery Board of Scotland, I was enabled to get some plates made up similar to those in use at home, and am trying them out here. So might I make an appeal to readers: should any one catch a marked fish (bearing one of my plates) would they kindly note the following particulars for communication to me. Also, if possible, they might once more return the fish to the water. (1) Species. (2) Where caught. (3) Weight. (4) Length, tip of nose to centre of fork in tail-fin. (5) Girth, by a tape passed round body just in front of dorsal fin.

The plates, either silver or brass, are marked with L and a number (*i.e.*, L 1, L 16), and are fastened to base of dorsal fin. In England silver plates are used, this being done as other metals would corrode from the action of the salt water when the salmon migrated to the sea. In India, however, there is no danger of this latter with the mahseer; any way personally I am experimenting with both brass and silver. The plate is as per diagram, and is fastened by the wires being driven through the base of dorsal fin, then twisted together and ends cut off.

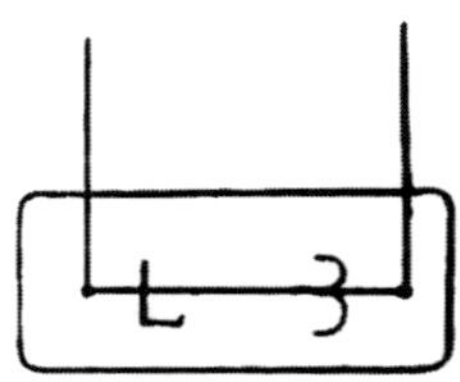

I may here remark, *en passant*, that it is no easy job to mark a fish, on a real hot day by a rocky river. Two hints: First, play and land any fish to be marked as quick as possible.

Second, while marking, measuring, etc., occasionally hold fish in water right way up, and do not let them turn on their sides, or belly up. Particularly do this when you have finished marking them, and see that the fish is pretty strong before leaving go of him."

Now, since writing the above, I have marked a good many fish, but so far with no result I regret to say. I have placed marked fish in the following rivers:—Cauvery, Pykara (near Ootacamund), Kalanadi (Canara), and Nerbudda, also in Bircha Lake near Mhow. If other anglers would try marking a few fish, each with their own distinctive plates, I am sure that the courteous Editors of the *Asian* and the *Indian Field* would willingly lend their columns to record any captures, and thus keep anglers in touch with each other.

CHAPTER IV.

LOCALITIES.

The Indus River.—Rises in Thibet, behind the great mountain wall of the Himalayas, and springs from the sacred mount of Kailas, 22,000 feet high. It is an enormous river, and runs 812 miles, before it enters the N.-W. Frontier Province. The chief features of interest in this portion lie in the immense gorges by which it breaks through the Western Himalayas. Near Skardu in Baltistan, the descent is said to be 14,000 feet sheer. Almost opposite Attock, it receives the waters of the Kabul river, a stream nearly as big as itself, and when both rivers are in flood, the junction is a magnificent sight. It is a river much given to sudden floods and freshets, in one of the biggest of which, 1858, it is recorded that the river rose 90 feet in a few hours, carrying away a part of Nowshera cantonment. Its total length is about 1,800 miles. Its delta is enormous, covering over 3,000 miles, and occupying 125 miles of coast line. It must not be forgotten that the Indus receives the waters of the Panjnad, *i.e.*, the united river formed by the joining of the waters of the five rivers of the Punjab, the Sutlej, Beas, Ravi, Chenab and Jhelum.

THE KABUL AND INDUS RIVERS.

By Bt.-Col. W. Norman, 22nd Cavalry.

THE KABUL RIVER.

This rises in the mountains some 45 miles west of Kabul, and just below the latter place takes in the Logar river. The main stream, then passing through open country for some 16 miles, enters the Tangi Garu Gorge, and at about two miles further on there is a magnificent waterfall, fully 100 feet in depth, where the whole stream careers over through one narrow channel. This fall is called the Mahi Par or place where "fish leap." From here the river flows through a series of rapids and gorges, till some twelve miles above Jalalabad it forces its way into the plain through the Darunta Gorge. Hence it widens out and continues in deep pools and rapids past Jalalabad, Girdi Kats to Dakka where it again enters a gorge and passing through the Mohmand Hills enters the Peshawar valley at Warsak, above Michni, and then after taking in the Swat river at Nisatha eventually joins the Indus at Attock.

Nothing is known as to its fishing capabilities above Michni, but the sight of the river about Girdi Kats is enough to make an angler's mouth water. Unfortunately, at the time I saw the river it was intensely cold and somehow I never took up a rod with me. To fish in the Afghan portion of the river will not be given to many, but it is as well to know that there is good water, and to be prepared to fish it.

From Peshawar as a centre there is very fair fishing obtainable when the river is clear, but unfortunately this is seldom the case. The river runs in several branches of which the principal, starting from Peshawar, are the Shah Alam, Naguman and the main stream. The best road to take is that leading to Charsadda. Riding or driving along this, reach the

Shah Alam at eight miles, the Naguman at nine and a half miles and the main stream at sixteen miles. There is good fishing at each place where the road crosses the stream. There must be big fish in the river, but it is seldom any above 10 lbs. are caught. The river is really very little known, this is probably due to the fact that it is somewhat disappointing to find it so constantly dirty. Given favourable weather and clear water, it would be worth while to take a boat at Michni and reconnoitre the river as far as the Charsadda crossings.

THE INDUS.

The Siran enters the Indus at Torbela and the junction looks a capital place, but I was there only once and then the river ran in red flood and I was unable to get even a bite, but according to "The Angler's Handbook" there is splendid fishing to be got. So far as I know it is never fished now, but should be easily accessible from Nowshera and the new cavalry cantonment at Mardan Road. The way to go would be by road, while the return journey might be by boat to Attock. At the latter place the Kabul river enters the Indus. There is good fishing above the junction, at the junction itself, and below the railway bridge. Nizampur and Dooga are other places in the vicinity. Besides the mahseer a kind of Salmon-trout called Pooa is taken; these run fairly large, I heard of one of 16 lbs. having been caught. It is not uncommon to take mahseer from 15 to 25 lbs.

Khushalgarh, some 30 miles from Kohat, is a favourite fishing place for the garrison at the latter place. Prior to the construction of the railway it used to be the custom to write to the Darogha at the bridge of boats for information as to when the water was clear and the chilwa running, but this useful official has probably now disappeared.

Another place is Shadipur, some fifteen miles above Khushalgarh. Here there is a village with supplies. The plan is to take a boat from Khushalgarh and fish up and down between that place and Shadipur. The boat should be of sufficient size to carry camp kit and servants, then one can fish and camp anywhere.

The best time of the year is March, when the chilwa are running. All fishing is by spinning chilwa or spoon, not by trolling. You locate the mahseer as they feed on the chilwa and then warily stalk him.

I have never heard of anyone systematically fishing the river from Attock down to Khushalgarh, but this is distinctly a thing to do if time can be spared. At Attock, boats can be easily arranged for to carry tents, servants, etc. The trip would include, besides the above places, fishing at the junction of the Hurroo and there are probably other places, virgin spots hitherto not known.

FISHING ROUND KOHAT.

The Kohat Toi rises near Hangu and there is a little fishing at Raisan, seventeen miles up the line, but it is not worth much unless combined with shooting. At Dodah, some twelve miles down the river, there is a very nice little rest-house complete with crockery, etc. Here some good fun can be got at times with a small fly-spoon. I have heard of a six-pounder being caught, but usually nothing bigger than two pounds comes to hand. In all probability there are better pools some distance below Dodah, and the natives declare this is the case, but I do not know of them myself.

THE KURRAM.

By Bt.-Col. Norman, 22nd Cavalry.

This rises in the mountains beyond Parachinar and flows down what is known as the Kurram valley to a point just below Thal. Here the river enters a gorge in the Waziri hills, and again enters British territory at the Kurram post, about five miles from Bannu. From the latter place the river flows on till it eventually joins the Indus. The gorge in the Waziri hills being transborder and hence not fishable, the river is practically divided into two portions, that above Thal, and that below the Kurram post.

There is capital fishing in the upper portion, though much destroyed of late years during the construction of the road up the valley. From Parchinar to Sadda fish up to three and four lbs. can be taken. Below Sadda the best fishing is from Mandori to Thal, here fish up to six and eight lbs. can be taken. In old days much bigger fish used to be taken, but there can be no doubt that road contractors and others dynamited the pools, and once this has been done to a river it seldom recovers its former fishing capabilities. Thal is connected with Kohat by railway, and Mandori is some twelve miles up the Parchinar road. In regard to poaching, it should be a standing order of the Thal post that this be prohibited. A little thought given to fish preservation would do much, but now and then a regiment turns up the sepoys of which run riot with casting nets and blankets.

Turning now to Bannu the fishing is poor as a rule, though there are some good pools. I have seen mahseer up to 20 lbs. brought into cantonments for sale but these were taken by nets in the gorge above the Kurram post; they do not come down to Bannu, probably because they prefer the rocky pools in the gorge. Still some fun can be got out of the stream below the Kurram post if one will be content with fish up to two and three pounds with the possibility of a larger one on exceptional occasions.

FISHING IN WAZIRISTAN.

There are a number of small streams in Waziristan, but two only are along routes held by our troops or militia. These are the Tochi and Zam. The fishing in both is practically the same, with small fly-spoon, atta and now and then with fly. The fish average one to two pounds, though now and then some just over three pounds are taken.

Swat and Panjkora rivers.—Very fair mahseer fishing is to be had in both these streams, and the fish run big. The snow trout begin to run up in October, when the mahseer fishing goes off. Spin with natural bait and use atta. Good fishing is to be had near Chakdarra on the march into Chitral. When the river is in flood, try live and dead bait picketting of the mouths of small tributaries, the mahseer run from 2 to 50 lbs., big ones predominating. The

Swat river is very strong and one is liable to get hung up a lot. The snow trout will take spoon up here, and run to 12 and 15 lbs., they do not give much play however.

There is fishing to be had at all the following stages on the march into Chitral, Sado, Robat, Warai, Darora, all on Panjkora river, mahseer and snow trout. At Dir, fish (snow trout) are fairly numerous, to be caught with worm. At Drosh on the Chitral river, there are small mahseer, though in other parts of the river they run big. Snow trout are to be caught up to six pounds in Sut Koh stream, fifteen miles from Chitral. A correspondent sends me the following :—

"Fishing in Chitral.—The best time is from the middle of March to the beginning of May, *e.g.*, when the water is not too dirty, and again about the end of September to beginning of November. Worm is the bait used; fish won't look at a spoon. The fish (snow trout) run up to about five pounds and are caught as a rule near the junctions of small streams with the Chitral river. The side streams, Turico river for instance, holds fish when the water gets very dirty, and in May this year about 200 lbs. of fish were caught in ten days, largest being about five pounds.

In the winter when the river is clear as a rule fish don't take at all, and apparently run down stream.

The best rod is a ten-foot one, with light tackle and a small hook."

A correspondent sends me the following additional information concerning the Swat river near Chakdarra :—

"Mahseer have been caught from March the 1st, till October the 31st, but the months of April and May are best. The fish run up to 40 lbs., but mostly from 10 to 20. The baits used are spoon and dead bait. A small black fish with a large head (Ophiocephalus Gachua) was found to take best, but chilwa or any silvery fish would do. Personally, I prefer gut traces and all silver spoons, and caught nearly all my fish with that tackle, but other men used Killin wire. Mahseer were also caught with atta. Snow trout were caught all the year round with spoon. The water a mile above and below Chakdarra used to be preserved. I should not call the Swat a very good river, and I think it was because we did nothing else but fish, living as we did right on the river, that we were fairly successful."

NOTES ON FISHING IN THE SWAT RIVER.

By Captain H. C. Kay, 8th Cavalry.

"The Spring fishing is much better than the Autumn fishing. Dead bait is the thing to use, and the best you can use is the Ophiocephalus Gachua, which looks like a diminutive murral, and can be caught in a net in any of the small tributaries such as the Chakdarra stream. It is very strong and lasts a long time on the hook. Pickle some in formalin and they will last for years, and are equally good as the fresh bait. As there are many small streams running into the main river, and this bait abounds in all, it follows that the mahseer are generally on the look out for them at the junctions, but they are killing bait anywhere in the Swat river. Spoon is not much good, unless when the water is very thick then use a 3 or 4-inch one. The following are the best sites :—

(i) The pool immediately above the Fort along the right bank, this is about the best spot in the river. Throw well out ; when the water is very clear the fish seem to stay in centre of pool, and a very long cast is required.

(ii) A good run which often holds a fish is just below bridge on right bank.

(iii) Under the bridge on left bank, a pool which always holds mahseer. Good place for atta fishing.

(iv) About 100 yards above this, cast out into junction, and the bait if well leaded will swing round to a deep hole, where mahseer lie well. Have caught all my best fish in the river here, and have been broken several times.

(v) About 100 yards below the bridge a small streamlet flows in from the fields. Here mahseer often lie.

(vi) On right bank, the junction of the Chakdarra stream, a very good casting place. Throw from up stream into junction, and as there is generally a good depth of water, you may expect fish of any size.

(vii) Not many good places up stream, though there are several small junctions; however, the fish are netted regularly and it is not worth making a pilgrimage far up. I have been five miles up stream and did no good.

(viii) Half a mile down stream from the Fort there is a good pool, best place, a strong swirl round a large rock, often a big fish here. Remainder of pool disappointing, though it looks excellent.

(ix) Down stream about two miles, just near where the river runs at the foot of some cliffs on right bank. A very good junction. Here large mahseer are often to be seen after the fry. If before casting you go up on the cliff, you can see what fish are moving. Cast from the centre spit of shingle into the junction, not from the shore where you can't reach the right place.

(x) About one and a half miles below this there is a deep pool under the cliff where, early morning and evening, monster mahseer can be seen near the surface. I have never heard yet of one of them being caught, though I and others have tried many times with every kind of device.

(xi) Khar junction, about two miles from Khar village, which is four miles from Chakdarra. One of the best places on the river. Very big fish have been caught here about three-quarter mile up stream, just below some large rocks on left bank. Fish from rock, but keep out of sight, a favourite place.

(xii) On right bank, nearly opposite this is a deep fast running pool; fish from rock which juts out, with a 6 to 8 oz. lead. Hold hard if you get into one here, the water is extremely heavy immediately below this.

(xiii) About one mile below Khar junction, another small junction.

(xiv) Below this point I have not done much good, though I have been four or five miles down stream on each bank, but had very little luck. Chief points to remember when fishing the Swat river are: weight your trace sufficiently to keep the bait about one and a half feet from the bottom, and the water usually being very

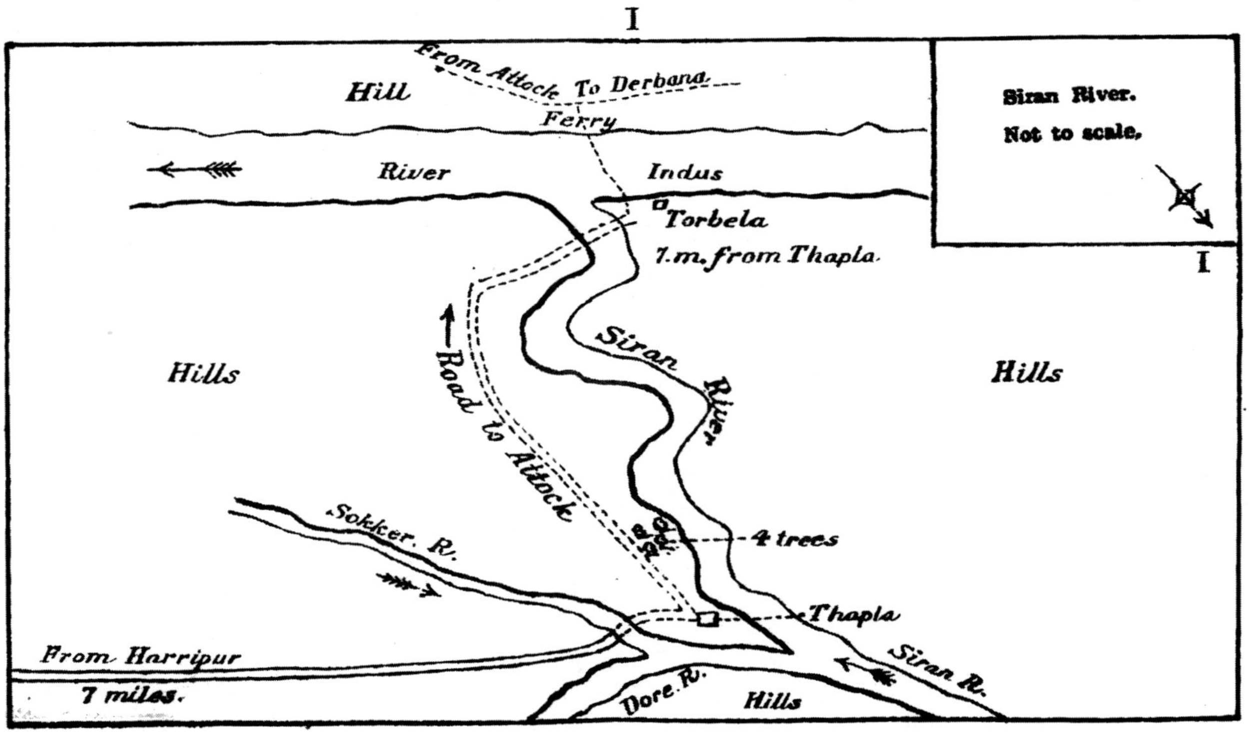
Siran River.
Not to scale.
From Attock To Derbana
Hill
Ferry
River
Indus
Torbela
7.m. from Thapla
Siran River
Hills
Hills
Road to Attock
Sokker. R.
4 trees
Thapla
From Harripur
7 miles.
Dore R.
Hills
Siran R.

clear, you must fish very fine. For dead bait one small treble only, up the vent. Spoon has very little success on this river."

The Siran River.—There are two points from which this river can be reached. First Hassan Abdal station, drive 20 miles to Harripur, the half way halting place for tongas on the way to Abbottabad. There is a nice dâk bungalow here, well furnished, with a khansama who will cater for you. From Harripur drive to Thapla village, seven miles, in a tum-tum, charge Rs. 3 per day. For first six miles the road is metalled, then comes the crossing over the Sokker Nadi, across which there is no pretence at a road. Walk this bit. The place to begin fishing is either at the junction of the Dore and Siran rivers, or go about three-quarters of a mile beyond Thapla to where four trees stand on river bank, near a small ruined cemetery. There are two A-1 pools just below this. From here right down to the junction with the Indus, all the water is good. The road, a species of hill track, driveable, starts again at Thapla and follows the river five miles to Torbela, a small town on the left bank of the Indus, crossing the Siran, a little before the bigger river is reached. A ferry here crosses the Indus, on the opposite bank, the road dividing, the north branch running to Derband and south to Attock. Fly-spoon and natural bait both seem successful, and I have a note of a one pound mahseer caught on a blackamoor fly. One must wade to fish properly; in a normal year the river can be waded without difficulty at intervals. The Siran is affected by snow water, but not badly. April and May are the best months, and then September and October, though I had fair sport when I visited the river in June. May and June, however, are very hot. The junction of the Siran with the Indus should be fished, *vide* the bag made by General Dandridge in 1887, noted in "The Angler's Handbook." I had not leisure to visit Torbela myself, nor was I very successful in gathering any definite *khabar* about the place.

The second spot on the Siran to make for is Sheri Shah village, 22 miles from Abbottabad. The road goes *viâ* Gadda 13 miles, and is nothing but a rough stony track, barely rideable in places. It is all up and down across the mountains, rising at one spot to over 6,000 feet. Some fine views of the snows are to be had, and once or twice a distant silver streak betokens the Indus. The only place to pitch a tent is in the bed of river, which is about one-quarter of a mile across here, opposite to Sheri Shah village. The Mangal stream runs in here. The heat in May and June is something terrific, and a visit to the river is not recommended at this time of year. There is lot of very good water, and I fancy one could fish all down to Thapla, but there were signs that the river is very badly poached here; I saw one man with a net who dissappeared as if by magic, also a boy with a string of small snow trout in his hand.

The Kalapani Stream near Abbottabad has been stocked by the Goorkha officers of the station with English trout (Fario). They

II

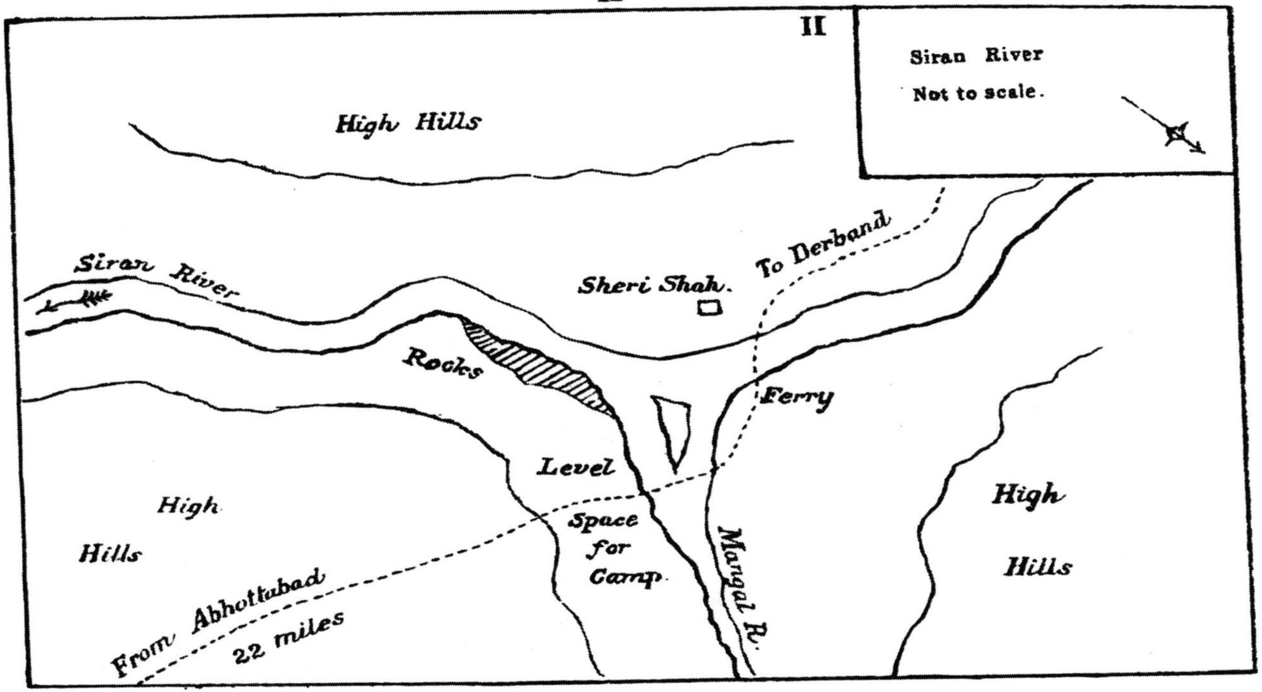
II
Siran River
Not to scale.
High Hills
Siran River
Sheri Shah.
To Derband
Rocks
Ferry
Level
Space
for
Camp.
Mangal R.
High
Hills
High
Hills
From Abhottabad
22 miles

were first put as fry into a tank near Abbottabad in 1895; and in 1896, 356 yearlings were turned out into the stream. Thanks to the untiring energy, backed with the requisite knowledge, of Lieutenant-Colonel Kemball of 5th Goorkhas, the trout have done well the last few years, and of the fact that they have bred freely there is no manner of doubt. It is just possible that the extraordinarily heavy rains of 1908 may have done some harm, but it is to be hoped not. In the hot weather of 1908 the stream was abnormally low and there were few big fish to be seen, probably these had taken refuge in deep holes, and were not to be tempted to feed during the day. But fish of up to three-quarters of a pound were fairly plentiful, and rose well to the fly, fighting most gamely when hooked. The Kalapani is a small mountain torrent, rising under Thandiani, 9,000 feet, the summer hill station of Abbottabad, and falling into the Dore river, under the Abbottabad-Murree road. The best fishing is from the Kalapani staging bungalow down to where the road from Abbottabad first approaches the stream. Above the bridge, near bungalow, a tributary the Safedpani runs in, and the fish work a short way up this also. Higher up lie the spawning beds. To reach the stream, drive 4 miles to Newershahr on the Gali's road, after this one must ride or walk up the Thandiani road. The staging bungalow is at the tenth milestone from Abbottabad, and possesses a khansama who can provide meals at short notice. Below the fishable portion of the Club water, snow trout are to be caught, but the stream here falls so rapidly that it is almost impossible to follow its course down. It could be fished up from the Gali's road, but the bag would not repay the labour. Since writing the above, I hear that the Club have successfully imported 3,000 ova this year, from Cashmere. One sincerely hopes that the fry will hatch out satisfactorily.

The Dore River, which is crossed near Sultanpur, on Hassan Abdal-Abbottabad road by a big bridge, and again on Abbottabad-Dungagali road by a second bridge, is simply one continuous shallow rapid, and holds, I fancy, practically no fish.

NOTES ON THE FISHING ROUND RAWALPINDI IN THE RIVERS SOHAN, KORUNG AND CHIBLAT.

By C. Boyce, Esq., S. and T.

"The rivers near Rawalpindi are the Sohan and Korung, the nearest points on each river being about five miles distant from cantonments; then there is the Chiblat near Hassan Abdal Railway Station, 30 miles from Pindi on the main line to Peshawar.

I would here like to point out to any one intending to fish any of the above rivers, that they are preserved by the North Punjab Fishing Club whose head-quarters are at Rawalpindi; the subscription to the Club is only Rs. 16 per annum, and anyone fishing these rivers should feel it a duty to send the subscription to the Honorary Secretary, care of the Rawalpindi Club, who will forward maps, etc.

The Sohan.—The nearest point to cantonments is five miles down the Jhelum road where the Grand Trunk Road crosses the river; from here right down to Moorga, the river is a

III

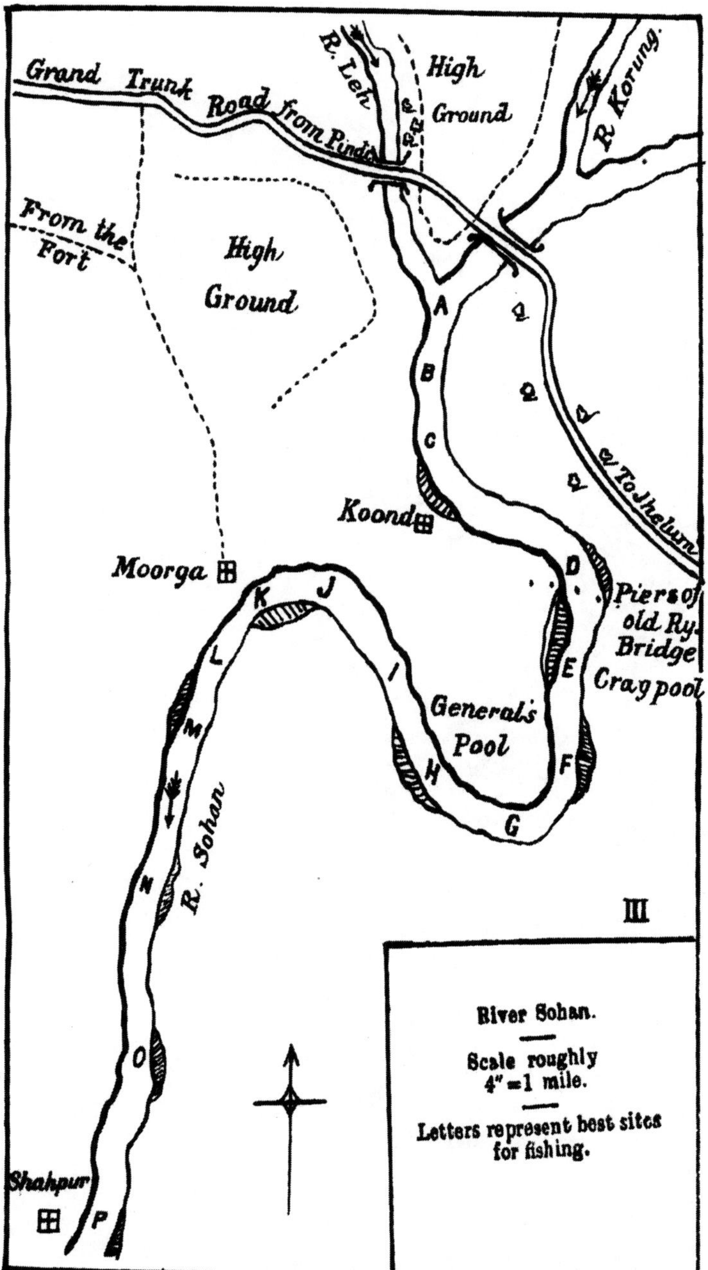
Grand Trunk Road from Pindi
R. Leh
High Ground
R. Korung
From the Fort
High Ground
A
B
C
Koond
Q
To Jhelum
Moorga
K
J
D
Piers of old Ry. Bridge
L
E
Crag pool
I
General's Pool
M
H
F
G
R. Sohan
N
III
River Sohan.
Scale roughly 4" = 1 mile.
Letters represent best sites for fishing.
O
Shahpur
P

IV

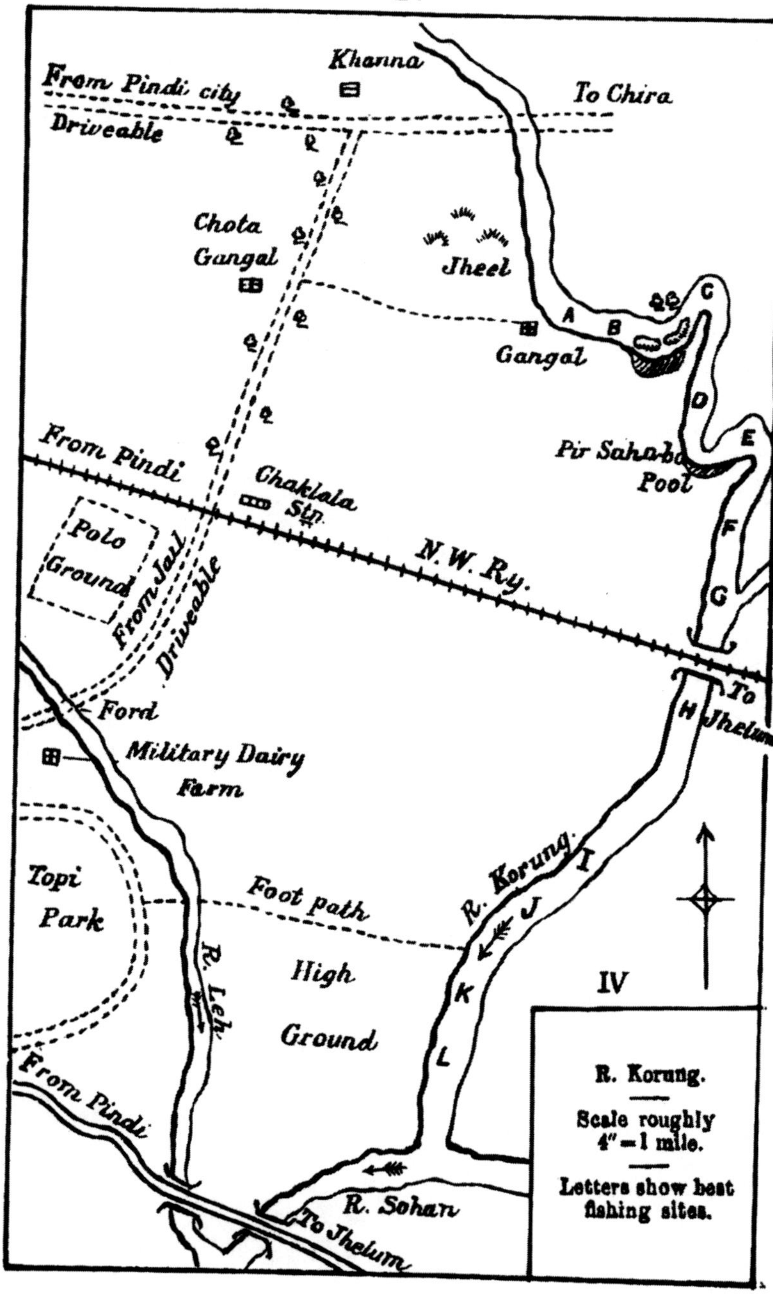
Khanna
From Pindi city
Driveable
To Chira
Chota
Gangal
Jheel
Gangal
A
B
C
D
E
Pir Sahab
Pool
From Pindi
Chaklala
Stn.
Polo
Ground
From Jail
Driveable
N. W. Ry.
F
G
To
Jhelum
H
Ford
Military Dairy
Farm
R. Korung
I
J
Topi
Park
Foot path
R. Leh
High
Ground
K
L
IV
From Pindi
R. Sohan
To Jhelum
R. Korung.
Scale roughly
4" = 1 mile.
Letters show best
fishing sites.

series of runs and pools and fishable all the way. There is a large pool immediately below the old Railway bridge piers, which holds enormous fish but they are seldom caught. I have three times taken fish of over 10 lbs. from it and in April 1908 one of 16 lbs. There is a Club boat kept near this pool at the village of Koond, and if any one cares for it, there are several pools large enough to troll in. Lower down the river at Moorga, one must troll and there is another boat kept here. Unfortunately, the water of the Sohan seems to take a very long time to clear and a very little rain or a duststorm makes the river quite unfishable; this is, I think chiefly the reason that the fishing here is run down.

The baits I recommend for the Sohan are, for trolling a one inch or one and a half inch silver and brass spoon, or a two inch brass Devon Minnow; and for fishing from the bank a three-quarter inch all gold fly-spoon, or best of all a small natural bait, this latter is deadly, particularly late on a hot weather evening when I have sometimes taken fish of over 10 lbs. The morning up to midday, and then from 5 P.M. till dark, seem to be the best times for the Sohan. I have often fished during the early afternoon but never did much until it was nearly sunset.

The Korung.—This is, in my opinion, the best of the rivers near Rawalpindi; the fish seem to take the bait better than in the Sohan, they will often take the artificial fly well and sometimes ravenously, and one occasionally gets quite a heavy fish.

The highest point on this river where I have fished is in the Rawal pool eight miles along the Murree road and the river is 100 yards to the right of the road. At the upper end of the pool above the dam the fish take a small Coachman very well, and although the average weight will be under half a pound one can get 20 or more fish in a day, with here and there a one-pounder among them; then below the dam good fish can be killed on parched Indian corn—a handful is thrown in to attract the fish and then a single grain threaded on a bare hook is thrown in among the feeding fish, much as a fly is cast. The best fish I got in this way was 4½ lbs., but I have heard of much larger ones being taken.

The next point where the river is fishable is from just below Khanna village, five miles from Rawalpindi. This can be reached by driving or riding along the Murree road to the Parsee Cemetery, and then branching off to the right, one can drive right up to Khanna; another and shorter way is to go past the Jail and Military Dairy, fording the Leh, across the railway crossing and on to Chota Gangal: from here the fishing is only half a mile distant, and the total distance from the Club is only four miles, it is possible to drive but the road is rough.

The reach from A to B on the map occasionally affords splendid fishing with the artificial fly. The fish average one pound, but on the 16th May 1908 I took 31 fish weighing 104 lbs. here, all on the artificial fly; my next best day was 30 fish weighing 37 lbs., but these were exceptional days and I have never approached these bags since. In the spring of 1908 this reach fished very badly, partly owing to dirty water, and I did not get a decent bag but took one nice fish of 5¼ lbs. on a Jock Scott in March. If the fish are on the feed they seem to take the two following flies as well as anything—(*a*) Jock Scott on No. 8 Limerick hook, (*b*) Grey Drake on No. 10 Limerick hook. The larger fish, *i.e.*, from three pounds to five pounds take the first named fly best : the largest fish taken by me from this reach was 5¾ lbs. and was caught on the first named fly in May 1908.

Below this bit of the river the spinning bait is a better lure than the fly ; however, it is occasionally worth while trying the fly, specially in the morning about 9 A.M. In May 1908, I got a fish of 7½ lbs. in the Pir Sohaba Pool on a Durham Ranger (grilse size). After the monsoon, when the river first clears, is the very best time for the Korung, and the best bait is a small chilwa mounted on Lacy's spinning tackle. The best way to make this is as follows : take a small double ringed treble hook, a No. 1 Limerick-eyed single hook and a length of gut, tie one end of the gut to the single hook, pass the other end through the lower eye of the treble, take two turns round the shank and pass through upper eye, the end of the gut is made fast to the trace. The method of baiting is to pass the single hook through the mouth of the bait and out of the gill and embed it firmly through the tail ; the treble hook is then manipulated down the snood to give the bait a curve and one of its hooks passed through both lips of the bait. This is a very simple flight and very effective in hooking a fish as well as spinning the bait ; another great advantage is that the snood need not be detached from the trace to re-bait and no baiting needle is necessary.

The Korung is fishable from the village of Gangal right down to its junction with the Sohan; and although the general run of fish taken will be under four pounds, one occasionally gets into a fish of over four pounds, particularly when spinning a chilwa late in the evening, and as the riverbed is all rocky ledges I recommend the use of traces made of Killin wire. From below the Railway bridge the pools cannot be commanded from the bank, and it is advisable to bring up the Club boat from Koond and troll with a one inch spoon. In the late hot weather when the river is very low and clear, the spinning bait is not of much use during the heat of the day, but fish will then take parched Indian corn well and one occasionally gets a good fish.

The Chilbat.—The nearest point to fish is under a mile from Hassan Abdal Railway Station, 30 miles from Pindi; from this point to its junction with the Hurroo the river is fishable all the way, the distance being about four miles. The junction itself does not appear to be worth fishing, at least I have never heard of anyone doing any good there.

The best bait for this river I found to be a one inch or one and a half inch brass Devon minnow and a chilwa late in the evening; with the latter bait one is certain to run a good fish about 7 P.M. if the water is in good order. Parched Indian corn and bits of melon are also good baits for this river, I am told, but I do not speak from actual experience.

The Chiblat is a disappointing river, as although it holds quantities of fish, they sometimes go off the feed in the most aggravating

V

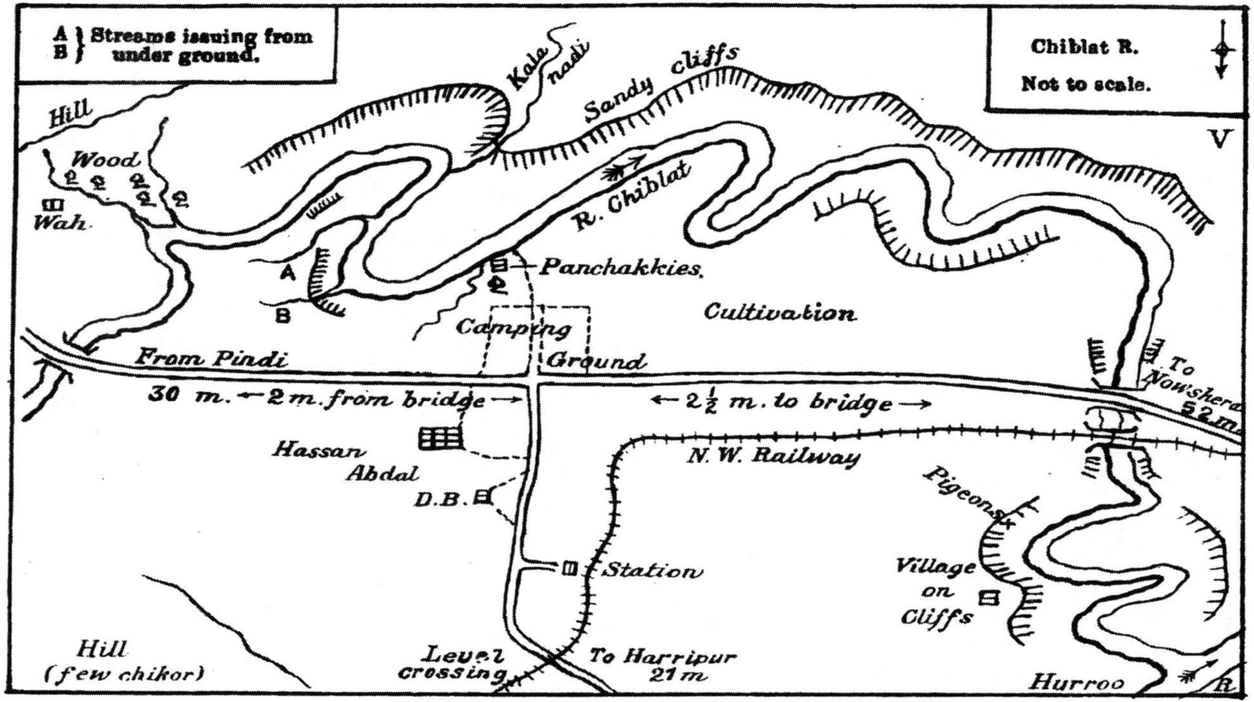
A } Streams issuing from
B } under ground.
Chiblat R.
Not to scale.
V
Hill
Wood
Wah
Kale nadi
Sandy cliffs
R. Chiblat
A
B
Panchakkies.
Cultivation
Camping Ground
From Pindi
To Nowshera 52 m
30 m. ← 2 m. from bridge →
← 2½ m. to bridge →
N. W. Railway
Hassan Abdal
D.B.
Pigeons
Station
Village on Cliffs
Hill (few chikor)
Level crossing
To Harripur 21 m
Hurroo
R

way. I have noticed this more in the Chiblat than in any other Indian river, in most of which the fish will take, though perhaps not well, if the water is in order.

For any of the above rivers a rather stiff twelve foot fly rod is sufficient, but I would recommend 100 yards of line, which on a three inch aluminium reel weighs very little, as one may at any time find one's self into a game fish of over 10 lbs., which it would be a pity to lose through want of a little more line."

The Hurroo river rises in the Murree hills, and is crossed by ford between Hassan Abdal and Abbottabad. It has a broad shingly bed here, and its only claim to notice is the great inconvenience to which it puts tonga passengers between the above named places, whenever it chooses to be in flood. There is no fishing to be had in the river till below Hassan Abdal, where the Chiblat joins it, and then it only really becomes a river by courtesy of the latter stream, which, except in the monsoon, supplies practically all the water there is. Below the junction for two or three miles, there are some excellent pools and runs. Also the natives say that there is good fishing at the junction of the Hurroo with the Indus.

The Chiblat river rises north of Janiki-Sang, and joins the Hurroo river south of Hassan Abdal. It is a wonderful little river for its size and length, and holds quite good fish. It is largely fed by underground springs, which well up as fully fledged streams, and pour sudden volumes of water into the river at unexpected places. Two of these there are, just north of the Panchakkies by the camping ground, at Hassan Abdàl, and it behoves one to walk carefully on the cliffs here, as there are a couple of open shafts, at the bottom of which can be heard the running waters of these underground tributaries. The higher waters of the Chiblat run just below the bungalow at Jani-ki-Sang, the half way camp between Pindi and Hassan Abdal, and here can be had quite pretty sport with fly using a small rod and very light tackle, soon after the rains, catching mahseer up to half pound in weight. Just after the monsoon the stream seems to be full of fish. My own experience of the Chiblat is limited to only a few days' fishing in September, and this should be borne in mind, when reading the following notes, as the stream probably fishes very differently in the hot weather. The Chiblat is an exceedingly pretty little river, twisting and winding over a shingly bed among yellow sand cliffs, the banks in places being lined with reeds. The best place to fish it from is Hassan Abdal, two or three stations beyond Pindi on the line to Peshawar. By the Grand Trunk Road it lies 30 miles from the former cantonment, and with the aid of a motor a very pleasant day's picnic could be made to the river. There is a nice dâk bungalow at Hassan Abdal, between the station and the Grand Trunk Road, and within half a mile of the river. The fishing begins at the first road bridge, two miles towards Pindi and is good for the whole six or seven miles down to the junction with the Hurroo river, which lies about one and a quarter miles below the second road, and railway bridges. Fly-spoon and fly seemed to meet with success, and I was told that melon seed was the lure to use towards the end of the hot weather. To bait with the latter. Take an unripe melon, and scoop out the seeds together with some of the pith. A piece of this about an inch long should be fixed on the hook, tying with thread if necessary, and the lure gently slung into the river. I believe fish of up to 20 lbs. have been caught in the Chiblat, though not recently; now-a-days they seem to run between one and six pounds with an occasional fish up to 10 lbs. The pool by the Panchakkies near camping ground is one of the best in the river, both the junctions of the two small streams being likely spots. Just below the second road bridge is a good pool, and below this again comes some broken water and an excellent rapid A little further down is a long deep pool, above which tower some high sand cliffs, where one can get some pretty sport shooting blue rocks. Below the first bridge is a lot of nice water, especially good if tried with fly, and half a mile down comes a splendid pool, where two small streams join from left bank. There are a lot of eels in the Chiblat, also I fancy there are kalabanse. The river is liable at times to temporary discolouration owing to numbers of buffalo and cattle being driven into the water. For this reason, very often the river is crystal clear below the upper bridge, whilst almost unfishable further down at the second bridge. After rain the Chiblat clears extraordinarily quickly.

The Leh river lies within easy reach of Pindi. Drive up past the Jail along the Khanna road till you reach the Military Dairy Farm Near by is the village of Topi. Below this are some falls, and from here right down to the junction with Sohan is all grand water that ought to hold any number of fish. It is nothing but great rocky pools and runs, some of the former deep and large enough to shelter fish of up to 100 lbs. But it struck me that the river was very destitute of life. Below the road bridge, some four miles from Pindi, and just above the Sohan junction, when the water is clear, large numbers of fish can be seen in the Leh, mostly kalabanse. Possibly the fact that the Leh helps to drain Pindi bazaar may have some bearing on the absence of respectable fish!

The Ling river is a small tributary of the Sohan, and is seen from the railway, on the right of the line as the train approaches Rawalpindi. It is best reached from Riwat, ten miles from Pindi, down the Grand Trunk road. From here it is about three miles across country, lying a short distance the further side of the railway. *En route* to it a small rocky stream is passed which holds quantities of fry. The Ling is hardly worth making a pilgrimage to, but to anyone on the march down the Grand Trunk Road, with nothing better to do, it might be worth the ride out for an afternoon's fishing. It is a pretty little stream, with occasional nice runs. I fished it one afternoon in September, with very indifferent success, though I saw one fish of about 10 lbs and moved one or two smaller ones. I was told however that about two miles down, at its junction with the Sohan, very fair fishing was to be had.

And only the other day a man told me that about ten miles up, there are some big pools in the Ling, which hold quite decent fish. This I presume would be where the Pindi to Kahoota road crosses the river.

NOTES ON FISHING IN THE SOHAN RIVER.

By Bt.-Col. W. Norman, 22nd Cavalry.

"It is not generally known that the Sohan can be reached from Murree with but little trouble, but to any one whose leave expires about 15th October it will be found a pleasant trip. The first march is some 20 miles to Kotli, where there is a good civil rest-house situated on a hill and surrounded by pine trees. The first four miles from Murree are along the Kashmir tonga road, after which there is a riding path through the woods to the right just beyond the first tonga stage and below Lower Topa. Thence through the woods to Kotli. At 10 miles from Murree is a place called Bani where there is a bania's hut, and where, if required, a suitable camping ground can be found. From Kotli it is about ten miles to Pihot where the Sohan is first reached. Here there is a shady camp. The next march is Chirah. The next Khangota or Sihala. At the latter place the N.-W. R. is struck, Sihala being a station on the line. From Chirah, Rawalpindi is sixteen miles distant. The river is fishable from Pihot with small fly-spoon as far as Chirah; there are some very fine pools, and they may hold larger fish; but I only got them myself up to four pounds. From Chirah downwards the fishing is excellent at times. About one or two miles below Chirah the river runs through a gorge, passing the old Ghakkar fort of Farwala. There are some splendid pools in the gorge especially near Farwala. One pool, in which I was not successful, was crowded with fish up to ten and fifteen lbs., and I believe there were two or three of nearly 20 lbs. Nearing this pool I saw a large tail fin cruising about in a shallow rapid. I cast forward but there was a swirl and nothing more Climbing over the rocks, after several fruitless attempts to entice the owner of the fin, I saw the pool below the rapid simply swarming with fish. From behind a rock I cast into the rapid and allowed my bait, a chilwa, to float down the pool. Time after time I repeated this and each time with the same hopeless result. As the bait entered the pool the fish simply bolted as if terror-struck. When I withdrew the bait they again moved up *en masse* to the head of the pool and lay like a flotilla of submarines, heads towards the rapid, only to bolt when the bait came down again. This is an example of what happens when one cannot see into a pool. Several of the pools had a weir trap at their lower ends where the shallows began. There is no doubt that the stream is badly poached, but there is also no doubt that it is well worth preserving being so near Rawalpindi."

The Jhelum river rises in a spring called Vernag, in Kashmir territory, where a pool of deep blue water wells from the bottom of a high scarp of a mountain spur. Fifteen miles from this uniting with three other streams it becomes navigable and continues so right down to Baramula, 102 miles. It receives many tributaries, the best known of which, in its higher waters, is the Liddar stream which comes down from the everlasting snows, overlaying the head of the Liddar valley and from the mountain lake of Tarsar. Below Baramula 5,000 feet, the placid Jhelum leaves the valley and rushes headlong down a deep gorge between lofty mountains of the Kazinag range on the north and the Pir Panjal on the south. At Kohala its bed is only 2,000 feet above sea-level.

NOTES ON FISHING IN KASHMIR.

Trout fishing.—The Dachigam (or Arrai) river affords very excellent sport, but as it is inside the limits of one of His Highness the Maharaja's Game Preserves, or Rukhs, a day's fishing can only be enjoyed by special permission, obtained at present from His Highness through the Home Minister. This permit will allow, under present regulations, the holder to fish for one day in the Rukh (eleven miles from Srinagar) with artificial bait only, and if no number of fish is specified on the permit, only one of a minimum limit of 16 inches may be killed, all the rest must be returned to the river. There are also various regulations, such as the angler not being allowed to take a Srinagar Manji or boatman into the Rukh, coolies being obtainable in the village of Harwan, where the Hatcheries are, just outside the borders of the Rukh. A Rukh guard has to go with the permit holder.

Other streams, not in game preserves, are however coming on (*vide* Fishing Rules—Trout waters), and a three and a half pound trout was killed this year in the Upper Veshoo. This promises to be a very good trout stream, as also the Achibal river, both of which can be reached comfortably in a day's march from Islamabad, 38 miles from Srinagar.

Fishing for trout in these waters, and also in those mentioned as Trout Waters in the regulations, is at present obtainable by license, Re. 1 per diem, or Rs. 10 for ten days or any number of days up to ten, *pro rata*. Full information of the rivers that are being stocked with trout, and which will be gradually opened for fishing, is contained in the accompanying Trout Report for 1908-09, and in the enclosed extract from the Jammu and Kashmir State Fisheries Regulations of March 1909, which, however, as stated, may be changed at any date.

Fish in Dachigam Rukh have been caught up to 7 and 8 lbs., and this year, 1909, two fish were supplied from the breeding tanks for a banquet given by His Highness in honour of the King-Emperor's birthday, weighing respectively 15 lbs. and 13 lbs.

Trout in Kashmir, except small ones, do not readily take the fly until August or July, in which months very pretty sport may be had. Up to these months Phantoms and Devons seem to succeed well; but a disgorger should always be ready at hand for fish that have to be returned to the water.

The Salmo Hoochen or Fresh Water Danube Salmon are only yearlings at present in the Hatcheries at Harwan, and their produce will not be ready for some years to come.

Mahseer.—The only place in the Kashmir Valley where mahseer fishing is at all reliable is from Ningal at the southern outlet of the Woolar Lake to Sopor Bridge. The best time of year is August, but the conditions as regards heat, flies and mosquitoes are most unpleasant. One requires to be a very keen fisherman to put up with all the discomforts.

Occasionally, however, mahseer run up and give good sport at Sambal and Shadipore, where the surroundings are much more enjoyable.

Gold Spoons (Luscombe pattern) are as good a bait as any, but dead bait, Phantoms, and Devons are all successful at times.

Chirroo and Choosh.—These indigenous fish are common throughout the rivers and streams in the valley, and at certain times and places they afford good sport. The Veshoo is the river most favoured by sportsmen, for there the Choosh take the fly freely in May and June. The Sind river, above Gunderbal, is another good locality for Chirroo, but as it is the chief spawning bed for these fish they are now protected during the months of May and June.

Fairly good sport, however, can be obtained in these reaches during July. During the mulberry season a good basket of Choosh, averaging about three to the pound may be caught under almost any mulberry tree on the main river and its tributaries.

Snow trout.—On the upper waters of the side streams the humble worm is the best bait for the snow trout which abound everywhere.

Licenses.—For all fish except the trout, licenses for which are mentioned elsewhere, a Rs. 5 license obtainable from the Agencies in Srinagar is necessary. Trout licenses and Special Licenses to fish for country fish in Trout Waters under Rule 4 of the Fishery Rules are obtainable from the office of the Secretary of the Game Preservation Department.

The following is reprinted here by kind permission of the Kashmir Authorities:—

EXTRACT FROM THE JAMMU AND KASHMIR STATE FISHERIES REGULATION.

Amended to Sambat 1966 under His Highness the Maharaja Sahib's Order No. 2870, dated 3rd March 1909.

Under the provisions of the Kashmir Fisheries Regulations, His Highness the Maharaja is pleased to notify that the aforesaid Regulations shall extend to the following local areas.—

(1) The whole of the Kashmir Province.

(2) The Poonch River only in the Jammu Province together with all its tributaries.

1. **Definitions, etc.**—Water means and includes all rivers, streams and lakes, all ponds belonging to the State and all tanks constructed by or under authority of the State.

Trout Waters mean and include all waters which are now being stocked with English Trout, in which no fishing shall be permitted except under a special license issued for the purpose under these Regulations.

Reserved Waters mean and include waters where fishing shall not be permitted, except under special license issued in that behalf, nor shall the capture of fish be allowed by means, other than rod and line, or single casting net, which shall not exceed 20 feet in diameter, with meshes not smaller than one inch from knot to knot.

N. B.—The ordinary landing net and bait-net used by fishermen is permitted to be used provided that the owner holds a license for rod fishing as laid down under Notification 7.

Sanctuaries mean and include waters where fishing, because of the sacred nature of the place or otherwise, shall not be permitted under any circumstances.

Protected Waters mean and include waters where fishing shall not be permitted, except under a license issued in that behalf, in the manner indicated hereafter, nor shall the capture of fish be allowed, except by one or other of the recognised modes of fishing.

Fixed Engine means and includes any net, cage, trap, sluice, or other contrivance for taking fish fixed in the soil or made stationary in any other way.

N. B.—The erection of dams for the working of mills, etc., is permitted but in all cases a free channel must be left open for the passage of fish up or down the river.

2. Reserved Waters.—(*a*) The following waters shall be deemed to be "Reserved Waters," the fee for fishing in which shall be—

	Rs.
(*a*) By rod and line for a period not exceeding ten days	10
(*b*) By rod and line for a period of one year from the 1st of January ...	20
(*c*) By casting net as defined above, which includes the right to fish with rod and line	20

1. (*a*) The Poonch River, from Kotli to Tangrot, including the Junction Pool and the Chukker on the Jammu Bank of the Jhelum, and Tangrot ; and,

(*b*) the following waters shall be deemed to be Reserved Waters, the fee for fishing in which shall be—

	Rs.
(*i*) By rod and line	5
(*ii*) By casting net as defined above which includes the right to fish with rod and line under (*i*) ...	15

2. The Liddar, from one mile above the junction of the Liddar and Tannin to the junction with Jhelum.

3. The Sindh, from Kangan to three miles below Ganderbal Bridge, and again from one mile above Utkhurro village to the junction with the Jhelum.

4. The Pohroo, with its two branches, the Lolab and Kamil streams.

5. The Vishoo, from its source to the village of Khudwani

6. The Kishanganga at Gurais from the dâk bungalow to Kanzalwan.

7. Biroo, stream.

N.B.—Except the portions of the above waters which are specially defined as Trout Streams.

8. The following waters on the Jhelum :—

(*a*) The Dalgate Pool and the channel from Dalgate to Gagribal.

(*b*) Shadipore, from the junction of the Sindh to half a mile below Shadipore.

(*c*) Sumbal, from the bridge to half a mile below Shadipore.

(*d*) Baramulla do. do. do.

(*e*) Sopore do. do. do.

(*f*) Ningle from the Woolar to the boundary pillar.

All the tributaries of the above, from the junction with the main stream to three miles up stream as far as the boundary pillars.

N.B.—All places, on the above rivers, that are defined under Notification 2 as sanctuaries are closed.

The following places on the above waters are reserved for Rod Fishing only, from April 15th to September 15th :—

(*a*) The Sindh river at Ganderbal from half a mile below the old bridge to half a mile above the Chinaars on the left bank at the village of Mulpora, and including the Island Pool ; also from Utkhurro village to the Chinar tree, 300 yards below the village.

All fishing is strictly prohibited at Ganderbal within the limits of His Highness' Camping Ground.

(*b*) The Dalgate Pool and the Canal Gate Pool just above the Library.

(*c*) The bridges at Baramulla, Sopore, Sumbal and Bijbahara from 100 yards up stream to half a mile below the bridge, and Ningle

3. Protected Waters.—The following waters shall be deemed to be protected waters, the fee for fishing in which shall be—

	Rs.
(*a*) By rod or line	2
(*b*) By Walraz, Narchoo and Tokri Jal	6

(c) General License for fishing by net which includes (a) and (b) and also the Khuri-Jal, the Thorang-Jal, the Khuksha-Jal, Kishup-Khuri-Jal and Bislai.

(1) The Nala Bringi in Tehsil Anantnag, Kashmir Province.

(2) The Dal Lake in Srinagar Tehsil, Kashmir Province.

(3) The Anchar Lake in Srinagar Tehsil, Kashmir Province.

(4) The Nala Shala Boog in Srinagar Tehsil, Kashmir Province.

(5) The Nala Makhama in Sri Pratap Singhpura, Kashmir Province.

(6) The Hokar Sar in Sri Pratap Singhpura, Kashmir Province.

(7) The Khushipura Lake in Sri Pratap Singhpura, Kashmir Province.

(8) The Nala Talar in Uttarmachipura Tehsil, Kashmir Province.

(9) The Nala Haihama in Uttarmachipura Tehsil, Kashmir Province.

(10) Wahgam Kuel in Uttarmachipura Tehsil, Kashmir Province.

(11) The Woolar Lake in Uttarmachipura Tehsil, Kashmir Province.

(12) Nala Madmati in Uttarmachipura Tehsil, Kashmir Province.

(13) The Nala Anderkot in Uttarmachipura Tehsil, Kashmir Province.

(14) The Nala Naidkhai in Uttarmachipura Tehsil, Kashmir Province.

(15) Doorak Kalan in Uttarmachipura Tehsil, Kashmir Province.

(16) The Watlab Ghat in Uttarmachipura Tehsil, Kashmir Province.

(17) The Dar Nambal Ghat in Uttarmachipura Tehsil, Kashmir Province.

(18) The Makdam Yari in Uttarmachipura Tehsil, Kashmir Province.

(19) The Khud Lab in Uttarmachipura Tehsil, Kashmir Province.

(20) The Nala Sir in Uttarmachipura Tehsil, Kashmir Province.

(21) The Nala Banyari in Uttarmachipura Tehsil, Kashmir Province.

(22) The Nala Kanihama from Batpura to Kausa in Uttarmachipura Tehsil, Kashmir Province.

(23) The Buda Marg in Uttarmachipura Tehsil, Kashmir Province.

(24) The Chaku Dab in Uttarmachipura Tehsil, Kashmir Province.

(25) The Sugand Naraknuh in Uttarmachipura Tehsil, Kashmir Province.

(26) The Tahas in Avantipura in Uttarmachipura Tehsil, Kashmir Province.

(27) The Khawaja Bagh in Baramulla, Kashmir Province.

(28) The Hajin Bagh in Baramulla, Kashmir Province.

(29) The Nala Sandran in Anantnag, Kashmir Province.

(30) The Nala With-Watroo, Anantnag, Kashmir Province.

(31) The Verinag stream, Anantnag, Kashmir Province.

(32) The Jhelum river from Khanbal to Domel in Kashmir, except the portions which have been declared as "Sanctuaries" or "Reserved Water."

(33) Nullah Bahan in Tehsil Kotli above Boundary Pillar.

(34) The Nullah Ranghar in Tehsil Kotli above Boundary Pillar.

(35) Triplabal Ferozepore.

(36) The Remiara.

(37) The Ramshi in Avantipur.

(38) The Tral stream or Chandarhar.

N.B.—All places on the above rivers that are defined as "Sanctuaries" and "Reserved Waters" are closed to holders of this license.

4. Trout Waters.—The following waters shall be defined as Trout Streams, the fee for fishing in which shall be—

		Rs.
(*a*) By rod and line for 10 days	...	10
(*b*) By rod and line for 1 day	...	1

(1) The Lidder and its tributaries above Bhatkote Bridge.

NOTE.—Visitors to the Lidder and Pahlgam will be permitted to fish as at present for country fish on the understanding that any Trout taken must be returned to the water, unless the fisherman is in possession of one of the Trout Licenses above laid down.

(2) The Achabal and Arput rivers.

(3) The Vishu from its source to one mile below the tehsil of Koolgam.

(4) The Arrah river from the Dachigam Rukh to the bridge at Telbal.

(5) The Kishanganga river and Gorai stream from their junction at Kanzalwan to their sources.

(6) The Wangut stream.

(7) The Erin and Sirander streams.

(8) The Ahan waters at Sopore.

(9) The Desoo and Nowboog branches of the Bringhi river above the junction.

NOTE.—Sportsmen holding a Rs. 5 License for "Reserved Waters" wishing to fish for country fish only in any of the foregoing streams can obtain a special permit for the purpose from the Secretary, Game Preservation Department, on the distinct understanding that any English trout taken are immediately returned to the water.

The following are the sanctioned methods of fishing in the Trout Waters :—

(1) By rod and line.

(2) With artificial baits.

(3) No fish of less than 12 inches to be taken.

Anglers are requested to make use of disgorgers so as to avoid injury to small fish if caught.

N.B.—These Rules regarding Trout Waters are experimental only and liable to revision at any time.

5A. **Prohibitions**.—No fishing, whether under a license or not, shall be allowed in any of the Reserved Waters between the hours 7 P.M. and 5 A.M. from October 15th to April 15th.

5B. Fishing on the Poonch river in the pools of (1) Jangoo, (2) Palak, (3) Potah, (4) Lower Arno, and (5) the Junction Kool, including the Chukker on the Jammu Bank of the Jhelum at Tangrot, (6) all tributaries of the above which are defined in these Regulations as "Reserved Waters," is prohibited during the periods and in the manner noted below :—

(*a*) All trolling, or fishing other than by casting with rod and line, from November 15th to February 15th.

(*b*) All fishing by net from November 15th to July 15th, except in Jangoo Pool where the prohibition will be from October 15th to July 15th.

(*c*) Whereas the tributaries of the Poonch river defined as Protected Waters are the chief spawning beds of the Poonch river, no fishing by rod or net shall be allowed in the portions so defined from March 15th to June 15th ; and

(*d*) Whereas the Reserved Water on the Sindh river and (*vide* para. 2 to clause 3) from Kangan to 3 miles below Ganderbal Bridge is one of the chief spawning beds of Kashmir, no fishing by rod or net will be permitted in this water from May 1st to June 30th.

6. Penalties.—*Regulation* 6.—Whoever is found fishing in any sanctuary shall be liable to be punished with imprisonment, with or without hard labour, for a term not exceeding two months, or with fine which may extend to Rs. 100, or both.

Regulation 7.—Whoever is found fishing in any "Trout Reserved" or "Protected Waters" without a license as herein laid down ; or

Regulation 8.—Whoever uses dynamite or other explosive substance ; or

Regulation 9.—Puts poison, lime or other noxious material into any water ; or

Regulation 10.—Whoever erects any fixed engine on the banks of or in any water with intent under any of the above headings to destroy or capture fish, or uses for that purpose any instrument or net other than herein specified ; or

Regulation 11.—Whoever in any Reserved Water shall be found fishing between the hours of 7 P.M. and 5 A.M. from October 15th to April 15th ; or

Regulation 12.—Whoever shall capture English trout in any form whatsoever, except under the conditions laid down ; or

Regulation 13.—Whoever not being a license-holder under the terms of this regulation shall be found in possession of nets for the illegal capture of fish ; or

Regulation 14.— Whoever shall aid and abet the committal of any of the offences herein laid down, or shall in any way contravene or attempt to contravene the provisions of this Regulation or of the rules made thereunder, for which no special punishment is provided : shall be liable—

to be punished on first conviction with imprisonment not exceeding one month, or with fine which may extend to Rs. 50, or both, and for a second or subsequent offence shall be liable to be punished with imprisonment for a period not exceeding two months, and with fine which may extend to Rs. 100, or both, except that for a second or subsequent conviction under Regulation 6 he will be liable to be punished with imprisonment for a period not exceeding six months, or with fine which may extend to Rs. 500, or both, and in addition to the above, any fixed engine or other illegal article used for the capture of fish, as well as any fish captured, shall be liable to be confiscated by the Durbar.

Regulation 15.—If the offence is a continuing one, in addition to the above punishments, with a fine that may extend to Rs. 10 for every day after the date on which he has been warned by any authority against a continuation of the offence.

N.B.—The possession of nets is illegal except in the hands of license-holders, who, according to the terms of their licenses, are permitted to keep nets of the dimensions defined under the Kashmir State Fisheries Regulations.

NOTE.—Imprisonment in the case of fishing in "Reserved Waters" may be either simple or rigorous, but it shall only be simple in case of fishing in "Protected Waters"

7. Licenses and methods of obtaining them.—*Draft Rules, Notification VII.*—Licenses for fishing in Trout Waters can be obtained from the Secretary, Game Preservation Department, or Frank Mitchell, Esq., in charge Trout Experiments, Harwan, care of P. O. Srinagar.

Licenses for fishing in "Reserved Waters" can be obtained from the Secretary, Game Preservation Department, Srinagar, Agencies issuing licenses, the Motamid Durbar and all the principal riverside Post Offices. The license will carry with it the privilege of fishing in "Protected Waters." A license thus granted will run for a period of one year, commencing from the beginning of the Sambat year, *viz.*, April 12th, except at Tangrote where the license shall run from January 1st.

The Post Masters authorised to receive applications and issue licenses under these rules shall get an allowance of 5 per cent on the receipts of licenses issued by them.

Licenses for fishing in Protected Waters can be obtained from the Secretary, Game Preservation Department, or the local Tehsildars. This license shall entitle the holder to fish in Protected Waters only. It will run for a period of one year from beginning of Sambat year.

Licenses granted under these rules shall be of general application in respect of all the Protected Waters in the State.

Licenses granted under these rules for "Reserved Waters" shall be of general application and shall entitle the holder to fish in all the waters in the Jammu and Kashmir State, except in those for which, under Regulation 5 (2), a special license is necessary.

N. B.—Tehsildars may employ license-holders to net fish for His Highness' Guests, or for Members of the Ruling Family at any time within their own Tehsils, but a report of this should be made at once to the Secretary, Game Preservation Department, stating the daily amount of fish supplied. This rule does not apply to Trout Streams.

The above licenses shall be in triplicate, one copy of which will be given to the licensee, and the other transmitted in the case of—

Reserved and Protected Waters, direct to the Secretary, Game Preservation Department ; the third foil shall remain with the issuing officer for record.

A license for fishing by net shall entitle the holder to fish by rod and line as well.

Any license-holders in possession of a license for Protected Waters, who shall wish to exchange the same for a Rs. 15 license for Reserved Waters shall be permitted to do so on payment of the difference between Rs. 15 and the amount already paid, on application being made to the Secretary, Game Preservation Department.

8. **Control of waters.**—The grant of licenses, appointment of watchers and all matters of control, whether financial or executive, in the State Fisheries, shall be under the Secretary, Game Preservation Department, who is hereby authorised to close any river or water at any time should he consider it necessary.

9. **Restrictions regarding license.**—The State reserve to themselves the right to refuse to issue any license, or to cancel any license at any time, if circumstances render it necessary.

The following notes have been supplied me from the Office of Director of Trout Culture, Kashmir, with kind permission to reprint :—

REPORT ON TROUT CULTURE FOR SAMBAT 1965.

By F. J. Mitchell, Director, Trout Culture.

The enclosed report is sent for the information of those who may be interested in trout culture.

Any further information which may be useful to those wishful of stocking lakes or streams in the Himalayas (over 5,000 feet) will be gladly supplied.

A limited number of ova will probably be available for delivery at Rawalpindi next winter from Kashmir.

Letters on the subject should be addressed to—

F. J. MITCHELL, Esq.,

Hony. Director of Trout Culture,

Srinagar, Kashmir.

As I shall be leaving Kashmir shortly for England, and shall not return till autumn, I am obliged this year to make my annual report earlier than I should otherwise have done.

The season has been so far favourable that there has been no difficulty about water, and I think that fair progress has been made in all directions.

Without considering the question of licenses for trout fishing which will, I hope, shortly be proving a source of revenue to the State, we have gone far this year to prove that the revenue from the sale of ova and trout can be made to cover the outlay at Harwan. Apart from the cost of distribution, the State may congratulate itself on having got some three-quarters of a million ova turned out in its streams, free of cost. A list of the ova distribution is given in Appendix A., along with a list of the yearlings turned out in the autumn. To these I have added a cutting from the *Field* of November 28th, which bears strongly on the contention I have always maintained of the advantages of stocking our streams with ova. Three months old fry cannot be safely distributed in this country. Yearlings are excellent for stocking our lakes, but my fry pond results have so far been so very much below those obtainable in England, that I think that for streams we shall be well advised to stick to ova only.

The trout sold were from 6 to 7 years old, and averaged from 11 to 13½ lbs., the sales having been made from the older cock fish when in the top of their condition, and of this class some 25 have been set apart from which sales may be made from next June. These are being replaced by three-year-old fish of 2 to 3 lbs. in weight.

The foreign despatches of ova have been—

(1) To Gilgit, 30,000 ova supplied free of cost.

(2) To the Punjab Government at Nugger, Kulu Valley, 30,000 to be paid for.

(3) To the 5th Gurkha Rifles at Abbottabad, 3,000 ova also to be paid for.

The first of these proved unfortunate, as from the day it crossed the Tragbal we had a fortnight of the worst weather of this winter. The ova was delayed 5 days at Minimarg, and again 7 more on the other side of the Burzil Pass (14,500 feet). On its arrival at Gilgit, the trays were found to be frozen solid and, the thawing out being done by inexperienced hands, it was improbable that so delicate an operation should prove successful. Major Dew says that at one time some of the eggs seemed to have life in them, but that none of the little fishes had the strength to hatch out after what they had gone through. It is to be hoped that better results may be obtained next year, when the experiment is to be again tried.

The other two despatches were quite successful, if one may judge from a letter received from Colonel Kemball and a telegram from Mr. Howell, Deputy Commissioner, Kulu. The former says that, apart from the upper tray having been crushed down on to the top tray (an accident which must have resulted from his cooly trying to cram in too much snow at Garhi Habibula) the loss was practically nothing. Mr. Howell's wire reads. "Ova arrived intact. Great performance. Congratulations." I believe this journey is probably a record one for ova, as after the 200 miles of road to Pindi and 20 hours of rail to Pathankote it had to be carried another 90 miles by tonga to Palampore, and then about the same distance on coolies to Nugger.

The local sendings apparently all reached their destinations safely, though the men taking up the Upper Veshu and Gungabal sendings must have had a trying time. Twenty thousand ova put down at Minimarg have been since buried under an avalanche, and the report when the snow melts will be interesting. Of course the box should not have been placed where an avalanche was likely to come.

The total ova output this year is nearly double that of last year, and I have re-sorted the stock trout in the ponds lately in a manner which I hope may again result in an increase of ova next winter. Further experiments are also being made with the idea of getting a better percentage from the fry ponds. The enormous number of frogs which keep coming in from the paddy fields is probably responsible for a great deal of the loss incurred. It seems impossible to keep them out. The frogs are rare in the upper valley streams where eyed ova is usually put down.

The Huchen continue to grow satisfactorily, and there are now about 700 well grown yearlings in ponds Nos. 1 and 2, which should give a good breeding stock in 1911.

I append a copy of the report of the Alberta (Canada) Fish and Game Protection Association, which bears out what I have previously written in reports of the advantages of having a Spring spawning fish in this country. Of the Cut Throat Trout I know nothing beyond what I have read, but I hope the Huchen will prove as fertile a spawner in the rivers into which he will be turned later on. He is very like the Brown Trout in appearance but grows bigger and is by all accounts a very sporting fish.

The surroundings in Alberta are so similar to those in Kashmir that the report can hardly fail to prove interesting to those who have the future of Kashmir fishing at heart.

There seems little doubt that the trout are spreading naturally in the Kashmir streams where poaching is rendered impossible by nature or by the strong arm of the Law. Colonel Kemball writes that he has heard of trout being caught at Uri, and I myself had a most detailed account of a capture made at Garhi with a description of the fish. I should much have liked to authenticate this, but when I asked for the captor's name, I could get no further than that it was Colonel Sahib. There is a general feeling that such captures are against the Law and I cannot get names or dates. If trout can go as far down the Jhelum as Garhi with the snow water, it adds a great field to their possible spread in India. It is not likely that they will breed so far down, but with plenty of water to move in, they can always get back to a more suitable climate when the time comes for them to do so.

During the summer of 1908, I was able to visit a fair number of the high lakes of Kashmir, and was specially struck with the capabilities of Lakes Gungabal and Nunkol. They certainly lie very high in the hills, about 12,000 feet above the sea, but the feeding is good and the flow of water out of them is constant throughout the winter, proving that a considerable amount of their water-supply is from springs.

Both lakes were still open when the yearlings were sent up in November, and the temperature of the water was then 43 degrees, so that the period of their being completely frozen over is probably very much overestimated. I can see no reason why, in time, they should not be as good fishing lakes as any in Scotland or Norway. Lakes Tarsar and Marsar are also very promising. The former is by far the better of the two, and will one day give grand sport to His Highness' guests. The latter will, I hope, at any rate form a reserve from which the Lidder will be kept stocked. The number of yearlings sent up is of course at present insignificant, as Lake Gungabal with its one and a half square miles of water would require 100,000 yearlings annually for some time to stock it thoroughly. However, a beginning has been made and we can only go on slowly.

Lake Konsar Nag proved a disappointment as a prospective home for trout, but is invaluable as the source from which the Vaishoo gets the greater part of its winter supply of water. The lake appears to be the outcome of that peculiar disintegration which is always going on in our hills. The great boulders from each side of the valley must have kept rolling down and meeting, till they formed the embankment which now holds up the lake. That this embankment has never become quite water-tight is shown by the fact that the water never reaches the top, but leaks through it, the principal outlet being some 500 feet below the bed of the lake. That the lake is entirely fed by snow water was pretty clearly shown by the water marks on the precipitous banks on each side. The northern shore showed a high water level mark some seven or eight feet above the surface of the water at the time of my visit on October 27th, while the southern shore showed where the water had stood when the last snow had fallen about a month previous. This marked a fall of three to four feet and it would be curious to know how much further the fall went before low water was reached, probably in January. The leakage of the lake probably accounts for many of the springs for a considerable distance down the Vaishoo, and the natives maintain that there is also a big outlet on the Punjab side of the range of hills to the south, but this seems highly improbable. At any rate the Upper Vaishoo is thus rendered one of the most promising streams for trout rearing, as every spring seems full of insect food. Unfortunately, the snow falls very early in the valley and it is difficult to get the ova up as no tracks are kept open in the winter.

The Upper Sind between Baltal and Sonamarg, of which I saw the lower stretch after a flood in August, seems more easy flowing than some of our hill streams and, therefore, more promising, but I hardly feel justified in doing too much here until I am more satisfied as to the effect of the avalanches in the narrow valley during the winter. There is a rumour that the water is sometimes absolutely dammed up for days at a time.

I was very much pleased with the appearance of the Ferozepore Nala, which I visited in August. Though rapid it contains excellent pools and its proximity to Gulmarg makes it specially suited for a fishing stream. One hundred thousand ova were put in at Sonapatri and Hafkadan, four to five miles above Gorevan, from where the fish will work down.

When at Gungabal I had a look at the upper waters of the Bandipore Nala, where it takes its source from the Pundit Lake Buttar and from springs in the fine Salnai valley (according to Guzers and Chopsus wrongly marked Chitradoor on the map). The short length through the valley is as good as could be, but on leaving it the stream becomes rapid for a long distance, and I had not time to explore it downwards or to look at the other branch of the stream taking its source in Lake Chitra Nag (or Mansar). There is, however, plenty to do for a year or so stocking the rivers already taken in hand and this one can wait its turn.

A report from a reliable source has reached me to the effect that a fine trout of 2 lbs. was seen in the Reorso river, two miles above the village of that name, where 14,250 fry were sent in season 1906-07. It will be interesting to get a reliable report from this stream, as if the trout are really doing well, the stocking might be continued. Captain Stewart has promised to visit it in early April, and if he gets fishing weather then, will no doubt be able to get a fair idea of what fish there are in the stream.

APPENDIX A.

The yearlings shown as sent out from Harwan Fry Ponds are the residue of 50,000 ova hatched out and turned into them. This gives a return of about 19·31 per cent, which at home would be considered very bad indeed, in some cases as much as 50 per cent being obtained there. I do not know what the final results obtained by Major Wigram at Achibal were from 55,000 ova sent to his fry ponds there, but the last I heard was that he had got 3,000 yearlings and there was still one pond to empty. This was a first experiment. Good results could hardly be expected before the ponds had been thoroughly tested. Some trout and also some chiroo got into the fry ponds which must have depleted them sadly.

This year, his indent for 100,000 ova has been complied with, and I hope that he will be able to get better percentages than I have got so far.

Yearling despatches from Harwan were as follows :—

For Lake Gungabal	3,000
For Lake Tarsar	1,000
For Lake Marsar	1,000
For Lake Ahan Water	2,000
For Rivers above Achibal	2,300
For Darrah	250
For Gurais	40
For Pond No. 9	65
Of 50,000 ova 19·31 per cent	9,655

Despatches of ova from Harwan—Season 1908-09.

Date		Destination		Number
16th December, 1908,	to	Gilgit ...	... ...	30,000
" "	"	Kishengunga	... ...	40,000
27th "	"	Upper Vaishoo	... ...	100,000
30th "	"	Lidder ...	... ...	100,000
15th January, 1909	"	Sonamarg	... ...	40,000
" "	"	Stream above Nunkol	...	40,000
19th "	"	Ferozepore Nala ...	...	100,000
30th "	"	Lidder ...	... ...	100,000
3rd February	"	Achibal Ponds	... ...	100,000
15th "	"	Nuggar Kulu (Punjab)	...	30,000
" "	"	Buniar Nala	... ...	10,000
" "	"	Abbottabad	... ...	3,000
8th March	"	Kishengunga	... ...	50,000
" "	"	Fry Ponds, Harwan	...	50,000
				793,000

Extract from the Field, dated November 28th, 1908.

Stocking with Trout.—In the new issue of the Howietoun Fishery Company's handsome prospectus (Stirling N.B.) there are some hints on stocking which are worth reading. It is stated that rivers, lakes, or ponds may be successfully stocked with ova, fry, yearlings, or two-year-olds, according, of course, to the circumstances of each case. If there is any depth of water, two-year-olds are recommended as being safest and giving quickest results. If, however, the extent of water is great, and a large number of fish are required, "in the interest of due economy time must be sacrificed." If there are plenty of small gravelly streams with clear water suited to very young fish,* then ova sown in redds will give the best results; if the streams are not sufficiently clear for this, then fry three months old are advised. As to this the paragraph goes on, "But our experience is that there is no half way house between ova sown in redds and three-month-old fry. Younger fry are too risky; they *may* do, but only where ova would do as well, and at half the cost."

Since writing this Report I have had a letter from Kulu saying that the 30,000 ova had arrived on February 24th, and that up to the first of March when all had been examined and picked over, only 251 bad eggs had been found or a loss of under 1 per cent of the number sent. This is a wonderful result after such a

* *N. B.*—As in the upper streams of Kashmir.

journey, and speaks volumes for Pundit Sudhama's careful packing and attention to the ova *en route*.

APPENDIX B.

Extract from Rod and Gun and Motor Sport in Canada, dated November, 1908.

Facts about the trout and trout streams in Alberta.

The Streams.—These are mountain streams flowing down the eastern slopes of the Rocky Mountains, the Bow and its branches, and all other mountain streams south of this river to the boundary.

Character of these Streams.—Swift running, with rapids and falls, having rocky, stoney, and gravel bottoms. During fall, winter and early spring, these streams are at low water mark and perfectly clear. In winter during the coldest weather, many of the smaller ones freeze to the bottom. This does not mean that they stop running, but that the ice is forced to the bottom, and the water runs over it, making them uninhabitable for the fish and seriously interfering with the depositing and hatching of the fall spawn. During May, June, July, and August these streams are raging torrents, carrying down mud, silt, and even trees, and are very treacherous. During these floods these streams very often find a quite different course. A number of spring creeks join these mountain streams which are not affected by these floods and in consequence afford good spawning places.

Trout.—There are two kinds.

(*a*) *Salmo Mykis* (commonly called the cutthroat). This is a real trout of good formation and attractive colour. It is a very game fish when caught in season, which is during September and October, when it is at its best, and readily rises to the artificial fly. It spawns in the Spring, during April and May, ascending the different streams for the purpose. It is very prolific from the fact that it *takes but a short time for the eggs*

N. B.—This has not been noticed in Kashmir. On the contrary the water runs under the snow and ice.

to hatch, since they are deposited at the approach of the warm season of the year. All the above streams are fairly well stocked with these trout considering that they have never had any legal protection during spawning time, and that they have been destroyed by every device known to man at this particular time. The fish lives wholly on insects, and therefore does not destroy fish of its own or other species.

(*b*) *Salvelinus Malma (Bull Trout).*—This fish belongs to the Salvelinus family and is not a true trout. It lives almost wholly on fish of its own and other species. It spawns in the fall, and during that time has had legal protection. It is despised by fishermen as a game fish, and it does not rise to the artificial fly, and when caught on the hook with bait puts up no fight. It therefore has had every chance to increase in numbers, and these streams ought to be full of them. The reverse is the case, owing partly to the habits of the fish itself and partly to the difficulties of fall spawning as mentioned above, more particularly the latter.

(*c*) *Other Game Fish.*—*Williamsonii* (Rocky Mountain White Fish) popularly known as the Grayling is another game fish in these waters. It lives altogether on insects, rises well to the artificial fly, and puts up an excellent fight for life when caught. It spawns in the fall, and has also had protection, and like the Bull Trout is few in numbers.

CONCLUSION.

(*a*) These streams are not suitable for fishing during the Spring and Summer months owing to the muddy condition of the water.

(*b*) They give excellent fishing during September and October and sometimes in August, for the water in all the streams is low and transparent.

(*c*) They are not suitable for fall spawning fish, as shown by the two kinds which are not increasing in numbers.

(*d*) The Cut-throat (*Salmo Mykis*) meets all the requirements and conditions, and ought to be protected without consideration of any other varieties.

(*e*) It is not advisable to introduce outside varieties such as the *Salvelinus Fontinalis* of Ontario which belongs to the same family as the Bull Trout, with all its habits ; it is not a true trout, lives to a great extent on fish ; spawns in the fall and is liable to the same obstacles in spawning, but with this important difference that it is a great game fish with flavour of flesh unexcelled. It will be impossible to legislate so as to protect the Cut-throat which spawns in the Spring and is at its best in September and October, and the *Salvelinus Fontinalis* of Ontario which spawns in the fall and should have a close season in September and October. The latter fish should be taken during June and July, but at that time the waters are muddy and no fishing can be done. The natural increase of these will be interfered with by the frost the same as that of the Bull Trout.

Certain Kashmir streams in the hills though not very muddy at this season are so heavily charged with snow water as to be almost unfishable till nearly mid-August, notably the Wanget.

The Kaghan valley.—To any jaded travellers who are tired of Kashmir and wish to strike out some new route for themselves, the Kaghan valley has many attractions to offer. The climate is delightful and the scenery glorious. It is one of the routes from India proper into Chilas and Gilgit. Down the centre of the valley flows the Kunhar river, a swift mountain tributary of the Jhelum which rises in a lake, the Lulusar, lying 3½ miles above Basal, the third camp beyond Narang. Its water seems to vary a lot in colour for no apparent reason. There are plenty of snow trout in the river, running up to 5 lbs. and probably bigger. No mahseer have been seen or caught as far as I could gather. About Narung is one of the best spots. The trout will come for a fly-spoon occasionally, but are best caught bottom fishing. Use worms if you can get them, but they are not easily procured, otherwise use a small white caterpillar found under stones. For anyone who might be interested in this trip, the marches up the valley are as follows :—Abbottabad to Mansehra (B. and P. O.) 16 miles, along a good road fit for wheeled traffic. Next stage is Jaba, 3,750 feet high, thirteen miles, road still driveable for first nine miles, where main road is left at Uttarshisha village and a track eight feet wide goes off to left leading to Balakote (B. and P. O.) eleven miles beyond Jaba. Balakote could be reached by driving if the main road was not left at Uttarshisha, but by this route it is 30 miles from that village. Balakote is a large village on the right bank of the Kunhar river, crossed here by a suspension bridge. On to Kawai 5,000 feet (B.) is twelve and a half miles and from there thirteen miles takes one to Mandri (B). The bungalow here is half a mile this side of the village, and is situated at the junction of the Manur Nala with the Kunhar. On to Kaghan itself is eleven and a half miles, the road continuing an eight feet track, good with all streams bridged. Kaghan is a big village, elevation 6,750 feet. Narung 8,000 feet is the next stage, and lies fourteen miles on. Supplies such as sheep, eggs, fowls, etc., are procurable the whole way up. The views of the snows are grand, and once the first few marches are past the rainfall in monsoon is trifling.

NOTES ON TANGROT.

By G. N. Thompson, Esq., 43rd Erinpuras.

How to get there.—Train to either Dina or Jhelum and thence by road.

VI

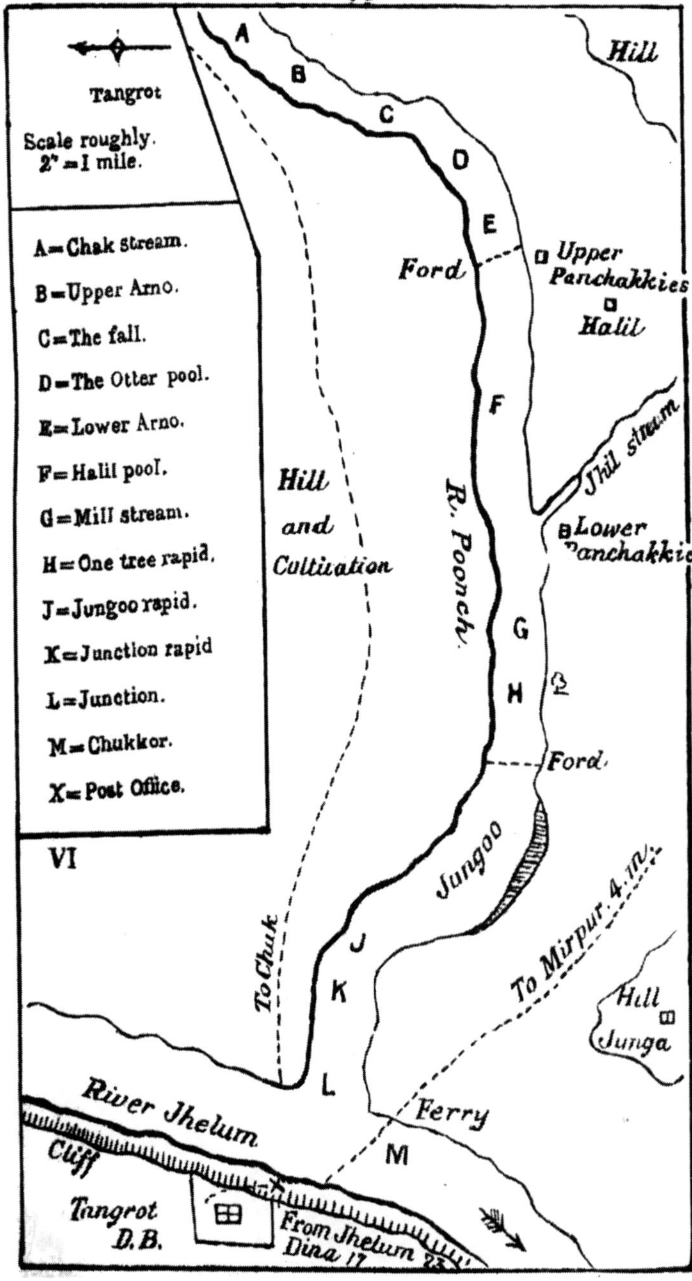
Tangrot
Scale roughly.
2" = 1 mile.
A = Chak stream.
B = Upper Arno.
C = The fall.
D = The Otter pool.
E = Lower Arno.
F = Halil pool.
G = Mill stream.
H = One tree rapid.
J = Jungoo rapid.
K = Junction rapid
L = Junction.
M = Chukkor.
X = Post Office.
VI
Hill
Ford
Upper Panchakkies
Halil
Jhil stream
Lower Panchakkies
Hill and Cultivation
R. Poonch
Ford
Jungoo
To Mirpur. 4. m.
To Chuk
Hill
Junga
River Jhelum
Ferry
Cliff
Tangrot D.B.
From Jhelum 23
Dina 17
A
B
C
D
E
F
G
H
J
K
L
M

Dina is 16 miles from Tangrot. Jhelum $22\frac{3}{4}$ miles.

Two Up trains (from Lahore direction) and 2 Down trains (from Rawalpindi direction). stop at Dina daily.

There is no waiting room at Dina, but there is a Railway subordinates' rest-house within a few yards of the station.

Jhelum station has refreshment and waiting rooms.

There is a dak bungalow about half a mile from the station.

The Up and Down Punjab and Calcutta Mails stop at Jhelum, and two Up and two Down Local Trains stop daily at Jhelum.

Transport from Dina can be obtained by communicating with the camel chowdhri, though it is well first to write to the Thanadar or Station Master at Dina a few days before arrival, stating one's requirements.

At Jhelum one should give the Tehsildar previous notice of one's requirements.

There is on the road to Tangrot a pretty little bungalow at Shekhopur (permission to occupy it should be obtained from the Deputy Commissioner of Jhelum) situated on the banks of the Jhelum. This is a good place to break one's journey. Distance from Jhelum 12 miles, from Dina about $4\frac{1}{2}$ miles.

The following are the charges for transport :—

Coolies—

Tangrot to Dina	...	As. 8
„ Shekhopur	...	„ 6
„ to Jhelum	...	Re. 1

Ponies or mules—

Tangrot to Dina (Riding or Baggage)	...	Re. 1
" " Shekohpur	...	As. 10
" " Jhelum	...	Rs. 1-8

Camels—

Dina to Tangrot	...	Re. 1
Jhelum to Tangrot	...	" 1-8 to Rs. 2 (apparently on fixed nerrick).

Accommodation—

There is a four-roomed bungalow at Tangrot. Charge for occupation Re. 1 per diem. A certain amount of crockery kept.

The chowkidar, Mohammad Ali, can cook a simple meal and, if he is given notice beforehand, will have a meal ready for one on arrival. No regular khansamah is kept, and one ought to bring all one's stores with one. On the bank of the river by the Post Office, where the boats are moored, there is room for three or four tents. Some kikar trees and the cliff give a certain amount of shade. If one should run short, stores can be obtained from Hazura Mull and Ram Chund, General Merchants.

Boatmen and Shikaris—

The following is a copy of the rules hung up in the bungalow regarding boatmen and shikaris :—

"The proper charge to pay for boats is Re. 1 a day, when plying in the Poonch in Kashmir territory. This is the charge for a boat with three men including a qualified steerer. If the steerer acts as shikari and is a registered man, he is entitled to four annas extra. If only two men are taken the charge for the third man, reckoned at two annas, may be deducted if the employer wishes.

A charge of four annas a day extra may be charged, if the boats are taken up the river beyond the limits of the Tangrot fishing. The proper price of the registered shikaris at Tangrot is 8 annas a day, or twelve annas when away from Tangrot up the river.

The boatmen and shikaris came before me on March 15th and accepted the above agreement.

The following shikaris are registered under the Kashmir State Game Laws, Fisheries :—

SHIKARIS.

Fukroo, Fakira, Mahomed Alum, Ghulam Mahomed, Nek Mahomed, Ghulam Hussain, Mankta, Ghulam Hassan, Khutab Din, Hassan, Sakkhi Mahomed, Sher, Satar Mahomed.

BOATMEN.

Hassan Din, Sakkhi Mahomed, Mankta, Mahomed Alum, Fateh Mahomed, Mahomed Hassan (son of Fakira).

March 15*th*, 1909.

(Sd.) H. R. WIGRAM, MAJOR,

Secretary of Kashmir State Game Preservation Department, Fisheries.

Of the above men I can thoroughly recommend Ghulam Hussain. I have employed him several times and have found him always thoroughly straight and very hardworking. He can use a casting net to catch bait, which several of the other shikaris either can't or won't do.

Licenses.—The cost of licenses are as follows:—

For any period up to ten days---Rs. 10.

For any period exceeding ten days up to one year—Rs. 20.

These licenses include fishing in the Poonch River as far as Leri, and any of the licensed waters in Kashmir (exclusive of Trout waters, for which, I believe a special license of Rs. 100 is required).

If a person goes to Tangrot for 10 days and then, in the same year, returns for a two months' fishing trip, one would first pay the Rs. 10 for the 10 days and on coming back for the two months' fish, would pay an additional Rs. 10 converting the original Rs. 10 license into a Rs. 20 yearly one.

Local Supplies.—Fowls, eggs, sheep, milk, etc., are obtainable locally at Tangrot. There is a bazaar at Mirpur in Jammu territory, where fruit and vegetables are usually obtainable.

Fishing.—The usual method employed at Tangrot in the Junction and Jungoo pools is "chuckering" or trolling from boats. There are also one or two good places for casting at the head and tail of these pools.

The Junction is the best place from spring up to the rains. From October to the middle of February, Jungoo is the best. A nice bit of water to fish is the Lower Panchakkies and One Tree Reach, as a rule the fish run small here but if the chilwa are running, one has the chance of hooking a big one, and he gives one plenty of fun for the stream is very strong there.

The best times are from the middle of September to the middle of November. March, April, May and June are good. During the end of March, April, and May, however, one has to take one's chance of the river being unfishable owing to snow water.

The places for big fish are—in the spring up to June, the Junction ; in the Autumn, Jungoo.

As to baits, when the fish are properly on the take one bait is as good as another. From the records in the Angler's Books the following appear to be the most successful.

Natural bait, $2\frac{1}{2}$ inch spoon (silver or gold and silver) and Devon minnows.

An Angler's Book is kept in the bungalow for anglers to record their bags, a study of this book, and the two old ones, giving records as far back as 1873, is the best guide as to what baits one ought to use at various times of year.

A staff of watchers is kept up by The Kashmir Game Preservation Department, consisting of a head watcher, assisted by four or five under watchers. Fakira is the head watcher.

How to return from Tangrot.—The best way to return from Tangrot is by boat to Jhelum. The journey on an average takes about six hours.

The charges are as follows :—

Large boat for over 8 maunds of baggage, Rs. 10.

Middle sized boat capable of taking 8 maunds of baggage, Rs. 8.

Small sized boats (similar to fishing boats), Rs 6.

Chowmook.—This place is 10 miles above Tangrot on the Poonch. There is a furnished bungalow there, consisting of two bed and bath-rooms and a dining room. No lamps, crockery or stores. The charge for occupying the bungalow is 8 annas a day. Chowmook is a good place to go to if Tangrot is overcrowded. There are some nice runs at Chowmook, but one is not likely to get the big fish there that one may get at Tangrot.

Record.—The record fish was caught by the late Capt. Lacy and weighed 62 lbs."

Further Notes on Tangrot.

As there is no doubt that the point most of interest to anglers visiting a place, is how others fared there : when I visited Tangrot in 1908 I took the opportunity of culling the following extracts from the Anglers' Book there. They are prefaced with one or two notes that may be useful.

The road Dina to Shekopur is quite undrivable. Dina to Tangrot, 17 miles, camels, mules or ponies, Re. 1 each. Camels very slow, ponies very tiny. Boats from Tangrot to Jhelum, Rs. 6 and 8. small with no awnings, take 5 to 8 hours. Post Office, delivery and collection every second day. There are some exceedingly fine illustrations of big fish on the

VII

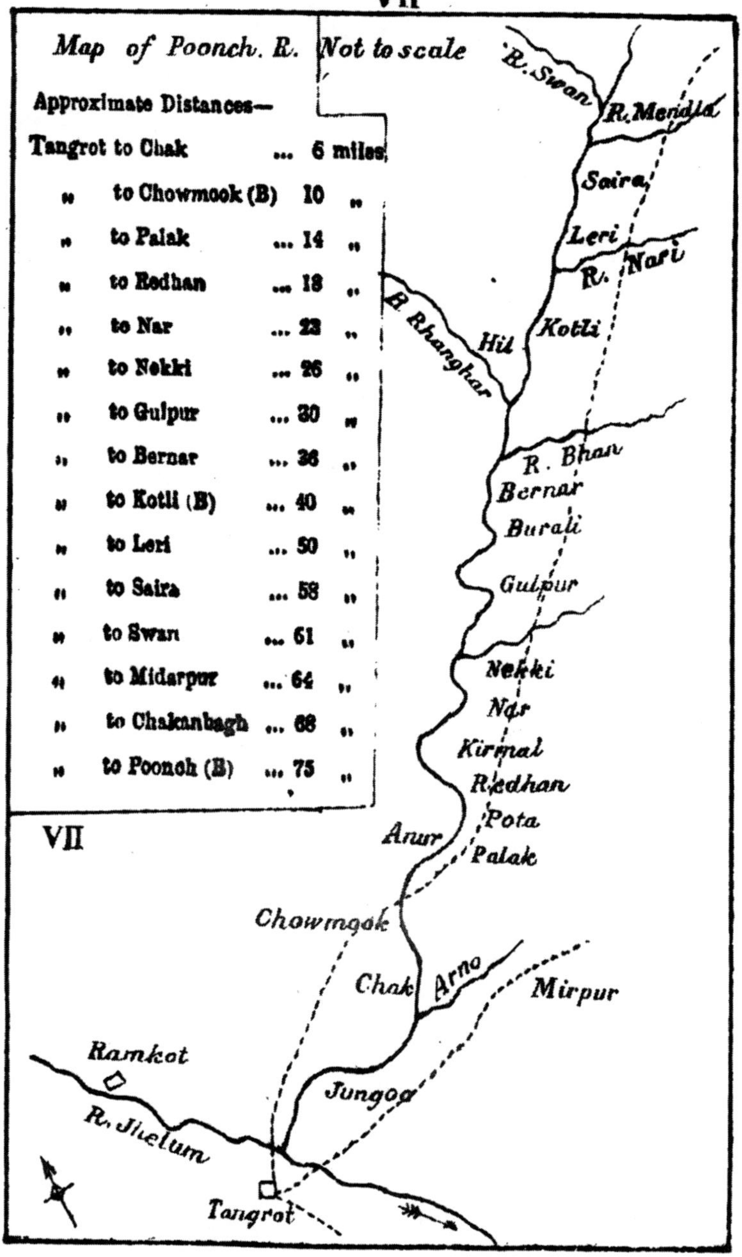
Map of Poonch. R.
Not to scale
Approximate Distances—
Tangrot to Chak ... 6 miles
" to Chowmook (B) 10 "
" to Palak ... 14 "
" to Redhan ... 18 "
" to Nar ... 23 "
" to Nekki ... 26 "
" to Gulpur ... 30 "
" to Bernar ... 36 "
" to Kotli (B) ... 40 "
" to Leri ... 50 "
" to Saira ... 58 "
" to Swan ... 61 "
" to Midarpur ... 64 "
" to Chakanbagh ... 68 "
" to Poonch (B) ... 75 "
VII
R. Swan
R. Mendla
Saira
Leri
R. Nari
R. Rhanghar
Hil
Kotli
R. Bhan
Bernar
Burali
Gulpur
Nekki
Nar
Kirmal
Redhan
Pota
Palak
Anur
Chowmook
Chak
Arno
Mirpur
Ramkot
R. Jhelum
Jungoo
Tangrot

walls of the bungalow ; a 45-pounder, caught by Fred Orchard in February 1908 being a real work of art, as is a 62-pounder caught by the late G. H Lacy.

After the Poonch has come down in flood, the shikaris as a rule seem to be able to make a fair guess from which tributaries the dirty water is coming, and the following is the number of days that must usually elapse before the river comes down clean again.—The Rhanghar and Bhan, known by their red waters, eight to ten days. The Nari three or four days; Mendla two, and Chakan Bagh one day.

The following notes are only for the last three years, except the first two bags which are inserted as worth noting :—

On 16th March 1903—Four rods got 384 lbs., 40, 40, 30, 28, 28 lbs., etc.

On 17th March 1903—Four rods got 363 lbs., 40, 40, 31, 25 lbs., etc.

On 15th November 1905—Col. C. Anderson caught, in Jungoo on single gut and 1″ fly-spoon strong breeze blowing, 24, 38, 40, in morning, and 42, 5, in afternoon.

On 1st January 1906—One 12 lb. mahseer and a 2 lb. kalabanse, caught in Jungoo on phantoms.

On 4th February 1906—Water very dirty, lots of fish showing, caught a 29-pounder in Junction on spoon.

5th to 9th March—Twelve fish all in Junction, biggest 18 lbs.

Rain set in 21st March till end of month. Poonch rose 20′ on 23rd.

2nd to 13th March—Twenty fish, biggest 22 lbs., all below Upper Arno ; a good deal of snow water in Poonch. Caught on 2½ and 3″ spoons. (15 couple of snipe on Mirpur jheel.)

18*th to* 25*th March*—Weather most unsettled, both rivers full of snow water.

1*st to* 7*th March*—Twenty-one fish weighing 248 lbs. Biggest 29 lbs. Mostly at Junction. On silver spoon, silver Devon and dead bait on Crocodile spinner.

17*th to* 23*rd April*—Thirteen fish, weighing 123 lbs., biggest 37½ lbs. Mostly Junction. On brass spoon and brass Devon.

24*th May to* 2*nd June*—All between J. & K. 54 fish, weighing 240 lbs., biggest 22 lbs. 24th to 27th, Poonch rather dirty, Jhelum in flood. Fished with 2″ spoons and 2″ and 2½″ Devons. Water getting a bit too clear, 2nd June.

7*th to* 10*th June*—Six fish 81 lbs., biggest 38 lbs. River clear, Poonch dirty on 9th, rain in hills.

14*th to* 20*th June*—Twenty-four fish, 176 lbs., biggest 21 lbs., nearly all about Junction; all on 1½″ to 2½″ spoons. Wonderfully cool for time of year. Poonch red but clearing on 15th. On 20th again came down red.

26*th to* 30*th September*—Eleven fish, biggest 14 lbs., one 1 lb. butchwa. All below Arno. Storm in hills 28th. Poonch clear all 29th, came down dirty 30th. Jhelum dirty whole time.

27*th to* 30*th September*—Eight fish, biggest 8 lbs. Arrived Junction Swan, September 14th, to fish down to Tangrot. It immediately rained for 24 hours and Poonch came down roaring flood. Even after cleared, fish off feed. Only got one decent fish, 14½ lbs, on 1″ brass spoon at mouth of Mendla. Arrived Tangrot October 5th. Total fish, 57—111 lbs. mostly got in tributaries and trolling pools on way down. Very few got spinning.

6th to 16th October—Nine fish, 90 lbs. Mostly about Jungoo. Got one mulley. On natural bait, spoons and Devon. Poonch dirty on 6th, seven rods, some of time, some got nothing.

17th to 28th October—Seventeen fish, 380 lbs., biggest 44, 38½, 18½, 33, 34 and 2 mulleys. Mostly Jungoo, natural bait and phantoms. Poonch dirty 22nd, clear evening 23rd.

29th to 31st October—Poonch very low and clear.

21st to 25th October—Ten fish, 97 lbs., biggest 39lbs. Natural bait and Devon in Jungoo, first two days (3 fish) then fly-spoon in Jhelum.

5th to 25th November.—Poonch dead low, Jhelum right but cold. Got 249 lbs. fish. Fishing during day useless. Got fish at Junction early morning and evening Fly-spoon or tiny phantom. Big fish all caught in Jungoo after dark.

18th to 20th November—Poonch very low and clear. Jhelum clear and too cold. Bag *nil*.

November 26th to 2nd December—Five mahseer, 53 lbs., one 35-pounder, all on natural bait in Jungoo. Also one mulley 5 lbs., one 35-pounder. Water not favourable, too clear and cold.

24th to 27th December—Eight fish, 34, 32, 16, water clearing after recent rain. A-1 sport on Christmas Day, 101 lbs. Casting 3" phantom in top corner of Jungoo.

January 1907.—Weather very bad all through this month. On 7th, Poonch very low; heavy rain 8th and 9th and both rivers in flood 9th to 14th and again 24th to end of month. In addition, wood contractor closed Jungoo with rope bunds to catch sleepers. However, got a few fish and think *January* not a month to be despised.

N.B.—Strict injunctions have now been given to wood contractor that Jungoo is not again to be bunded.

23*rd February to* 6*th March*—Up to Kotli and back. Thirteen fish, 19, 7, 7, on small Devon.

9*th March*—Arrived to find both rivers dirty. On 10th heavy rain fell, and also on 11th. No fishing till 14th. Snow water followed rain and sport till 18th, when I left, was poor.

6*th March to* 3*rd April*—Got a 30 lb. fish, tail end of Jungoo rapid first evening on spoon. After, a few up to 11 lbs. Broken in junction one day by a fish. Two days after this fish a 9 pounder was caught in Jhelum with my spoon and trace still in him.

24*th to* 28*th February*—Nine fish, 80 lbs. 19, 15; mostly junction on 3″ brass Devon.

1*st to* 20*th March* —Ten fish, 110 lbs., 31, 22, 17½; mostly junction on 3″ Devon; 7th to 13th unfishable.

21*st to* 30*th March*—Ten fish, 110 lbs., 31, 22, 17½; 7th to 18th unfishable.

5th *April*—Heavy snow water rendered junction unfishable.

31*st March to* 6*th April*—Seven fish, 6, 6, 6, 5, 3, 2, 2, lbs. All caught Panchakies on phantom and dead bait. Could do nothing elsewhere.

5*th to* 12*th April*—Went up to Chak. Poonch very high and coloured, heavy snow water, caught only few small fish. Hooked a 30 lb. fish on frog in Upper Arno, he broke me.

On return Tangrot 12th, Poonch very high and fishing hopeless.

6th and 7th May—Poonch rather high, Jhelum snow water. Got a 10½-pounder junction rapid on spoon.

Fished Poonch down to Tangrot 23·5 to 18·6, and stayed Tangrot till 26th. Coming down poor sport, only 11 fish 22½ lbs. Good deal of rain at Tangrot, 29 fish, 24, 12, 12, 9, all at junction on—— ?

Fished Poonch to Tangrot 23·5 to 18·6, only 10 fish—18¾ lbs. Stayed Tangrot 18th to 26th. Jungoo full of rafts; bag at Tangrot 38 fish—298 lbs. 22, 21, 10, nearly all junction on 2″ silver Devon.

On 21st Poonch unfishable in morning, on 23rd Poonch came down red.

7th to 10th July—Nine fish, 17, 9, 8. Poonch rather too clear.

29th June to 17th July—Ten fish, 59 lbs., and one 25 lbs. turtle.

23rd September—Tangrot to Chak, 13 fish, 21½ lb. on 1″ fly-spoon.

24th September—Chak to Palak, 16 fish, 30½ lbs., fly-spoon.

25th September—Above Palak, 20 fish, 69½ lbs., fly-spoon.

26th September—Above Palak, 5 fish, 26 lbs., fly-spoon.

27th September—At Palak, 4 fish, 10 lbs., fly-spoon.

28th September—Redan to Pirmal, 26 fish, 102 lbs., fly-spoon, an 18½ pounder large spoon.

29th September—Palak, 10 fish, 38 lbs., fly-spoon.

30*th September*—Palak, 4 fish, 31 lbs., fly spoon.

1*st October*—Returned to Tangrot, no sport on march down. Fish apparently very plentiful about Pirmal, and less and less down river. (Lt.-Col. Russell and Lt. Underwood).

21*st September to 3rd October*—Poonch to Tangrot, 129 lbs. of fish. Water clear the whole time, weather hot and dry; mostly spoon, all smallish fish.

7*th September to 9th October*—Twenty-three fish, 93 lbs. Poonch to Tangrot.

3*rd to* 12*th October*—Tangrot to Palak and back, about 38 fish, 71 lbs., on spoon. Poonch very low and clear.

N.B.—It must be remembered that the rains of 1907 were very scanty.

6*th to* 12*th October*—Eleven fish on natural bait and phantom, mostly Jungoo, 37½, 29, 20, 20,15, 13, etc. Poonch as low as *December*. Fish taken in Jungoo 5-30 to 6 A.M. and again 6-30 to 7 P.M. Could not move fish anywhere else.

2*nd to* 4*th December*—Two small fish, Pauchakkies. Poonch very low and clear, Jungoo full of rafts.

11*th to* 13*th December*—Nine fish, 77 lbs. 17, 13, 10, Jungoo, fishing under difficulties as pool full of sleepers.

11*th January* 1908—21, 12, 19, 15, top end Jungoo, 3″ blue phantom. Poonch slightly dirty, strong wind blowing.

12*th to* 23*rd January*—River dead low, fishing off.

24*th January*—Twenty pounder Junction, 3″ blue phantom, river pale coffee colour.

26th January—10, 10, Junction, dead bait.

3rd February—Twenty-three pounder, Bihari junction, 3" brown phantom, the only decent fish I got in three weeks, from Tangrot to Kotli and back, though I did not fish much, as river so low.

Poonch hopeless all *February*, dead low and clear and cold north wind every day. Hardly a fish taken below Jungoo whole month. Plenty of fish showing in chukker, but could not catch them. Jhelum dirty whole month. 3rd February to 12th March, 52 fish, 425 lbs. 45, 28, 25, 22, 18, almost all in Jungoo on dead bait. Hardly a blank day. Water slightly coloured and low. Lost two or three in chukker.

Arrived Tangrot March 8th. Jhelum in red flood, Poonch so low that only 2′ of water at junction. Jhelum cleared on 11th, and between 13th and 18th we caught fish in chukker 36, 35, 27, 23, 20, 20, 20, 19, 15, 10, 7½, 6, 4, lbs. All on 3 and 2½″ spoons. On 17th and 18th Poonch rose a little. The 36-pounder caught casting from stones half way down chukker. (Mrs. Crawford caught a 27 lb. mahseer.)

March 31st to April 1st—7, 13, 6, 6, 9, Jungoo to Junction, on 2½ and 3″ spoon; water coloured.

March 22nd to April 1st—Twenty-nine fish, 224 lbs. From Jungoo to Chukker.

Arrived Tangrot 16th February to find river very low, at last melting snows from early and unusual heat began to tell, but fish could not get up Poonch and began to collect and show in reach in Jhelum below chukker. This gave some fishing, but many blank days, owing to wind and storms making the Jhelum dirty.

21st February to 3rd April—Forty-four fish, 907 lbs. 48, 46, 43, etc., all on dead bait and spoon.

The above interesting note is by I. Z. Allan, and I would recommend the study of the full record in Angler's Book.

3rd to 6th April—Five fish, 110 lbs. 48, 25½, 19½, at L. and K. on phantom and spoon.

18th to 25th April—Twenty-four fish, 255 lbs., 25, 24, 18½, etc. Fish taking well.

3rd April to 1st May—Ninety-six fish, 521 lbs, 31, 29, 20, 15½. River unfishable 7 to 19th April. Towards end of April Poonch too clear. Nearly all caught at K. on spoon.

17th to 21st May—Twenty-three, 230 lbs. 30, 25, 23½. on 2½ and 2″ silver spoons. Nearly all at K. River muddy but clearing.

21st April to June 1st—One hundred and one fish, 549 lbs., 42, 34, 22. One kalabanse and one tengara. May 20th to 26th, had 96, 321 lbs. May 10 to 16, water too muddy to fish. Big fish caught early morning and evening. All on spoon, mostly at K. (J. D. Inverarity).

19th April to 29th June—Eight hundred and sixty-six lbs. fish, between Tangrot and Swan river, 37, 33, 29¼, 17, mostly on spoons. (G. N. Thompson.)

N.B.—Above is a most interesting bag and should be studied.

15th to 18th June—Water good order, 6 fish, 16 lbs. at Junction; silver spoon.

25th to 29th June—Five. 32 lbs., water clearing after 27th.

21st to 29th June—Fourteen, 144½ lbs., 37, 27, at K. and L., all on chilwa.

After a careful study of the Anglers' Book for the last six years, the following is the conclusion I arrived at. May and June, and September and October seem to be as good months as any. March seems very uncertain. April even more so. December and January have occasionally given good results. The Jhelum and Poonch seem to be as uncertain as any river could be, but given one month on the rivers, one might expect, say, 13 blank days, 15 indifferent to good days fishing, and 2 A-1 days. And it is those two red letter days, that make Tangrot such a Mecca to the Indian Angler.

About eight miles up from Tangrot the Casi stream joins the Jhelum, and might be clear if the latter was dirty. However, it does not carry much water and is almost impossible to fish near the junction without a boat, as it flows in down a glen with perpendicular cliffs.

There are a lot of wild pigeon in the rocks up the left bank of the Jhelum above the bungalow.

At Shekopur there used to be fishing according to "the Anglers' Handbook", but latterly I have never heard of any one fishing here.

Notes on the Poonch River.

By Bt. Colonel Norman, 22nd Cavalry.

This river can be reached either from Kashmir, or from Jhelum. To reach it from Kashmir, a start has to be made from Uri whence the stages, *vide* the Kashmir route book, are—

			Miles.
Hyderabad	...	...	... 10
Aliabad	...	...	... 7
Kahuta	...	...	... 8
Poonch	...	...	... 9
		Total	... 34

A new road has, however, been lately made which is slightly longer.

		Miles.
Uri to Aliabad	...	... 18
Aliabad to Poonch	...	... 19
	Total	... 37

There is a rest-house at Aliabad, and also one at Hattar about 7 miles from Aliabad. These are available to travellers but only after application to the Governor of Poonch.

From Jhelum on the N.-W. Railway, or from Dina one station higher up the line, roads lead to Tangrot, a famous fishing centre, at the junction of the Poonch with the Jhelum. From Jhelum it is 24 miles to Tangrot, this distance being divided into two stages, each being 12 miles, with Shekopur as the half way house, where there is a very good little bungalow. There is a fair driving road from Jhelum to Shekopur, thence a riding one to Tangrot. Carriages are obtainable at Jhelum. Taking it all round, the best way to reach Tangrot is from Dina. Here, there is a small Railway rest-house of one room, which the Station Master at Dina places at the disposal of travellers if not required by the railway officials. A contractor living close to the station supplies some very diminutive riding ponies and either mules or camels for baggage, and a letter to the Station Master will have the transport ready to meet the train. It is usual to do the distance to Tangrot in one day, as it is hardly worth while to stop at Shekopur, about four miles from Dina, unless one happens to arrive by a late train.

No matter which route is taken into Poonch, it is customary to obtain the permission of the Raja of Poonch to enter his territory and fish in the river. This act of courtesy should not be forgotten, for the Raja, who is himself a good sportsman, can give much assistance. Tangrot itself is in British territory; here there is a four-roomed bungalow and a post office. There is, however, no khansamah. Fishing in the Poonch is permissible only by license, under the Kashmir Fisheries Act, the fee being Rs. 20 per season or Rs. 10 for one month. Licenses are obtainable at Tangrot from the water bailiff or from the Superintendent, Kashmir Fisheries, Srinagar, Kashmir. At present this officer is Major Wigram, but it is better not to address him by name as he may be absent at the time.

It is most important that all anglers stick closely to the tariffs laid down for boatmen, shikaris, etc. The present rates were decided by the Superintendent, Kashmir Fisheries, in consultation with these gentlemen and all agreed to them. They are—

A boat with three men Re. 1 per diem, with two men only, 14 annas. If the steerer acts as a shikari and is registered as such, he is entitled to 4 annas extra. If the shikari does not act as a steerer, he is paid 8 annas a day at Tangrot and 12 annas if taken up the river.

There is really no necessity for a shikar at all, but some of them are very useful at times in landing big fish and several of them are good at making up tackle. The registered shikaris (in 1909) are—Fakroo, Fakira. Mahomed Alam Ghulam Mahomed, Nek Mahomed, Ghulam Husain, Mankta, Ghulam Husain, Kutab Din, Hassan, Sakhi Mahomed, Sher and Satar Mahomed.

The boatmen are Husain Din, Sakhi Mahomed, Mankta, Mahomed Alam, Fateh Mahomed, Mahomed Hassan (son of Fakira), Jecadar is Fakira.

It is advisable to write on ahead to one of these men and engage his services, as at times there is a great rush of anglers to Tangrot and neither boats nor shikaris are available.

In regard to the best time for fishing the Poonch, there is no doubt that March, April, September, October and November are the best months, but there is often very good fishing at other times in the year. The following précis taken from the Angler's Book in the Tangrot bungalow, shows the number of fish of 30 lbs. and upwards taken from 1875-1895, and it is perhaps the best guide as to the best time for fishing.

January	3.	1 in Jungoo, 2 at H, all on 2½" spoon.
February	2.	1 at H, 1 at L, on 2½ and 3½" spoon.
March	68.	1 in Jungoo, 4 at H, 4 at J, 7 at K, 21 at L, 26 at M, and 5 up the river. Of these 44 were caught on spoon mostly S and G, and 3 to 3½". Five were taken on natural bait.

April	15.	1 in Jungoo, 6 at J, 6 at L, 1 at M and 1 at N. Of these, 5 were taken on spoon, one on bait and one on 4½″ "Glass Bait" (?). A 62 lb. was taken at N, on 3½″ G and S spoon.
May	7.	2 at J, 2 at K, 3 at L, all on spoon.
June	2	Place not stated. One being a 50 lb. on natural bait.
July	*Nil.*	
August	2.	Up river at Mendli.
September	13.	1 at K, 2 at L, 1 at M, 1 at N and 8 up the river. Nearly all on large spoon.
October	38.	1 at K, 2 at L, 1 at M, 1 at N and 8 up the river, at places not stated.
November	25.	9 in Jungoo, 1 in Arno, 5 at J, 5 at H, 1 at M and 4 at Nar. Of these, 8 were on natural bait and 10 M spoon.
December	1.	At L on spoon.

Total ... 176 in 20 years.

The above cannot be considered a perfect record of every fish caught during the period stated, probably many anglers did not enter their catches, certainly not those who, starting from Tangrot, fished up the river.

From Tangrot to Poonch the distance is 74 miles, and this can be divided up into as many stages as there may be leave available, but the following may be taken as the most suitable :—

Tangrot.		Miles.	
Chak ...	...	6	
Chowmook	...	4	(Rest-house)
Palak ...	...	4	
Kirmal ...	...	5	
Nar ...	...	6	
Chak ...	...	8	
Thatli ...	...	5	
Hil ...	...	3	(Good junction.)
Kotli ...	...	3	
Leri ...	...	9	
Mendli ...	...	7	
Madaarpur	...	6	
Poonch ...	...	7	
Total	...	73	

Supplies are now and then difficult, so a good stock should be laid in according to fancy. The best place to camp in at Poonch is in the Raja's gardens, for which permission is of course required. There is no postal arrangement up the river, though a post does go through to Poonch, arrangements to bring along one's post must be made personally with the Post Master at Tangrot, who will forward letters if coolies are arranged for.

It is useful to take a boat up the river from Tangrot, and the boatmen at the latter place wile do so as far as Kotli for an extra charge.

It is well to know that if the Poonch comes down in flood it takes a good 5 days to clear at Tangrot.

Jhelum Canal.—Headworks at Rasul, eight miles on trolley from Bahadari station, Canal bungalow, permit required from Executive Engineer of Canal. Like at Rupar, the dam here is constructed across a gap between low hills, with weir 4,100′ in length and canal can take 3,800 cubic feet of water per second. I am told that the fishing here is indifferent, as it seems to be a matter of much difficulty to find the water clear. This is a pity, since with a good flow of surplus water (see note on Chenab Canal) always going down, the fishing here ought to be better than at most of the other headworks.

At Jhelum itself there is, I believe, some fishing to be had in the river, using atta for mahseer, and a fly-spoon for butchwa.

By driving about four miles up the river from Jhelum, to where some saw mills stand, there are two or three good rapids, and if fished from a boat, by spinning either before the snow water comes down, or in the autumn, occasionally one gets a couple or so of good mahseer in an afternoon.

Two or three men have told me that they have had good sport stopping a day at Kohala, *en route* to Kashmir; spinning when the water was clear, and using atta if coloured. There seems no doubt that the Jhelum here holds plenty of good fish.

Concerning the Mahl and Goon rivers, I have not been able to procure any information that throws further or later light on these streams, than that given in the Angler's Handbook.

The Chenab River—Rises in Lahoul and is formed by two streams ; one, the Chandra, issues from a large snow bed on Bara Lacha, 16,000′ high, the other, the Bhaga, which rises on the north-west slopes of the pass. Both streams unite at Tandi, and the river now known as the Chenab sweeps through Chumba into Cashmere territory. All along this portion it flows between immense cliffs, and high mountains. At Akhnur it becomes navigable.

At Khanki.—Eight miles from Wazirabad are the head-works of the Chenab canal, where I am told good fishing is to be had. Probably, it is much the same and governed by the same conditions as the head-works of Sirhind Canal at Rupar. Reached *viâ* Wazirabad and Mansurawala station, whence it is two miles by trolly. Canal bungalow, for use of which permission should be asked from Executive Engineer in charge of canal. The river runs in a very broad sandy bed here, nearly one mile across, and the canal takes all the water in the cold weather, its capacity being 11,000 cubic feet per second. Fishing is in the canal, or in pool in river below sluice gates. A most interesting scheme of canals has, I believe, just received the sanction of Government, and will be carried out in the next three or four years. At Rasul on the Jhelum Canal, a lot of water runs annually to waste, whereas the Chenab Canal wants all it can get, and has none to spare for Montgomery district, where water is badly needed. Hence the following scheme. Above Jhelum and below Tangrot a canal will be taken off from the river, down which the surplus water now passing the shutters at Rasul, will flow. This canal will join the Chenab river just above Khanki. Then some miles above Wazirabad, an equivalent amount of water will be taken from Chenab down a canal into the Montgomery district. So Government, in its wisdom, may make another two fishing localities for us !

Near Wazirabad.—In the Chenab itself some fishing may be had by anyone who marches up or down the Grand Trunk Road. The river generally seems dirty here, so use atta or worm. Go two miles back along the road to where the road and rail bridge crosses the river. Fish under the bridge itself, and also about 200 yards up off some rocks is a good place. The Pulkoo stream, half way to the Chenab, could also be tried, it is about 15′ deep near the bridge of boats, and a lot of fish were moving the day I crossed it.

Also, in the smaller runs of the Chenab near Multan, quite good sport is to be had with butchwa, using, as a bait, clotted goat's blood.

Notes on the Chenab.

By Bt.-Col. W. Norman, 22nd Cavalry.

"This river rises in Kashmir and enters the Sialkote district some nine miles above Beni Sing, where it takes in the Jammu Tawi. And concerning this river—the Jammu Tawi—a correspondent writes me 'I have only tried it once, without success, and from what I saw of the river, was not much impressed with it from an angling point of view'. Some twenty miles north of Beni Sing is Riassi, Kashmir territory, and now and then reports are circulated of wonderful fish taken here by the villagers with nets. It is not improbable that, allowing for exaggeration, there may be some truth in these reports. From Riassi to Akhnur the river flows through the mountains and there must be some good places, but so far as is known, these have not yet been visited by anglers. Below Akhnur, the river breaks up into a number of channels which eventually form junctions with the main stream. Beni Sing is thirteen miles from Sialkote, by the Chaprar road, which is drivable but rough. There is a fair camping ground and supplies from a village close by. The fishing is from boats which can be got from the Guzar Pul ferry, about a quarter of a mile down stream. The next place to fish at below Beni Singh, is Sikka. The latter is a group of hamlets opposite the Gangwal Ferry. The latter is some thirteen miles from Sialkote *viâ* the Gondal road, also drivable but rough. Crossing the river at the Gangwal Ferry, camp should be pitched on the high bank just below the junction of the Miran Khor nala. Some six hundred yards above this, there is another junction where the Bhag nala comes in. Fishing is from boats at the two junctions, and from the high bank below the Miran Khor junction. About one and a half miles below this the Khano Bhao nala comes, also on the right bank, and before joining the main stream it takes in the Bhimber Tawi. Here again the fishing is from boats which can be obtained from the from Kooree-ka Pattan Ferry. The latter is the ferry by which one crosses the river in order to reach Minaor on the road to the Tawi. About a mile below the latter junction is Marala, the head-works of the Upper Chenab Canal, which, it is believed, will be completed in 1912. When completed, the weirs at Marala should rival those at Rupar. About thirty miles below Marala is the Alexandra bridge, over the railway, and here there is fishing from the bank. Lower down stream again is Khanki, the head works of the Lower Chenab Canal. Here there are undoubtedly fine fish but they are very shy. Alexandra Bridge is some two miles from Wazirabad station, from whence one can bicycle along to the bridge on the Grand Trunk Road. Khanki can only be reached with the assistance of the Canal Engineer, who would provide carriage by rail or trolly.

In regard to the fishing itself. There is no doubt that there are good fish in the river, for they are constantly caught by the natives with nets, but do not so easily come to hand by rod and line. The river is undoubtedly poached in all directions, especially near Wazirabad and at Khanki, so that it is hardly worth while going to these two places. At Beni Sing and Sikka some good fish have been taken by rod and line. The capabilities of the river are undeniably great, but they want consideration, and this should be paid when the Marala canal is completed."

THE NOWSHERA OR BHIMBER TAWI.

By Bt -Col. Norman, 22nd Cavalry.

I have not fished this from Nowshera, and can only give an account of the lower portion of the river, accessible from Sialkote. Leaving Sialkote cross the Chenab about 12 miles from cantonments at a ferry just above Marala. The latter is the head-works of the Upper Chenab Canal, which is in process of construction and should be opened in 1912, and then perhaps, if proper steps are taken, Marala may become a second Rupar. Crossing the Chenab ride to Minaor, about 9 miles, here there is a lovely camping ground in a mango grove. The next ride is to either Chokla, or Baro, the former being on the right bank and the latter on the left bank of the Bhimber. The preference should be given to Baro, distant 9 miles from Minaor. Leaving Minaor, the road strikes the river at Chamb and here, near some panchakkies, a small fly-spoon can be used. Fording the river at Chamb, ride to Samoo and then re-cross to right bank till opposite Baro, when re-cross. It is not worth while wasting time at Baro, though there is a little fishing both above and below. If horses are previously sent across the Chenab the day before, it is advisable to ride the 30 miles to Baro in one day. The going is capital the whole way. From Baro the next march should be Seripla, about 8 miles, but over very stony country. Seripla is not marked on the map and, as a matter of fact, it is almost impossible to recognize any of the places named on it, the inhabitants profess utter ignorance of the places named. The camp is on the left bank of the river, opposite a small village on right bank. From here there is no further road up the river, and the kit would have to make a long circuit over the hills to the next camp at Kaholian. The natives say that in parts the road is so bad that mules would have to be unloaded, this being the case it would be necessary to send coolies along with the kit. Above Seripla, the river is one succession of long deep pools, some of which are over 800 yds. in length and flanked by difficult hills and cliffs. The scenery is magnificent, and the passage up the pools and rapids on *mussuk* rafts most exciting. The inhabitants are Dogras, a wonderfully cheerful and willing lot of folk There is no difficulty in getting coolies and arranging for rafts. Each raft requires four men to propel it, and they are well content with four annas a day. There are absolutely no supplies to be got except milk, so one should take a supply of fowls. A short distance beyond Baro, is a village called Ausirn, there is another just below it, and from these two the shikaris and coolies should be obtained. From Kaholian the next march would be Nal, but I have not been up as far as this.

Now, in regard to the fishing there is a capital little run above Baro where the track crosses the stream, and from here on to Seripla there are a succession of runs and pools, though we only got small fish up to two and three pounds, there are in all probability very much larger ones. I was broken, when fishing with single gut, by a large mulley, about 10 lbs , who simply took my spoon like a mahseer. Above

Seripla the two biggest taken by anglers from Sialkote, were 14 and 20 lbs. About half way between Seripla and Kaholian is a difficult gorge called Machi Bawan, where there are some grand pools but full of rocks, and one has to be skilful in playing one's fish. The best lure is silver and copper spoon, but the fish take natural bait also.

To anyone fishing from Sialkote on a ten days' trip, the thing to do is to make straight for Seripla, make that a centre and on occasions, leaving the camp there, move up some three miles to Kaholian. Here there is a nice camp, plenty of shade and good water, a couple of blankets and some washing materials will have to suffice, for the rafts cannot well carry more in addition to one's own weight. The Khansamah would go on another raft, and he can only take a couple of cooking pots, teapot and a minimum of supplies. In case it is desired to stay at Kaholian more than one day, coolies can go back to camp for supplies.

The Ravi River—Rises in Kulu, passing immediately into Chamba. It runs for some miles along the Jummu boundaries, the mountains here rising straight from the river bank. At Shahpur it leaves the hills but still continues to run through high cliffs.

There is fishing to be had below Dalhousie, if one knows where to make for, but one must go before the snow water comes down.

At Madhopur—About 8 miles from Pathankot, is the head of the Barin canal, with weir 2,370′ long and taking 8,000 cubic feet of water per second, but about the fishing here I could get no definite *khabar*.

Between Shahdara and Lahore, the Ravi is crossed by a bridge of boats. There is a small P. W. D. rest-house here on bank. Opposite it is a mud flat, off which several local anglers were fishing when I passed. They were using worm and catching butchwa and small rohu. One boy fishing off bridge of boats caught a seetul of 1 lb. on worm. This was in October.

The Beas River—Rises in Kulu on the south side of the Rohtang Pass, at an elevation of 13,000′ above sea-level. In its higher reaches it is an extremely swift stream, its fall being something like 125′ per mile. A correspondent kindly sends me the following.

"Always use him if you can get him, Sadharu of the village of Sansarpur, Post Office Tal Wara, District Hoshiarpur. He is a high class Rajput, and quite a decent native and companionable. A second man (a shikari) in some ways a better man, but a sycophant and beggar, but knows the river well; also a good class Rajput is Mian Changan, Post Office Pandain, District Hoshiarpur. Best months for fishing—(*i*) end of September, or in October when water is clearing (but not too clear); (*ii*) in March after winter rains.

Places on river—1. Dera Gopipur. 2. Nariara Paltan. 3. Purana Pultan. 4. Gul Bahar. 5. Duk-ki-Pultan. 6. Cherra. 7. Bainta. 8. Khetra. 9. Sathana. 10. Simle (Sadharu lives close here). 11. Hora (near flour mills). 12. Rey. 13. Bogrwan. 14. Suruwan. 15. Bahadarpur.

16. Nowshera (quite close to Gurdaspur). Recommend telling Sadharu to meet you at Gopipur; get *mussak* raft (Kutnao), and go down river gradually fishing best places, ending at Nowshera, thence by ekka to Gurdaspur. Best part of river from Cherra to Bogrwan; 6, 7, 9, 1, 12 are excellent pools and pay best when hurled from a boat. This would have to be brought and a man arranged to work it, very few on river. Sadharu knows names. Jhanda at Rey, and Chowratta at Nowshera are excellent boatmen and know the river. Alternative way would be to go by ekka or tonga to Nurpur or Kotla and across to Katrah by road with mules, crossing the river at Duk-ki-Pultan. Katrah is two long marches, a small police bungalow is at Chandari about half way.

Supplies.—Milk, butter and fowls not got easily: you can get sheep in most places. Grain, also, generally dear. Live bait also difficult to obtain. Spoon is easiest and most used, also Devon minnows, the weighted ones being best. For bait I always use the Crocodile spinner. Small fly-spoons and fly rod give excellent sport. Excellent run from Sathana to Simle. Must have tent. Bungalows only to be got at Dera Gopipur (dak bungalow, no supplies); Talwara, near Hora, District bungalow; Nowshera, forest bungalow. Road along river best for mules. Camels can be taken but, above Bogrwan, give trouble, grazing, etc. Must use Malloch or Hardy casting reels to get best results if casting from bank, but in any case to be preferred to ordinary reels. Pay of fisherman should not be more than 8 annas a day, or Rs. 10 to Rs. 15 per month.

Bazar Chowdry at Pathankot or Gurdaspur; or by Kangra, by tonga and ekka to Dera Gopipur.*

Another correspondent sends me the following: "The Beas near Hoshiarpur, used to be one of the best rivers in India, but for the last six years the netting and poaching that has been going on is appalling. The formation of the bottom, all round smooth stones makes it quite easy to net. There used to be no netting or poaching in Bruere's time, when he was D. S. P. Hoshiarpur, but now they have wiped the river clean !!!"

Then again, the Beas river is crossed lower down by the railway bridge and road ford, half way between Girana and Raya, two stages on the Grand Trunk Road. Good sport may sometimes be had, fishing under the railway arches. The two pools nearest each bank, are, or were, the best to fish in, as through both there was a fair current in 1908. Use a fly-spoon. Fish mahseer up to 5 lbs. (and probably much heavier) and butchwa. In October, if river is clear, one might make quite a good bag of the latter. I do not know if the new bridge for second line of rails will improve or spoil the fishing, probably the former.

The following note by Yuba Bill, on the Beas river appeared in the *Indian Field* of July 4th, 1907, and is reproduced here by kind permission of the Editor of that paper :—

"Strange to say, the river which stands first in my estimation as a Mahseer river, is barely mentioned in books on the subject, per-

---

* Note—Dera Gopipur is spelt Deihreh on Ordnance maps. –S.D.

haps because owing to the difficulties connected with carriage and supplies, it is less frequented than other well known rivers. I refer to the Beas, which flows through Kulu, and later on forms the natural boundary between the Kangra and Hoshiarpur districts, Panjab. Some years ago, I supplied Mr. G. H. Lacy with some brief notes on this river, which he included in his book 'The Northern Punjab Angler's Handbook,' and, as far as I am aware, this is the only book which contains any mention of this charming river. The best place to make for, in order to start fishing, is Dehra Gopipur, and the easiest way to get there is to go to Jullunder by rail; thence to Hoshiarpur, 25 miles along a metalled road by dâk ghari; and on to Dehra Gopipur by dooly or ekka. I forget the exact distance of this part of the journey, but a dooly takes about 13 hours to accomplish it, and it is most conveniently undertaken by night. At Dehra Gopipur there is a dâk bungalow just above the river. For about ten miles above this, the river is a fishable, but the best fishing is for some four or five marches down, as far as Surawan. Below this, the river gets into flatter country and breaks up into several streams, in which only small fish will be taken. Doolies can be obtained on application beforehand, to the Deputy Commissioner of Hoshiarpur. Mules are necessary for carriage, for the marches along the river, for which application should be made to the Deputy Commissioner of Kangra, and also for "drays" or "kutnaos," which are the only means of getting at the best water. These consist of country beds tied on inflated buffalo hides, which only draw about two inches of water and can be taken over almost any rapid. Tents are necessary, as there are no bungalows below Dehra Gopipur. The most comfortable way of travelling is to send your tent and luggage off on mules when starting in the morning, send off a servant on one kutnao, and take another yourself, stopping to fish all the likely places on the way. You you can thus arrange to have breakfast ready for you on arrival at your next camp, 8 to 10 miles distant, at about midday, and your luggage—bedding, etc.—will arrive during the afternoon The best fishing place on the river is the Sitana pool, which contains monsters, and where you can camp under a magnificent banian tree on the cliff above the river, on the right bank. A gold and silver spoon is the best bait, with a change to a fly in the smaller runs. Supplies should be taken. From Surawan go across to Pathankot railway station."

Concerning the upper waters of the Beas, I have not been able to find out as much as I could wish, but as it is a river of big tributaries in the higher reaches, there should be some good fishing to be got. However, it is a curious fact, related to me by more than one angler, that above Mandi the mahseer appear to cease altogether taking a spinning bait. When the recent Mandi expedition was on, the troops found the Suketi Nullah to be full of fish, but owing to lack of tackle were not as successful in catching them as they could have wished. The natives, however, at Mandi, fish with rod and line. The Suketi, as the hot weather progresses, becomes a chain of deep pools, practically still water, and overgrown to a great extent with weeds. In the pool below the suspension bridge, the fish could be seen in large numbers, and of all sizes. They took atta, and, if a big one was hooked, it was generally a case of being borken in the weeds. Also, they soon got shy, but this was only to be expected in still pools. Several of the streams in Kulu are now being stocked with English trout; the experiment is new, but, from what I hear, gives every promise of being a great success.

Mahseer in Kulu seem to be rather a doubtful quantity, but a correspondent writes me that they are certainly present in May and October at the junction of the Parbati and Beas Rivers. The same correspondent kindly gives me the following information: "Below come the Tirthan and Sainj rivers, and lower down the Pandoh Nullah and the Ool River. No one has ever fished these systematically. But the Beas all the way is full of good pools, and should be worth trying. Use live or dead bait, but atta is *the* thing in the Beas anywhere above Sujanpur-Teerah. The Ool river would appear to be affected by snow water. At Sultanpur, fish of three and four lbs. (Himalayan barbel) have been caught in May, on atta, and in the rains, worming with trout tackle is good fun.

Since writing the foregoing notes, on the Sutlej and Beas rivers, I have been fortunate enough to receive the following most interesting contribution from Lieut.-General W. Osborn, (late of the Indian Army), than whom there is probably no better or more experienced angler to-day in this country.

"The two most accessible rivers of the Punjab, for mahseer fishing, are the Sutlej and the Beas, but before noting the fishing localities on either, it is well to say a few words as to their respective merits. I will take the Sutlej first as being the larger of the two.

The Sutlej is of immense length as compared to the Beas, and its great length is a positive disadvantage to it as a fishing river. It rises in far off Tibet in the Mansarowar Lake, and, from its long course, it is much subject to those small floods of discoloured water, which are the bane of the mahseer fisherman. For if upon any section of this river, high up or low down, storms of rain, sleet or snow should occur, down comes a small flood which spoils the fishing, and the constant nature of these floods is very tantalising, for, generally speaking, when they come down the river takes a long time to clear. More than once I have lost nearly a whole fishing season while wearily waiting for the Sutlej to get into order. This is bad enough for a man whose time is his own, but to a fisherman whose leave is limited, it is fatal to his prospects of sport. Of fish of course there are many, for the river is well stocked with mahseer of all sizes, and, while the water is clear, sport is certain, but the fickle nature of the Sutlej as I have described makes it a disappointing river.

The Beas in its nature as a clear water river is very different from the Sutlej. I consider this to be the very best fishing river in the Punjab. Compared to the Sutlej it is quite a short river, taking of course its length where mahseer fishing may be practised, and it holds grand fish of all sizes. The Beas rises in a clear pool on the very top of the Rotang Pass, the Pass over which runs the road to Ladakh, Yarkand and Central Asia. From its source, which is a sacred spot among Hindus, it takes a southerly direction, running down the face of that range of the Himalayas known as 'Beas Khund' till it reaches the head of the Kulu valley at Rahla. From here the river winds through the whole of the Kulu valley, its volume increased by very many tributary streams. Of course some of these latter are glacier fed, but many are not, and those that do come from the glaciers, do not in any very great measure affect the colour of the main stream of the Beas, which remains in a fishable condition for a much longer period than the Sutlej.

Fishing localities on the river Sutlej.—Those that I have personal knowledge of are as follows: First five miles to the south of Bilaspur as you approach that town from Kalka, there is a tributary of the Sutlej known as the Gumbar Khud, or Gumbar Nullah; this stream is much affected by mahseer during the spawning season, and, at its mouth where it enters the Sutlej, there is good fishing to be had. The next place is at the town of Bilaspur itself. The straight run from above the dak bungalow, up to where a large tributary stream debouches from among the low hills, is good fishing ground, but only from the bank where eddies occur. The next march from Bilaspur as you approach Suket and Mandi, is Dihur (as spelt on Ordnance map). There is good fishing ground all about the right bank above the ferry here. The left bank is precipitous, there is a very good fishing place and a good pool surrounded by large rocks at about $1\frac{1}{2}$ miles below the ferry. It is close to some temples and a grove of trees known as 'The Ram Bagh.' In fact there are many fishing places in the vicinity of Bilaspur and Dihur, where a fisherman, who knows his way about, can easily find sport, but of course the Sutlej must be clear.

Fishing localities on the river Beas. The first and highest point on this river where mahseer fishing may be tried is at Largi, about 11 miles from Bajaura in Kulu, on the Simla road. Here where the tributary river, the Sainj, enters the Beas, is a good fishing place, between the mouth of the Sainj and the Largi Bridge, close to some large rocks, below which there is an eddy and a pool. The Sainj itself is a good small mahseer river, when its waters are clear.

The next fishing place that I have any knowledge of, is on the Beas at Mandi, in the large pool above the suspension bridge, where the Suketi Nullah enters the pool. This used to be a splendid pool, but it has been ruined as a fishing place by frequent dynamiting, which was permitted of course, and could not be stopped as Mandi is a Punjab Hill State under its own Rajah. Just above the bridge at Mandi, the Suketi Nullah enters the Beas. This small river, considering its size, was the most remarkable river for good mahseer running up to 30 lbs. and over that I ever knew. It used to abound in good fish for two miles or so up in the direction of Suket, but this river, too, and its many good pools, has since been ruined by daily dynamiting. The river Beas at Mandi, and its tributary, the Suketi, will take at least three years to recover from the damage done to them by poachers and dynamiters of high position.

The next fishing place that I have any knowledge of, is at Dera Gopipur. This is a well known spot renowned for good sport, though rather too much frequented now-a-days. There is a dak bungalow here. It is the head-quarters of the Tahsil, and the fishermen shikaris of the town will show visitors the best places to fish. There are now, I believe, one or two boats on the river. It may be taken for granted that every point on the river Beas, where tributary streams from the Himalayan range (right bank) enter the river, good fishing is to be found near and about the mouths of these streams.

Proceeding down stream now we come to 'Dada Siba,' the headquarters of Rajah Jye Singh. There is a good camping ground here but no fishing that I know of quite near. About half way between Dada Siba and Sunsarpur, both on the left bank of the river, the Beas runs close below some high cliffs, at this place there is a large pool which holds good fish. It would be a good plan to encamp in its vicinity as I once did. From this pool going down stream we arrive at Sunsarpur, a good place for a camp, and about a quarter of a mile above Sansarpur there is a very good mahseer pool. Sirdaru, the Shikari of Sansarpur, is a very good fellow, and a great ally of mine. He knows all the good fishing places on the river in his neighbourhood and, while at Sunsarpur, it would be well to cross the river and fish at Satna on the right bank, not far off. About a mile or so below Sansarpur is Talwara, where there is a police or district bungalow.

There is no fishing at Talwara that I know of, except in the bulrush swamp below the right bank, close to the bungalow. In this swamp there are deep weedy pools, which are full of murral, which can only be caught if you know the Southern Indian way of catching them called 'Taptana.' A long bamboo rod is used, almost any dry bamboo will do if it tapers and is light enough. About two yards of strong line hangs from the point, the end of this line should bear a medium sized hook snooded with Hercules wire gimp. I mention this snood as it is the strongest. Hook a small live, or even dead, fish on to the hook through the back fin, a chilwa is best if you can get him. Then go dapping between the weeds as you would for chub. When you get a run strike, and heave the murral over your head into the next parish behind you, or he will dive into the weeds, from which you will find it difficult to dislodge him. Fastidious 'Record Breakers,' I won't call them fishermen, who turn up their noses at anything less than a 50lb. mahseer, would not soil their hands with this style of fishing, but there is fun to be got out of it, and a murral is a good fish to eat. For how to cook him see 'Thomas's Rod in India.' One march below Talwara we come to Ray, this is a good fishing place. I have known a 56lbs. mahseer landed here. I don't know the Beas below Ray, so that as far as fishing localities within my own knowledge goes, my fishing notes of the river Beas end here.

The Ool (this is the spelling on Ordnance map) river is a good-sized tributary of the Beas. It enters the main river some five or six miles above Mandi. I have never caught in it anything but Himalayan barbel. Mahseer, I should say, run up the Ool to spawn, but it is probable that they do not remain in it, as the Ool is cold, being a glacier-fed stream."

The two Beyn rivers pass one on each side of Jullunder, and in both, I believe, bottom fishing is to be had. The western I am told is the best, being dammed into deep pools in places, it is necessary, however, to be on the look out for quicksands. The Tommies from Cantonments visit these streams occasionally. Both rise in the Siwaliks, the Eastern (or white) Beyn passing within five miles of Jullunder flows into the Sutlej, the Western (or black) Beyn distant 18 miles from Cantoments, runs into the Beas.

The Sutlej River—Rises in Thibet, near one of the Manasarowar lakes, at a height of some 15,000′. Before reaching Bilaspur State N.W. of Simla, it flows through some immense gorges in the Himalayas. As a fishing river it is not very well known, owing probably both to its size and the fast volume of snow water that starts early from its sources up beyond the Himalayas, and to the fact that so much of its fishable course in India lies among the higher mountains, inaccessible to the casual fisherman with limited leave who must hit off the very brief time when the river is in order, either in March or when the rains have cleared off and before the icy waters from Thibet have chilled the mahseer's blood and put them permanently off their feed. Down below Lori bridge, about six marches from Simla *viâ* Narkanda the natives tell of enormous mahseer, and probably this portion is freely poached for the Simla market. And for those who may be marching up the Sutlej, or who, being stationed in the Simla hills, would like to give the fishing a trial, the following few notes about some of the tributaries may be of interest.

The *Nauti Gad* well known in connection with Simla's new water supply, flows in on the left bank. A short way up above its junction with the Sutlej, however, occur some falls which probably preclude fish of any size being found higher up the river. In the stretch below the falls there are one or two nice pools that hold a lot of snow trout. This junction, as well as all the junctions of Sutlej tributaries, is worth trying for big fish. The best route to Nauti Gad is probably either to follow the Suni road direct, or else go *viâ* Naldera, and one would have to find one's way as best one could to the stream from the nearest point the road passes by it. From Suni it lies about three miles, and Suni from Simla is some 17 miles.

A stream, rising above Jangi and flowing in from the right bank, about six miles below, is, I am told, of fair size but dynamited to death.

Almost opposite a small stream runs in past Senj, which sometimes hold fish of quite decent size for a mile or so up, if the tributary is carrying water.

The Sher Khud—Lower down on right bank, its junction only a mile or two below

Gamber river, is a fair sized stream but has a sandy bed with enormous pools, which are probably netted in the hot weather.

The Gumrola and Ullay—Tributaries on the left bank, carry no water to speak of, though from the map one would imagine them to be of fair size.

The Arni River—Flowing into Sutlej on right bank below Lori bungalow, should be worth a trial, as it has a fair sized catchment area and receives another big tributary, the Bisna stream.

Also midway between Lori and Suni, a big stream rising in Shikaradevi, over 11,000′ high, flows in on right bank. About this I can get no *khabar* however, and it is off the beaten track, and probably would not be known of unless a trip was made to it deliberately. There is a village marked Barlog at junction.

The Gamber River—Probably the best known and most accessible tributary the Sutlej receives. Though its course is short it has a large catchment area, and, if the winter rains are good, carries quite a large volume of water, equal to, if not greater than, that of the Giri at Kharganu. It can be reached both from Simla or Sabathu. If from Simla, one can make for either the upper reaches or the junction. In the former case proceed *viâ* Jutogh to Sairi, 10 miles, the road leaving Simla at Boileauganj and passing by Jutogh on the right drops steeply down to Sairi, which is a small village with a bazar and a bungalow. Thence through Haut to the junction of the Kani and Gamber rivers, being about 9 miles, leaving the Kakarhatti and Sabathu road at about two miles from Sairi. In latter case go *viâ* Jutogh (five miles) to Erki bungalow 16 miles from Simla, this is a large village with a bazar. Thence to Namuli bungalow is 14 miles. From here to Bilaspur is 12 miles, a lot of climbing being necessary at the start, and then road makes a long descent to Bilaspur. The track is some seven to eight feet broad with some very steep gradients. Bilaspur is a town on the left bank of the Sutlej and there is a bungalow here. From Bilaspur quite a good road runs to the junction of the Gamber river, about 3½ miles.

If going from Sabathu, proceed down the road through Kakarhatti, two miles and continue along the Erki road leaving this at about seven miles from Sabathu and asking your way to the village of Bagara. From thence below the junction of the Kani stream, the river begins to hold fish. Some few miles down below Bagara a stream runs in on the left bank, coming past Nari. Though this only carries apparently a trickle of water, there are some fine pools holding quite big fish for a short way up. Camps can be made at intervals anywhere down the river, whenever any suitable place occurs. The Gamber appears to be rather heavily poached in one or two of the small States through which it passes. There are some good pools down near the mouth, and the junction with the Sutlej is A—1. The water of this latter is heavy, and it is hard to do it justice from the bank. I heard of a 52-pounder and a 40-pounder being caught here not long ago. The water of the Sutlej below the junction is glorious, deep and rocky, with one magnificent run just below the junction itself; and should you, fishing from Simla side of Gamber, hook a big fish in junction and he elects to plunge down this rapid, your few seconds of leisure, while reel screams out its frenzied protest, may well be employed in deciding the next trace and lure you mean to mount, meanwhile, lowering your rod to save the top joint.

Next comes Rupar.—The headworks of the great Sirhind Canal, and a truly delightful spot to put in a few peaceful days. There are two canal inspection bungalows here, to occupy which leave should be asked from the Executive Engineer, Sirhind Canal, Rupar. The larger bungalow is fully furnished with lamps, crockery, cooking utensils, etc., the smaller one is furnished but has no accessories. There is also a police bungalow fully furnished, to use which permission might, perhaps, be got if other two bungalows are both occupied, but if the canal people have lent their bungalows to parties coming to fish, you would only be *de trop* to say the least of it. There are two ways of getting to Rupar, by water or road. The former is by house-boat up the Canal. There are three boats, to use which permission must be asked as above. Numbers one and two, at Rs. 4 and Rs. 2 per trip, are fully furnished with lamps, crockery, etc., and are fitted up most comfortably. Number three is Rs. 1-8 and is not fully furnished. Railway station is Doraha, on N. W. Ry., here two trollies will be found awaiting you (provided of course you give full information when you want house-boat) one for yourself and other for your kit. These take you to Rampur, about two miles away on canal bank, and here you board the house-boat. While this latter can come down of itself with the current, to go up, bullocks or coolies are necessary, the former are best and cheapest. Four relays are required at Re. 1 per pair, and are wired for at Garhi, Bhilolpur and Muzra. But the head boatman arranges all this for you. By leaving Rampur between 3 and 4 P.M., one should reach Rupar next morning by day-break. Your kit is taken from the house-boat to bungalow by a bullock cart belonging to canal authorities. It is very pleasant moving quietly up the canal, and each house-boat has a nice platform in front where one can sit. Going up in the cold weather, one often gets a shot at duck or teal in the evening. The second way to reach Rupar is by road to Sirhind station, and then tonga 30 miles, which takes about 4 hours and for which a charge of Rs. 6 is made. The servants and kit can come out in ekkas (Rs. 2-4 each) taking about twice the time the tonga does. For the benefit of those who might wish to motor out, a class to be reckoned with in future, I give the following Notes : Ambala to Sirhind 33 miles along the Grand Trunk Road, parts of which are very bad. From Sirhind to Rupar bungalow is another 33 miles *viâ* Morinda and Kurali. The latter is seven miles from Rupar, and in this last bit are three bad chohs (or sandy river beds), generally necessitating the help of coolies to pull one through. The middle one is a long way the worst, but usually a sufficient number of wayfarers can be got together to help. Most of the road from Morinda to Rupar is considerably better than the Grand Trunk Road. After crossing the bridge near Rupar town, turn sharp right and follow the canal road, round to bungalow. An alternative route which might be used coming back, is to get permission from Executive Engineer, Rupar, to use the canal road, which runs along the left bank. Here only two chohs have to be crossed, and the canal authorities can usually arrange for plenty of willing helpers to be ready to give a hand across. The road, unmetalled but quite a fair track, runs to Garhi 24 miles (N. B. to 25 milestone, as canal miles are only 5,000′). Here you strike the metalled road from Machiwara to Khana. Garhi to Samrala three miles, the road is very bad, thence 10 miles to Khanna, it is good. The latter place is 44 miles from Ambala by the Grand Trunk Road. Rupar is a big town and all usual supplies can be got there. There is also a nicevegetable garden belonging to canal authorities from which they kindly allow the mali to supply visitors. The time to visit Rupar is in March, and again in October. Towards end of March, the snow water begins to come down, and fishing becomes hopeless. The canal is closed usually from 15th April for one month, for cleaning purposes, andis of course shut down in the rains. It opens again about 15th October and then is the time to catch fish, if only the water is clear. As gate after gate is closed, the fish seem to know, by instinct, that they are being cut off from above, and a regular rush takes place, especially up the fish ladder, which during the day is packed with shoals of small fry trying to run up. The weir here is 2,370′ long, and the canal can take 8,000 cubic feet of water per second. The places to fish at Rupar are—(i) in the canal itself; (ii) in the pool below gates ; (iii) in pool below shutters under opposite bank ; and (iv) up at spur No. 3.

(i) To fish in the canal, spin with natural bait both from the platforms on each bank and off the bridge itself walking along and drawing one's bait through the eddies by each arch. The fish, mahseer only as a rule, lie everywhere, both close up under the spans and away down to opposite the house-boat moorings. We used to think the evenings the best time but much depends on the weather. It is worth trying a fly-spoon off the bridge if you see any fish moving and they will not touch natural bait. One evening two men using the latter did not even move a fish, while a lady using a fly-spoon and fishing in the same water caught two mahseer and had another run, from fish up to 5 lbs.

(ii) In the big pool under the gates.—This is a splendid pool and holds enormous fish. Despite the fact that it is practically still water we managed to catch lots of fish therein, and this at the end of March when canal had been unfishable for nearly a week with snow water. In the early morning up till 8 or 9 o'clock, use a fly-spoon from off sloping stones below the road, or off the two spits of sand that reach out, or—did do so in 1908 and 1909—from the opposite bank. The fish are mahseer, murral and mulleys and run big ; another man fishing there with me, was twice broken in one morning by real big ones. When fish stop rising here, go up on roadway over gates and spin between the arches. Mulleys are the fish that will respond most freely here, they seem to haunt the foot of the piers in large numbers. If they show a reluctance to take your spoon, try with live bait.

We caught lots of the latter by letting down a basket the other side of roadway between it and gates, as, usually where a trickle came through, small fish jumped freely at certain times of the day. If not jumping here, send a man across canal bridge to lock to see if any chilwa are jumping at the trickle that comes through the lock gates, very often large numbers can be caught here. Use a gut cast and not too big a single hook, drive it gently through back near dorsal fin and let down your small fish between two piers and let him play about, and you should not be long without a run. When hooked, you must go along roadway and climb down by fish ladder, where a man will have to reach down and net your fish. Which, by the way, reminds me that a long-handled, big landing net is a most useful and, one might almost say, necessary article at Rupar. Also, I slung my live bait over roadway into Sutlej above gates and hooked a 3½ pounder here. There are a lot of kalabanse in this pool, and I have seen some enormous mahseer. A 40-pounder was caught on gut and fly-spoon here in October 1907. All down this pool fish lie, though one does not catch many in the narrows. All the water, from the sluice gates down to the peepul tree about 200 yards down on left bank, is protected, below this it is leased annually to a contractor.

(iii) The pool under opposite bank is almost still water, though sometimes when river is rising a good trickle escapes through one or more of the shutters, making a small run into the pool. Very often when this happens, you see the small fish in shoals trying to run up, and the bigger ones feeding on them. This is the time to drop in a fly-spoon and your first cast generally hooks a fish. This pool is packed with mahseer, kalabanse, olive carp and mulleys. In March 1909 I caught an 18 lb. mulley here on a fly-spoon, just below the high bank.

(iv) Lastly spur No. 3, about 2½ miles up the river. There is a good run off this with a nice backwater, and this must hold fair fish. I have often heard it talked of, but have known of no really decent fish caught here; 4 lbs. was the best I took, but I did not give it a really fair trial.

Rupar is a very favourite spot for parties to go for Christmas. This is not a good time for fishing, however, though I caught a fair number of fish there in December 1908. In old days, when the canal was not so big, a lot of water always ran down river, but nowadays the canal takes it all, and only the trickles that pass through gates and shutters go to form the small stream that passes on down the Sutlej.

At Phillour—The N-W. Railway crosses the Sutlej by an enormous bridge. Under some of the arches big pools are left when the river subsides after the monsoon. One of these pools is usually deeper than the rest, and through it the current of the river passes. In this fish are to be caught, as is mentioned concerning the bridges over the other big rivers. I have, however, never fished myself at this particular spot, but it is worth a trial by any one on the march up Grand Trunk Road in October, November or March.

Also I am told that one can catch fish in the marshes that are caused by the overflow of the Sutlej near here, my informant added that one could spin in some of the pools.

The Jumna.

The Jumna rises near the lofty mountain of Bandarpunch (20,800′ high) and passing by the sacred shrine of Jumnotri flows some 80 miles through the Himalayas before emerging into the Dun. Just before it cuts through the Siwaliks it is joined by the Tonse, a larger stream than itself. The Jumna is not so big or important a river as the Ganges, and has insufficient water for its own canals receiving, therefore, through a cut into Hindan, some of the Ganges water which was formerly surplus. Now, however, the latter river is calling for more water for its own canals and a scheme is on foot to supply this from the Sarda river. The Jumna passes between Missouri and Chakrata, and to Mr. H. S. Dunsford I am indebted for the following notes, concerning fishing below Missouri :—

"Among the many sportsmen who visit Missouri, there must be some who are keen brothers of the angle, and who will be interested to hear that there is a certain amount of mahseer fishing to be obtained within a fairly easy day's walk of the station. There may also be some who are going across to Chakrata by stages, and who would be glad of the opportunity to wet a line *en route*. It is for the benefit of these that the following brief notes are written. The Jumna river is 12½ miles from Missouri by mileposts on the first stage out towards Chakrata, from which at least a mile may be taken off by those living in the Charleville Hotel and its vicinity. The march is an easy one, being all down hill with varying gradients with the exception of a short ascent on approaching Sainji bungalow, which is visible from the corner where the road passes above the Kempti falls, and another mild ascent for a short distance beyond Sainji. From the milestone at this corner, a short cut runs down to the bridge over the Kempti stream, which saves nearly two miles of winding road, but he who attempts this path must be surefooted and supple of joint. Another short cut between the 11th and 12th milestones brings the wayfarer on to the road again at a hut with a small patch of sloping ground, just above the river where there is room for a small tent, and from which a track down the hillside brings him to the head of the Jumna bridge in a couple of minutes. The journey can be done by a fairly active man in three hours, from the junction of the Simla road with the Mall down to the water's edge.

There are five pools within easy reach of the bridge, *viz.*, one immediately under it, two higher up and two lower down. During prolonged fine weather, the river is very fine and clear, while during the rains it becomes a muddy torrent; at both of these periods the fishing is at its worst, but in dry weather an occasional fish may be taken on fine tackle between 6 and 8 A.M. or from 5 P.M. till dusk, *i.e.*, before the sun gets strong on the water and when it disappears behind the western hills. The writer of these notes, who put in a day on these pools on 8th April 1909, when for want of rain the river was probably as low and clear as it ever is, took one fish of 7 lbs.

in the morning and one of 3½ lbs. in the evening, but when the river is clearing after rain, the sport should be better both as regards numbers and size. A trip worth trying would be to go on to Lakhwar dâk bungalow (where there is a most obliging khansama, who can knock up a decent meal at short notice) in the evening—2½ miles—sleep there and start fishing back to the bridge in the early morning. The river runs under the road for this distance, and mental notes can be made of likely places on the way up. This however is only an undertaking for an active man willing to work for his sport, as it involves a steep drop down to the river by hillside tracks in the first instance and a good deal of climbing off and on subsequently. The river-bed is hot, as is the camping ground above the bridge, and at the latter flies are troublesome, but these are drawbacks which attend most fishing expeditions. The mahseer take a small spoon fairly well, and would doubtless take natural bait equally well, perhaps better. Very large fish such as one would expect to get at Raiwala must not be expected, perhaps one of 10 lbs. would be the largest taken during three or four days' fishing, but for any one requiring a change from station life, an excursion for a day or two would be worth trying."

Tajuwala.—13 miles above Dadupore, is the headworks of the Jumna Canals. You can ride up either bank, but the proper road is up the left bank and is passable for wheeled traffic. The Some is crossed at Dadupore and the road runs more or less alongside the canal which here is more like a river (running as it does in one of the old beds of the Jumna). There are occasional runs which should hold good fish and which it might be worth while stopping to try. There is a furnished canal bungalow at Tajuwala, for permission to use which apply to Executive Engineer, Jumna Canals. Places to fish are in the canal heads, and in the runs in river above. It is an interesting fact that Tajuwala is one of the oldest canal works in Northern India, originating in 1356 when Firoz Shah III utilised the water to irrigate the royal gardens at Hansi and Hissar. The present weir is 1,700′ long, flanked at each end with a scouring sluice, the Eastern Jumna Canal on left bank taking 1,300 and W. J. on right bank 6,380 cubic feet of water per second. This latter, one may remark *en passant*, has thus a maximum discharge of more than three times average flow of the Thames at Teddington lock.

From Tajuwala one can fish right up to the junctions of Giri and Asan rivers: 3½ miles up the river lies Hatni Khund where there is a district bungalow (under D. C., Ambala) on cliff. The road, which though not good, is fit for wheeled traffic, follows along the river, passing into low hills almost immediately after leaving Tajuwala. The water varies considerably each year, sometimes the deep channel lying one side, and sometimes the other side of river-bed, while occasionally the river is shallow all over. But this is unusual and good runs and pools occur the whole way to Pounta, some 15 miles from Hatni Khund. *En route* Kalesar is passed, there is a forest bungalow here, usually, however, occupied by some forest official. The Batta stream flows into the Jumna from right bank some way down from Pounta; this stream is always worth a trial, both the junction and some way up, as I heard of a 20-pounder being caught in it. It is also a wonderful stream for murral, and one or two extraordinary bags of this fish have been made in the river. The Pounta pool holds very big fish. The time to fish here is after the rains or else in March before the snow water comes down, which is usually early in April.

Where the railway bridge from Ambala to Saharanpore crosses the Jumna, good fishing may sometimes be had under the spans, especially after the rains. The course of the river changes frequently, so that it is impossible to lay down under which arch to fish. Nearly always however it is one of the end ones. Fish are rohu, mulleys and butchwa. I also caught a kuggah and two turtles and possibly one might hook an occasional mahseer here. Try fly-spoon, but if not taking use worm altering the depth at which you fish till you find them biting; generally 2′ to 3′ for butchwa and mulleys. The main pool through which current passes is usually deep and holds some big fish. Bottom near arches is stony and one is liable to get hung up. Bridge is under one mile from Kalanour (small wayside station) and about four from Sarsawa.

Dadupur—Falls on Western Jumna Canal. Railway station Jagadri, 12 miles distant. Ekkas can be got at station. Rs. 1-8 per diem. The road is good in parts but some of it is very indifferent. Nice bungalow at Dadupore to occupy which permission must be obtained from the Executive

Engineer, W. Jumna Canal. Time to fish is in March, *i.e.*, before the snow water comes down and again in October and beginning of November when water has cleared after the rains. Fish are mahseer, goonch and trout (B. bola). Fish in the heavy water off two angles of bank, and down to the well on each side. Best lure natural bait, of which plenty can usually be got by hanging a basket just above rough water when chilwa are running up. A casting reel is an advantage here, as a good long cast is required to touch all the centre water from the banks. Pretty sport can also be had in October by using a fly-spoon below the dam in the Some river, where trout and mahseer up to 2 lbs. can be caught. This makes a variation from the continual chuck and chance it game one has to keep up in the Canal. Also by going a mile up the Some river, near right bank is a small jheel, off which a few snipe and a couple of duck are sometimes to be picked up in cold weather. A pleasant way to return to Jagadri is to borrow a canal row boat and drop down Canal. Takes three to four hours. It is worth taking a gun as below the bridge which carries the Ambala Saharanpore road across the canal are hundreds of blue rocks, and very pretty sport can be had for 10 minutes or so shooting them off the bridge while the boat retrieves the birds. It does not appear to matter what time of day one fishes, one hour seems as good as another. But when the chilwa are running then is the most hopeful time. Rafts coming down and shooting the fall on left bank are apt to be annoying sometimes. I have heard of mahseer being caught at Radaor in the Canal,

10 miles south of Jagadri. At Jagadri itself bottom fishing can be had in the canal just below the railway bridge, quite close to the station. There is a small furnished (no crockery) canal bungalow here, called Abdullapur bungalow. Fish with atta and weight your line well to prevent it drifting in to the side. The canal here is full of snags and one is constantly getting hung up. Fish occasionally run big, but are not plentiful and sport is not very exhilarating.

For the following notes concerning Karnal I am again indebted to Mr. Dunsford :—

"I happened to be at Karnal in the middle of March, when one of the periodical canal closures took place, and I tried the pool below the bridge regulators with a small spoon expecting to get some mulleys or possibly a small mahseer. I had no offers for about an hour, when shortly before dusk I had several bids from what were evidently small fish. I then put up a very small fly-spoon and took several trout. On the following evening I put up a white fly and took several more. I have no doubt that all the pools left under canal regulators during canal closures are full of these sporting little fish, from the canal head at Dadupore to 5 miles below Karnal, after which the canal gets smaller and the pools are insignificant. I was rather surprised at finding these fish so plentiful at such a distance (45 miles) below the canal head. There is a good pool at Indri, 12 miles above Karnal, where mulley up to 7 or 8 lbs. are taken, and in some of the silting reaches at the side of the canal there are plenty of murral up to 9 or 10 lbs. which take a small natural bait freely ; and at Abdullapur, 12 miles below Dadupore, fairly large mahseer have been taken on paste bait when the canal is running fairly clear, though the largest I have taken myself was only 8 lbs."

From Sarsawa station on the N.-W. Railway if one goes back along the line towards Ambala after a mile you will come to the first branch of Badi nala, continue for another mile to second branch where is a big pool on south side of line. In this I believe big fish have been caught, and there are, or were, one or two machans built out into the water. I tried here for a short time one day (too late in year) and had no luck, but I saw some fair fish rising and also some big turtles.

The Tonse River flows into the Jumna above the junction of the Giri. It holds extraordinarily few fish, accounted for perhaps from the coldness of its waters being as it is a glacier-fed stream.

The Pabar River, a tributary of the Tonse, which it joins just above Tuni forest bungalow can be reached from Simla, *viâ* Fagu and Chepal, to Tuni about 7 marches ; or from Mussoorie *viâ* Chakrata, also about 7 marches. But the reports that I have received concerning it are very conflicting and rather lead one to assume that though water and all is perfect the fishing is not very good. Also very large quantities of logs are floated down every year. Though from the map it would appear to be snow-fed this does not seem to affect the colour of its waters.

Okhla.—On the Jumna river and head-works of Lower Jumna Canal. There are two ways of getting to Okhla: drive from Delhi 8 miles, ghari hire for day Rs. 5-7, and ekkas Rs. 2-3; or go by G. I. P., Railway to Okhla station which is $1\frac{1}{2}$ miles from the bungalows. Coolies can be procured from a village almost opposite station, after a short interval, to carry your kit across; an ekka can be hired at Okhla to bring it back. There is a canal bungalow at Okhla for permission to occupy which some notice should be given to Executive Engineer, W. Jumna Canal, Delhi. It is a fair bungalow but used to be indifferently furnished, no baths, crockery, etc. All the fishing is in river below sluice gates, it is no use trying in canal. The fishing begins as a rule in April, when the snow water, which does not dirty the river here as it does at Dadu-pore and Tajuwala, begins to come down in sufficient volume to admit of some of the sluices being opened after canal has received its due quantity of water. Again after the rains when Jumna clears is good; in November usually too little water. There is an enormous variety of fish, mahseer, mulleys, goonch, butchwa, tengra, rohu and kalabanse all to my knowledge, and I am told that there are Mohi Catla, Murral, Silund and many other sorts. I believe that the canal is closed for a week some-times in April, for cleaning purposes, and this should be ascertained before visiting the place, as during this period the river would be unfishable owing to the silt carried down. Try natural bait and fly-spoon, also fly for butchwa, and if former fails try for the mulleys with live bait which can usually be procured without difficulty here. When I first visited the place on 1st June it was a bit late and thunderstorms had started to discolour the water. Also I visited Okhla, November 21st; this also was too late. In June it was a fine sight seeing the mulleys jumping, three or four fish of 20 lbs. and over in the air at the same time. There are in the hot weather enormous numbers of Gharial and turtles here, and trying a fly for butchwa one day I hooked a turtle of 30 lbs., managing to land him eventually. The places to fish are under the sluice gates, in big pool, in river below fish ladder, and in the runs that may be made by any shutters which may be open. Under the opposite bank is a very fine pool, and when any shutters are open that side, it affords about the best fishing. It may be fished from the high bank. The pool under sluice gates can either be fished from near bank, or from the lower end of fish ladder. In this pool I saw a native who was fishing with worm for small fry such as butchwa and tengra, catch a 24 lb. rohu, which was netted in the tiniest of nets amid great excitement. Some short distance down the river is Pier No. 5 (panch No. toka) where there is a deep pool said to hold big fish. It is hardly worth visiting however and is said to be netted to supply Dehli market with fish. After the monsoon, when the river falls, it is extraordinary to see all the pools left in the fields along river bank, simply teeming with fish, all doomed to die. The bigger ones are soon netted out, or hit on the head with *lathis.* I saw innumerable rohu fry in some of these pools. In April and May it is as well to remember that the place is very hot.

The Ghaggar River rises in Sirmur State in the lower Himalayas. Was once an affluent of the Indus, but now loses itself in the sands of Bikanir. It is not a perennial stream but depends on the monsoon rains. In its upper reaches it is largely tapped for irrigation purposes. Curiously the Ghaggar water in the hills is said to produce bad results if drunk, causing fever and goitre. Within 40 miles of its source it passes near Ambala city, a dry sandy bed without the veriest trickle of water. However it does hold a few fish higher up ; near Mubarakpur, half way between Kalka and Ambala, there is a pool known to the Tommies of the latter's garrison, and also there are places where native contractors catch fish for the cantonment market. Some few miles east of Chandigarh is Morni, in the hills. There is an old fort here, and below a long pool in the Ghaggar that used to be full of mahseer up to 2 lbs. There is also good shooting here.

THE GIRI.

The following notes are by no means official or exhaustive, the less so as I believe a well-known member of the Club is this year rewriting the Handbook. But they are penned as a small contribution to the literature on this most delightful river, and possibly may contain some points omitted in other descriptions.

First and foremost how to get to the river. The point to make for is the junction of the Ashni, Ussan or Simla stream with the Giri, Kharganu village lying nearly a mile beyond this and up the river. Two ways are open to one. First leave the train or tonga at

VIII

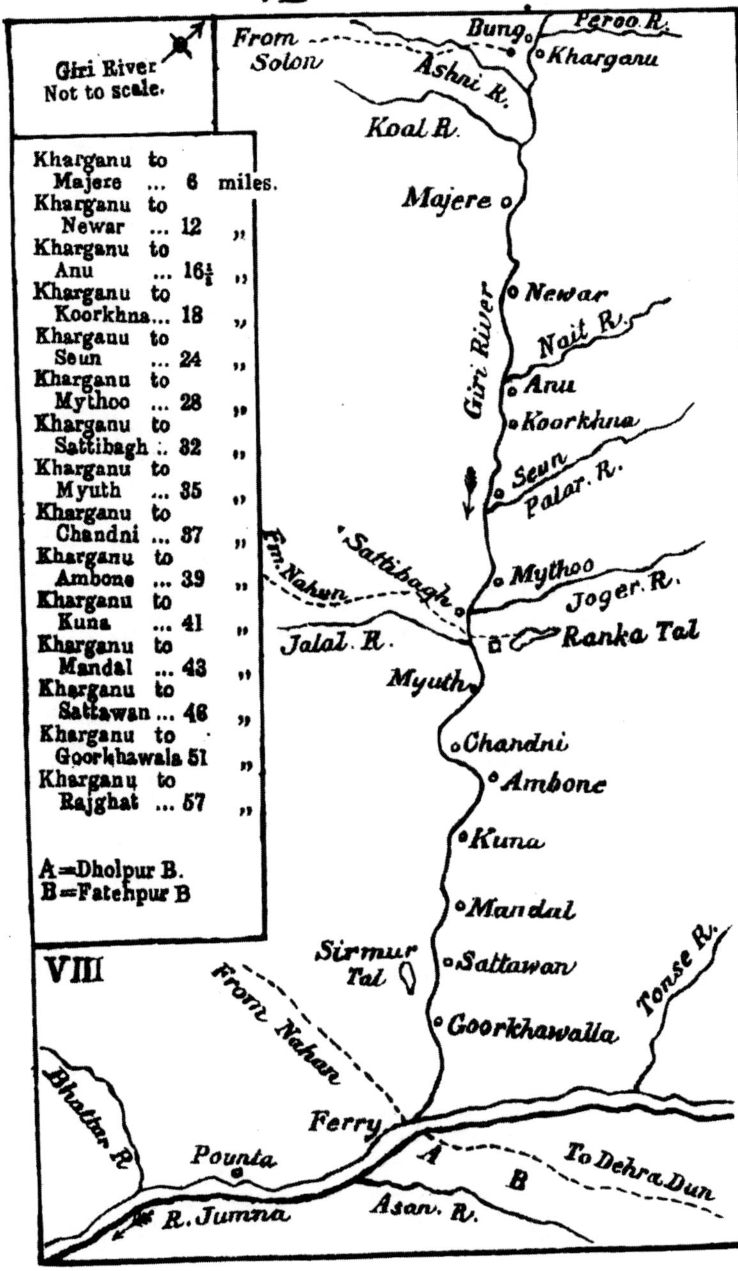
Giri River
Not to scale.
Kharganu to Majere ... 6 miles.
Kharganu to Newar ... 12 „
Kharganu to Anu ... 16½ „
Kharganu to Koorkhna... 18 „
Kharganu to Seun ... 24 „
Kharganu to Mythoo ... 28 „
Kharganu to Sattibagh .. 32 „
Kharganu to Myuth ... 35 „
Kharganu to Chandni ... 37 „
Kharganu to Ambone ... 39 „
Kharganu to Kuna ... 41 „
Kharganu to Mandal ... 43 „
Kharganu to Sattawan ... 46 „
Kharganu to Goorkhawala 51 „
Kharganu to Rajghat ... 57 „
A=Dholpur B.
B=Fatehpur B
VIII
From Solon
Bung
Peroo R.
Kharganu
Ashni R.
Koal R.
Majere
Giri River
Newar
Nait R.
Anu
Koorkhna
Seun
Palar. R.
Fm. Nahun
Sattibagh
Mythoo
Joger. R.
Jalal. R.
Ranka Tal
Myuth
Chandni
Ambone
Kuna
Mandal
Sirmur Tal
Sattawan
Goorkhawalla
From Nahan
Tonse R.
Bhattar R.
Ferry
Pounta
A
B
To Dehra Dun
R. Jumna
Asan. R.

Solan, where one can get breakfast at the dâk bungalow, and passing through the bazaar and under the Rana's palace, the road wanders round the wooded spurs of Bonfire hill, and then for some three miles runs along a high ridge with fine views of a deep gorge with a small rushing stream several hundred feet below one. Then a steep climb down some 600 odd feet to the bed of the Ashni and one comes to the fair sized village of Tikri. From here the path follows the bed of the stream, the remaining 4 or 5 miles to the junction. By this route the distance is about 10 miles. The second way is to alight at Salogra station, no refreshments to be had, and then walk from here about half a mile along the road to Simla.

Just beyond a small cutting through which the road passes, a path leads off down hill to the Ashni stream ; along the bed of the river, through some fine minature gorges, the track leads joining No. (1) route after about two miles just above Tikri village. This route is about 7 miles. There is no doubt that No. 2 is decidedly the quicker and pleasanter way. Both ways considerable wading of the Simla stream is necessary, and possibly just after the monsoon or a day or two's continuous rain it may be necessary to wade rather deep when passing through the gorges on route No. 2. Neither way can the road be called good, it being but a mere stony track. Ponies can be ridden, and all along the river-bed a lady could be carried in a dandy. The Ashni itself is a nice little stream, and I have seen fish of 2 lbs. and over more than a mile above the junction. Now formerly the spot to camp at was Kharganu village, and possibly it may still be advisable to go there if you require much in the way of supplies or many coolies to move your camp on down stream. The village is in Sirmoor territory.

But this year on the hillside above the junction, in Patiala territory, the Durbar of that State have built a most convenient little bungalow, fully furnished, and with the greatest kindness have put it rent-free at the disposal of members of the Giri Club, provided permission is first asked from the Superintendent at Chail. March till June, and again immediately after the rains till end of October, are all months in which it is worth paying a visit to the Giri. Like most Indian rivers it is uncertain, late winter snowfall may affect it in March and April, and a deficient monsoon of the previous year may mean too little water in May and June, while late continued rains may spoil the autumn fishing to a certain extent. Now for a short description of the river above and below the bungalow. Make the junction your starting point and first work up. In 1908 the junction changed its site, and gives now very indifferent fishing. However, if using a fly, a couple of one-pound fish will often succumb to you here. Above comes a shallow gravelly rapid, then a small pool. In the rapid at the head of this pool I caught a 4 lb. fish on fly, who fought most gamely. The pool and rapid above this, though water looks nice, I have never been able to move a fish in. Then below a bluff of the high hill opposite, which turns the water abruptly, comes almost the best pool in the river hereabouts. The rapid is very swift and the pool deep and it holds to my knowledge big fish. Stand well up in the rapid itself and fish just where it drops into the pool, the fish seem to lie right up at the head of the pool. For a quarter mile above this the stream runs fairly swift and of uniform depth, quite a good reach this for fly as a great many fish between 1 and 3 lbs. lie behind the rocks in this stretch. From here to the corner, though there are one or two good pools, I have never managed to catch a fish. But above this corner, where the river makes two almost right-angled turns, lies an excellent pool. If the water be clear wade up along the left bank till you can climb the great shale slope that comes abruptly down into the pool, from the footpath that you will see about 50′ above. Make your way along this and gaze down into the pool and several fine fish should reward your view. In fact this is the best spot to fish from. True, your position is a bit precarious and casting difficult, also landing your fish is a feat not easy in the performance, but there is a great fascination in watching the big fish follow up your bait, and they do not seem to notice one so high above them on the dark background. From here you must climb up to the path, and descending can fish the head of the rapid by standing well back on a big rock that juts out over the water. And in the rapid below this rock good fish often lie, but to fish it the river must be waded higher up and the spot approached down stream. Then just below the ford to Kharganu village, some big rocks jut out into a fair pool; especially at the head where two channels meet is a likely spot, in fact a certain one with fly for smaller fish. Above this again the river sweeps right away in a great bend, and in late years none of this water has been worth toiling round to fish, though next year the river may again alter its course here considerably. The best way is to pass through Kharganu village, and out the opposite side to where the path crosses an irrigation cut. Go along here to the river, and below you is a good bit of water and from here up to where the Peroo stream runs in is all worth fishing. Above this again for about two miles is indifferent water, though higher up again comes an exceedingly nice rocky bit of river. Back to the Ashni junction and below, the first pool and rapid are nice looking, though personally I have never been lucky here. Then there come one or two fair pools though not many fish seem to lie in this water. Lower one comes to the path leading to Majere on the right bank and here is a long good reach extending almost down to the Koal junction. Several quite decent fish lie under stones in this portion, although it does not appear very deep; the last bit just before the path debouches on to a level piece of green is worth a trial. It is best fished from off the rocks below the path and not from the opposite stony beach. The Koal stream junction is disappointing; below comes a long stretch of shallow stream, then an A-1 pool. In this pool the bigger fish lie deep round the large rocks in the centre. One evening standing at the head of this pool, in half an hour I caught 13 mahseer on fly, averaging over ¾lb. each. This was in June, and the water very low and clear. From this pool an irrigation cut is taken off and the river dammed almost across. Below here come several nice runs and rapids right down to where the piers of an old bridge stand desolate amid the rocks on either bank. Two particularly good spots there are. One is a rapid and pool just below where a small tributary makes a perpendicular fall of some 20′ on the left bank. The second place is a long deep reach full of good lies. The river becomes a sort of miniature Suez Canal here, making a broad curve, both banks open the right a good bit higher than the left. The right is the bank to fish from ; commencing at the top stand on the high ground, and casting across watch your bait swing round with the current and draw it slowly past the many big rocks that lie submerged in the stream. One cannot but move fish even if one fail to hook them in this reach. Then below the old piers of bridge the river still continues to fall fast, and about $\frac{1}{4}$ mile lower down where it makes a big curve comes some very nice water. About one mile below this, where there is a small wood on left bank, are some fine pools and rapids, though river here is liable to shift its course each year. Majere camp has nothing to show it, one pushes on past two lots of cultivation on right bank, to an open spot on the same side just before the stream enters into another gorge. No shade here but a nice enough camping ground, with one or two small natural caves useful for your coolies if it rains. Village some way back. There is a very nice run about a hundred yards above camp, and a splendid one just below. No spring actually near camp, but a small one about $\frac{1}{4}$ mile back, just above path. $5\frac{1}{2}$ miles this march. Leaving Majere the stream continues to fall fast and for half a mile there is some A-1 water. About 2½ miles down, two small tributaries run in, one on each bank, but do not however form junctions worth fishing. At about 3½ miles comes a nice open spot on left bank, with a good spring on opposite cliff; this might make a good camping ground, if one was not dependent on the usual villages, or if one wanted to do Koorkna in two marches. Just below this is some very fine water. Newar is 6 miles, and the camp is on open ground by a single willow tree on left bank, village being some way off on hill. No spring very near. Valley opens out somewhat here, and for a mile up and a long way down there are no really good pools or runs. According to the booklet the usual path between Newar and Majere is across the hills; mules can however be taken along river, but if water is at all high some of the crossings are a bit difficult as the stream has to be forded some 12 or 15 times. Newar to Koorkna is 6 miles good. The track is excellent between these places and mules can be taken comfortably. The river has only to be forded four times, the last crossing above Nait stream being the only one liable to be deep. If weather is very hot, it might be nice instead of camping at Newar to come on down half a mile and across stream to an open place where one could pitch a tent under a fig tree, quite a nice spot for a camp. At 3½ miles a nice stream joins from right bank. For five miles down though the ground falls fast there are no really nice pools or runs, but below this where the hills close in the water improves a bit. At six miles the Nait brook runs in on the left bank, a lovely little stream welling from springs out of the heart of the Chur, a hill nearly 12,000′ high showing snow on its summit almost the whole year round. Unfortunately the Nait, or Lojla as Ordnance Survey has it, usually breaks up into two or three streams at its mouth and so does not form a good junction with the Giri, but occasionally I believe it does form one mouth, and then as there is a good volume of water in it, excellent sport may be had at the junction. But the great merit of the Nait brook is that it holds quite big fish for some distance up, and in the event of the Giri being dirty very pretty sport may be had in it fishing with light tackle and a fly-spoon. Also it never dirties except after exceptionally heavy rain, in which it differs from all the other tributaries of the Giri. In the first half mile there are but two decent pools in the stream, then it gets good. About one mile up there is a splendid little pool with a sliding waterfall some 5′—6′ high falling into it, also it may be known by a small shingly island at tail of pool. Twice when I saw this it was packed with fish from 5 or 6 lbs. down, and is evidently very deep though quite small. It can be fished by climbing cautiously on to the rock at head and lying down on this cast into the white water, and especially just across in a small bay, and also away at tail of pool. Your first two or three casts are certain to produce swirls. One day the chilwa were running up and trying to jump the fall and the big fish were keeping the pool in a boil chasing them. While I sat there in the middle of day fish after fish up to half a pound cleared the fall and continued up stream. In a tiny pool among the rocks I caught two frogs and put them on alive, both were snatched off the hook at once, but a third they refused having, got suspicious apparently. I saw one fish in this pool that must have been nearer 15 than 10 lbs. He showed clean out of water in the shallows chasing a small fish. I tried natural bait also but they did not seem to fancy it like a fly-spoon. I was told that three miles up a landslip had formed a deep kund (pool) in which were lots of fish, and up to this I toiled one day. I found the kund (and they told me of a second another mile up), and though it was deep enough and big enough to hold anything, I never moved or saw a fish in it. I do not think it worth anyone's while to go up so far, as above the first two miles I caught very few fish and none over ¾ lb., and what is more I saw none on looking down from the rocks above. But in case anyone wishes to go up I will just give particulars. The kund is about 3½ miles up. After first 1½ miles going is very difficult in places, too hard work for a lady. Continue to where the stream makes two tremendous bends, and where is a lot of cultivation on plateaus. Then the hills close in. Above the last patch of cultivation cross below a deep cut where by the way is an A.-1 raspberry bush, to a quite good path you will see opposite. You will know you are right by a glimpse of a forest clad peak framed in the gap up stream. Follow this path about a ¼ mile to two huge rocks on top of one of which is a boundary mark like a chimney. Kund is just below this. I saw an 8 lb. mahseer that had been taken from a trap a long way up this stream, and I also took a 2 lb. kalabanse out of another such contrivance. Just across the Nait and on a plateau lies Anu village. Push on past this for half a mile and crossing another small plateau under cultivation on which stand two huts of Koorkna village you come to the camping ground of that name situated in a very pretty little wood. This is in my opinion the nicest camp on the Giri; there is a lot of jungle on the hill at back, and it is no uncommon thing to both see and hear kakur, hyæna and jungle fowl. Koorkna to Seun is 5 miles, the ground falls fast and all this is good water. The track is an excellent one most of the way, though in places landslips have wiped it out, and one has to go rather by guess work. In the first two miles a good deal of climbing is necessary for the baggage. At about 1½ miles a good track leads off over the hills to Nahan. River has to be crossed four or sometimes six times and two of the fords are a bit deep, especially No. 4, and if river is high and coloured some care must be exercised. Seun camp is in a nice little mango grove on a plateau, below the village, the only fault to be found with it being the flies which are bad. Just above camp is a white hut with tiled roof, a landmark for some distance. Below the camp are some large rocks, and a good pool in river in which are generally some decent fish. Not a hundred yards beyond camp the Paler Burn flows in. It, like the Nait, rises from springs in the Chur, and brings down quite a large volume of water, being in fact the largest tributary the Giri receives. It makes a splendid junction with the bigger river, quite *à la* Poonch at Tangrot, with miniature chucker and all. In the mango trees at Seun camp are generally to be found some green pigeon. And if the Giri is unfishable one may have some fair sport fishing up this tributary. I do not think that it is quite such a fascinating little stream as the Nait, and it has sometimes an annoying habit of being coloured the same as the Giri. About 200 yards above the junction comes the first good pool with a big rock in centre, and thence up are good pools at intervals. Some of the runs hold quite nice fish, and out of one not 2′ deep I took a 3-pounder one day. A mile and a bit up, the left bank of the stream suddenly falls back in a hollow sweep and two Panchakkies are built here. Up to here the going is very easy; above this spot commence a series of grand pools for so small a river, in the first of which a fish of over 10 lbs. followed my fly-spoon right across to my feet. About 2 furlongs up where some immense boulders have fallen into the stream, one large square rock is held up and forms an excellent little cave in which one can have breakfast under shelter from sun or rain. I fished the stream up some 3 miles, catching mahseer all the way, and from appearances one could fish on up another 3 miles and more. A very large number of fish, some of them running to 3 or 4 lbs., came short but the water was a bit coloured and the weather unutterably beastly, cold, thundery and wet. I enter thus minutely into the fishing of the tributaries, as now a days, I am sorry to say, it is no uncommon thing in the spring to find the Giri unfishable for days, in 1909 it was weeks at a time. I fancy fly fishing might have met with success in the Palar and Nait, but I did not try it, as a ¾" fly-spoon produced such pretty sport that I did not care to change. And if all else fails, and both the Giri and Palar are so dirty as to be quite unfishable, rather than waste day after day in watching a hopeless river, get some worms, easily procurable at Seun, and fish the junction, when you are almost certain of a run or two from fish up to 4 or 5 lbs. From Seun to Sattibagh is 10 miles, *viâ* Mythoo 6 miles The latter is usually missed out now as it is a bad camp down by the water's edge, and would not be known for a camp unless one was very much on the look out for it Below the Palar junction no very tempting water comes for about ¾ mile, so if making the fairly long march to Sattibagh, it would be better to follow the path up over the hill. Where it again descends to river there is a good run just below, and further on under opposite bank comes a fine crossway rapid. In the bends that follow this come some A-1 pools and runs. The ford here is deep and difficult after rain. The valley opens out a bit, but about ½ mile lower down come 3 or 4 splendid pools. If a camp was wanted between Seun and Sattibagh, it might be made here, about half way, where the track for the second time drops to river. A small open place among the rocks is suitable, as all this water is too good to be hurried over. A ½ mile down comes Badaria village on left bank, on a plateau, and below this is another very difficult ford when the river is high. Hence for some two miles or more down, though there are some occasional good bits the water cannot be described as very good. The track after this keeps zig-zagging across river, but the next seven fords are easy enough. The 10th ford, from right bank, which is some way below Mythoo (which is on left bank by the way), may be known by a tiny hut and wood on right bank, is crossed much easier by going 100 yards further down stream. After the junction of the Joger stream, which joins on the left bank within two miles of Sattibagh, the water improves again and is good down to the latter camp. Between Seun and Joger, Giri is crossed ten times, and between Joger and Sattibagh three times, the middle one of which is a real bad ford if river is at all high, being more than waist deep and the stream very swift. Coolies could avoid it by a very steep path over hill, but mules must cross here. The Joger is not a big stream but would have a fair junction if it did not split up at the mouth though in 1912 it formed one stream, and was good. A lot of water, too, percolates underground and wells out through the bank into the Giri for a distance of about 50 yards, clearly to be seen when the latter is dirty. Soon after leaving this stream the river swings round two corners, and then opens out, a large shisham wood blocking the end of the valley. Just round this last corner the Sirmur State is building a pukka bridge to replace the temporary one, which gets washed away every year. But it is not known when this will be finished, in fact I did hear its construction was to be abandoned. Sattibagh is above the river on right bank, a small ruined temple and some mango trees marking site of the camping ground. Sattibagh is only the name of the C. G. from the temple (Satti) and garden (bagh). A serai was under construction here, and one room was going to be set aside for Sahibs. As the old Giri booklet put it, Sattibagh stands at the meeting of the waters of the Giri and Jalal, but the latter is an utter fraud in its lower reaches and never has any water at all in it except in the monsoon. Even after heavy rain when the Giri was in high flood, very little water was coming down this tributary. There is a little, higher up in pools, but some of this is used for cultivation and rest runs away underground, which only proves one cannot go by maps. On the Ordnance Survey if one looks at the Giri tributaries, one would at once fix on the Jalal as the biggest by far. As a matter of fact they vary, but all the following hold fish :—Koal, Palar, Nait, Sattawan and Mandal tributaries, and Jalal. The Ashni, Toger and Peroo are inferior streams.

About ten miles up (where new pipe-line, Nahan water-works crosses stream), as is so often the way with these Himalayan tributaries, the Jalal is quite a respectable stream and there Mahseer up to 5—6 lbs. can be caught. All the water in Giri opposite Jalal delta is A-1 fly-spoon water. Above the camp lies the village with Tehsil and Post Office, the post arriving daily *viâ* Nahan and Barara about 8 P.M. and going out at 11 A.M., but it is as well not to put too much faith in it, and have nothing of importance forwarded to you. There are two or three bunniahs' shops, and atta, inferior kerosene oil and cooly rations can be bought here. Over the river across a temporary bridge often washed away and about one mile away through the hills lies the Ranka lake, a lovely piece of water set deep amid the hills. The path thereto leads one at first through an old orchard that must have been planted many years back by some former Raja. Then one comes to a small circular pond full of weeds in which are large numbers of Murral and three or four muggers. Over a small bridge and past a temple one arrives at the big lake. Here are some steps, the men's bathing place, with a closed-in place beyond for the ladies. Throw in some bread here, and heaps of mahseer up to 6 or 7 lbs. will rush for it. A path leads along to the further end of the lake, which is thickly wooded down to the water's edge. It swarms with fish, mostly mahseer, though one sees occasional murral, and holds some big mugger. Peafowl abound, also kakur, monkeys and jungle fowl, and a good many tracks of pig are to be noticed. If only the Rajah would put a boat on the lake and open it to fishing like Bhim Tal and the other Kumaon lakes, very pretty sport could be had. There must be enormous fish in the lake, by climbing out on to the overhanging branches of a big tree I saw mahseer of 12 to 15 lbs. cruising in the deep water.

From Sattibagh the river runs in a wide bed, the stream zig-zagging across, making a fair pool or run at each corner. Myuth camp, three miles is usually missed out now, and one can either camp at Chandni two miles on (before reaching this camp river is crossed by track seven times) or go to Umbone seven miles from Sattibagh. This is the nicest camp, as at Chandni a large number of mules kept by a bunniah there wander over the camping ground at will, and make it very dirty. Umbone camp is nice and shady and is situated 50′ immediately above the river. There is a village on the opposite bank, and it may be a convenience to some to know that a local mochi can do small repairs to boots, etc. In all this bit the river occasionally breaks up into branches, which rather spoil it from a fishing point of view. Umbone to

Kuna is two miles, where a camp could be made, while Mandal is again another two miles on. This is a nice shady camp high above the river. From Kuna to below Sattawan the water is all A-1. Mandal to Sattawan is three miles, and the camp is down near river with village some distance away. Or a camp may be made in shisham wood below Sattawan. All the water here is good. Below here, high up in the hills on the right bank, lies the site of Sirmur Tal, now dried up and under cultivation. There used to be a big pond near shisham wood separated from Giri by a high bank, but this is now dry, the bank having given way. Goorkawala, five miles below Sattawan, is a nice shady camp with village close by. There is an excellent run immediately below camp, then below this for about two miles is no really good water. Goorkawala lies about five miles from the junction, and from here down the river breaks up a lot, however fair sport is to be had in March and April in the branches. One can either camp near the junction with Jumna, or can occupy the forest bungalow at Rampur Mandi near the ferry, which is $\frac{1}{4}$ mile below where the Giri joins the bigger river. Charge, four annas daily. It is a nice little furnished bungalow, with chowkidar and sweeper.

Routes to the Giri.—From Simla about the best way to get to the river is to start the afternoon before your leave commences, drop down into the bed of the Ashni, go seven or eight miles and then camp for the night. This means a climb down of some 3,000′, all right to come down (there is no need to return this route as it is quicker to march to Salogra and train back).

Then the next morning continue march to Kharganu, which is 22 miles in all from Simla. This means that you are on the water earlier your first day than if you trained and marched from Salogra.

From Solan or Salogra the route has already been described.

From Dehra Dun, 22 miles by ekka, to Rampur Mandi. Cost Rs. 2-12-0 each. Ekkas procurable at short notice at Railway station or by previous application to the Tehsildar. The road is very good except the last 4 miles after it meets the road from Saharanpore. Rampur Mandi is on right bank of the Jumna, the ferry crossing to here from Rajghat opposite.

Or rail to Saharanpore and drive *viâ* Badshah Bagh and Timli Pass to Rampur Mandi, 44 miles. Write Tehsildar for bullock carts and tum-tums. Arrive Saharanpore early morning, and send off kit in carts to Badshah Bagh, at foot of pass, about 30 miles. Sleep here (getting permit to occupy bungalow from Executive Engineer, P. W. D., Meerut). Next day remains the 14 miles to R. Mandi, to use which bungalow permission should be obtained from Deputy Conservator of Forests, Dehra Dun.

From Tajuwala, *viâ* Jagadri, the route is described under former heading.

From Ambala *viâ* Nahan is 53 miles to Sattibagh. First 7 miles to Handesra are fair and drivable, but after that the road becomes very heavy and sandy as far as Naraingarh, 22 miles from Ambala. Nahan is 13 miles on, road becoming a superior hill track. To Sattibagh is another 18 miles, road being none too good. Coolies can be got at Nahan, where also Europe stores can be purchased, the place being the capital of Sirmur State. There is a motor road to Naraingarh from Barara on N.-W. Ry., but by an irony of fate Barara cannot be approached by a motor from any direction owing to an entire absence of metalled roads leading to the place.

As there is nothing more instructive than knowing how others have fared, I append a few extracts from two of the watchers' books.

21-11-05.—Have fished Giri down, leaving Kharganu 25th October and finishing Rampur Mandi 19th November. Result 72 fish weighing 247½ lbs., best 25½, 25, 21, 12, all on dead bait. Lost 4 others through tackle going.

Very few fish in river, will never be any use till kalabanse are netted or thinned out. (*Note.*—I hardly think scarcity of mahseer due to kalabanse; the writer of above apparently forgets that the greater number of mahseer would have returned to Jumma by November, the kalabanse not being so migratory, more of them stay up in Giri in cold weather.—S.D.)

4-4-06.—Sattibagh Snow water, river discoloured, caught a few fish at junctions, 14, 5, 3, 3, 1, 1, lbs.

9-4-06.—Fished Kharganu to Jumna, no sport, river too thick, a few fish at junctions.

24-4-06.—Have been on river since 31-3-06. Has only just cleared nicely. Sport poor, only about 150 to 160 lbs. between the two of us. Best fish 34 lbs., this does not include a 58 lb. goonch. Other fish 16, 12, 10, 8, etc. Small fish taking well now. Should have had much better sport if for three weeks river had not been filthy.

5-5-06.—Came to Kharganu 29-4, caught one mahseer of 7½ lbs., and 4 of 2 lbs. Lost a big one through rod breaking in pool 2 miles above Majere. Water in good order.

18-5-06.—Caught a 20 and 12 pounder to-day near Majere.

27-4-07.—Marched up from Rajghat to Newar, starting 28th March. River practically unfishable whole time owing to storms in hills. A big snow year on Chur seems fatal. Done fairly well at junctions, 20 fish with an average of 12 lbs. At Nait junction I caught in one day, 18, 3½, 4½, 19½, 4, and 31 lbs. All taken spinning natural bait.

28-4-07.—Fished with C. at Kharganu for 1½ days' Did best at Asan junction. Bag 12 fish, biggest 11 lbs.

3-5-07.—Came down to Kharganu for one day. Caught one fish 20 lbs., and 4 others weighing 24 lbs., also lost one good fish. Lot of snow water coming down and am afraid river will not clear this season.

13-5-07.—Two of us fished Giri for three days between Asan and Koal. Weather cloudy and thundery, fish not on feed. Each got an 8 pounder and some small ones.

13-5-07.—River very clear, caught 7 fish, biggest 25 lbs., all on natural bait, in four days, between Kharganu and Newar.

16-5-07.—Kharganu. River low and fish shy.

25-5-07.—Kharganu. River very dirty, caught nothing.

31-5-07.—Kharganu. River dirty and in bad order. In three days caught three fish, 7, 6, and 5 lbs.

10-6-07.—Think it's too late. River very thick for three days. Few fish 1 lb. down in Nait stream. One fish 3 lbs. Giri.

20-9-07.—Came down on four days' leave. First day river clear, caught 15 fish, none over 1½ lbs. Then river came down dirty; storm in hills.

9-10-07.—Water dead low. In five days between Kharganu and Anu only one fish of 7½ lbs. and a few small ones. Two trout on Zulu fly.

10-10-07.—Fished for 9 days Kharganu to Seun. River too low, all fish gone back to Jumna. Caught 9 or 10 fish, one of 20 lbs., two between 5 and 4 lbs., others under 3 lbs. Lost two good fish.

12-10-07.—River too low. Best fish 10 lbs. between Majere and Newar.

18-4-08.—Have fished down from Kharganu to Sattibagh. River coloured and low, very poor sport. Best fish 10 lbs. all on dead bait.

20-4-08.—Fished from Jumna to Kharganu. Sport poor, though river in order for some days. Best fish 19 lbs. and a 30 lb. goonch.

19-4-08.—Fished Sattibagh to Kharganu. Bag 7 fish, 7½, 9, 6, 9, 25, 2½ and 5 lbs.; possibly river too low this year for fish to have run up from Jumna.

25-5-08.—Three of us fished here Kharganu for three days. River very low and clear, and hardly any fish of over 5 lbs. to be seen. Caught 57 fish between us averaging just over ½ lb. using fine tackle and flies. Blackamoor, Zulu and Alexandra lake trout size all seemed good. Tried natural bait and fly-spoon without result.

The following note is interesting. 16-4-03. —Yesterday after fishing a pool a mile below Mandal, with natural bait I commenced with a small spoon, and throwing it into white water at head of pool, a few feet from me, a goonch of between 40 and 60 lbs. swallowed it as it reached the water. After hanging on for half an hour without moving him I put on a little extra strain and broke.

The following two brief accounts may prehaps be of use to those who visit the river in the hot weather, and find it either high and dirty or low and very clear. In April I went down for two days, followed Salogra route descending and Solan returning. The former took just three hours from the Tonga road, the latter a good four, the ascent up from Tikri being pretty stiff. I found the Ashni clear with plenty of water, the Giri high and very dirty, the result of heavy storms we had had earlier in the week. I camped on the bluff on opposite side of the river to Kharganu owing to difficulty of crossing the ford. I could get no supplies of any sort, the Sirmur villagers declining to supply anyone in Patiala territory. I decided that the water was too thick to fish that evening. Next day I moved across to Kharganu and camped this side of the village. The river had dropped nearly 2′ in the night and was beginning to clear, though still very dirty. Anyhow I was determined to start fishing. As Gokal, the local shikari, was absent with his cast net, I mounted a small preserved fish, a 5″ baril and fished down from the village, in the first hour moving nothing. I was just beginning to think it was hopeless when in pool No. 3 above Ashni junction a big fish rolled over my bait. The water was so thick that for a moment I did not know if he had even seen the small fish, and continued to reel in slowly. Suddenly came the welcome tug, and with one great swirl the fish was off. Straight down the pool he went, through the rapid below and was half way across the next pool before he consented to call a halt. For nearly 30 minutes he fought doggedly, never resting for a second, then at last he gave in and was lifted out by a cooly. The weight was just over 23 lbs., but he was a dissappointing fish, for by his length and size of fins he should have weighed a good 10 lbs. more. He was the nearest approach to a spent mahseer I've seen yet, however he fought splendidly and gave no sign of his condition till he was landed. In the afternoon I tried the same pool again, immediately rose another nice fish. However he came short as did two other smaller fish. About 200 yards below the Ashni junction stood a rock in mid-stream. I dropped the small natural bait behind this, and almost before it touched the water a 6 lb. fish sprang to meet it, was hooked and duly landed. The next day the river was still clearing, though by no means clear yet. I tried the Ashni junction, but with no success. I went up and tried Peroo junction, no result, but below the village I got another 6 pounder and two smaller fish. The next visit I paid to the river was in the end of May. The water was very low and crystal clear. I tried natural bait and fly-spoon, but the big fish would not move. Only a few minutes of excitement did I reap with these. In the pool below the village where the great shale slope descends to the water, I balanced myself and tried for two 10 pounders I saw. Time and again they followed the bait, then suddenly they shot away as a huge fish who could not have been less than 40 lbs. sailed out somewhere from the depths. Twice he came, then retired to his lair, and I saw him no more. Abandoning the big rod I put up a small trout rod with fine tackle. My first two flies were an Alexandra (lake trout size) for tail fly and a Zulu for dropper. Both seemed to find favour, though five out of six fished got hooked on the tail fly, no matter what combination I mounted. My bag the first afternoon consisted of 10 fish, a 4 and a 2 pounder among them. The next morning I caught eight more, two or three ½ pounders the best, and that afternoon had to leave or should have made a bigger bag. The fish, all mahseer, fought splendidly, some of them jumping just like trout. There is no doubt that small mahseer do fight well when hooked on fly, and when there is no punishing treble or flight of hooks to interfere with their breathing. Another fly I found very successful was a small salmon size blackamoor, and I have one minus the barb with which I landed 39 fish in the Giri, losing only one. So that the Giri is well worth a visit for a keen angler, any time between March and June, as long as the fisherman is not too ambitious, and if he finds the river too low, will content himself with light tackle and small fish.

A few notes are appended below, which concern the Giri.

The Giri rises from the Kuper Peak, south of Jabal, and gathering in several tributaries, the largest of which flows down from below Narkanda, it pursues its way passing 10 miles east of Fagoo on the Simla to the Chur road. From here downwards small fish are to be caught, though it is not considered to become a really fishable river till it reaches Kharganu. From here to its junction with the Jumna the Giri runs through the territories of the Rajah of Sirmur, whose capital is at Nahan, and from him the Club rents the fishing rights of the river and its tributaries. The yearly subscription is Rs. 50.

As regards tackle, a 14 feet rod and a reel to hold 100 to 150 yards of line, some fine steel traces and spinners or mounts for dead bait, single gut salmon casts, and an assortment of spoons $1\frac{1}{2}$ to $\frac{3}{4}$ inches, also some fine casts and lake trout size flies—dark for choice—for smaller fish, this will be practically all you will want.

Fish the mouths of all the tributaries, as there are generally one or two fish about waiting to run up, or who have just come down. When the river is coloured with snow water, these junctions are then the spots to try, as the fish congregate in the clearer stream to warm themselves after the colder waters of the main river. But when the Giri is coloured by storms only, this does not apply, as then the waters of the tributaries appear to be the colder of the two if anything. With regard to the clearing of the Giri it is hard to lay down any definite ruling, it can clear most extraordinarily quick sometimes, but watching the stream down below, one is rather in the dark on to what may be happening in the higher hills, and though the weather at Sattibagh be fine, disturbing factors in the Baghi range may check the rapid clearing of the stream. Four days may be taken as a general rule, after it has come down very thick, and on the third day one can fish, as often the best sport is obtainable when the water is just clearing.

Coolies sometimes seem to be a cause of difficulty on the Giri, especially in the higher camps, and a good many men take their own from Simla or Solan. Though this is a bit more expensive (5 or 6 annas a day or even more being paid), yet personally I think it is worth it, if one means to keep on the move, as it makes one quite independent, and allows of halting anywhere or moving off at a moment's notice.

There are a great many kalabanse in the Giri. This fish is of the Genus Labeo, to which also belongs the Rohu. They take no bait in rivers as a rule, though sometimes you will catch one on your spoon, but this is uncommon. Goonch also run to a large size in the lower waters. There are trout (B. bola) and also murral in the river, though I have heard of but few of the latter being caught lately.

Practically no supplies for yourself can be got along the Giri, but from most of the villages atta for coolies can be procured, and also an inferior brand of kerosene oil. No fowls or eggs to be got, but milk can generally be obtained.

The Giri in all the higher reaches, and as far down as Sattawan, will be found a very easy river to wade, as the bottom is mostly shingle, very different to the slippery boulders of the Ramganga and Kosi.

Concerning the shooting in Nahan, the old Giri booklet said, that it was always possible for members to get a permit for a week's shooting. But now I fear that a new regime has set in. Three men whom I know applied this year, two in March and one in June, but all got the same reply, *i.e.*, that it was close season for all game, including panthers! This must be good news to the panthers sitting on their nests, but it's rather hard on the villagers, who, so one of my informants told me, were complaining bitterly at the damage done to their cattle by the panthers, who appeared to be on the increase.

The Ganges.—The Ganges river issues under the name of the Bhagirati from an ice cave below a snow bed, nearly 14,000′ high, situated in the Himalayas above Gangotri, and runs a course of 1,500 odd miles. After the junction of the Alaknanda, a very large tributary, at Deo Prayag, it flows onwards under the name of Ganges emerging from the hills through a gorge in the Sewaliks near Hardwar. As far as Allahabad, 668 miles from its source, the river in the cold weather is a succession of pools, rapids and shoals, but after receiving its mighty confluent the Jumna, the two streams flow on a broad steady river. The tongue of land at the junction near Allahabad, called the Prayag, is one of the most sacred spots in India to the Hindus, and here every twelfth year (last 1906) is held the great Kumbh Mela, attended by over one million of pilgrims,

Though a big river where it runs alongside the pilgrim road from Gangotri to Tehri, it is believed that not many mahseer ascend far above the latter State. Snow trout are caught in the higher reaches, probably the icy waters issuing from their cavern of snow are too cold at first for other fish, till running two or three hundred miles of its course, the sun has had time to infuse some warmth into the tossing river.

The Barlganga River.—This tributary of the Ganges is quite one of the most delightful of Himalayan streams, only unfortunately cultivation is spreading on each bank and I fancy the river is a good deal poached. If only however the Rajah of Tehri could be approached with a view to his putting a veto on the building of a dam across the mouth of the river each cold weather, the fishing would continue to be grand. Why they build this dam is not quite clear to me, except for a trap or two in it to catch descending fish, because it prevents enormous numbers of fish from running up, and surely it would be better to leave half the river open? But the native poacher is an incomprehensible type of man. Occasionally heavy winter rains wash the dam away and then no better fishing could be wished for. The first time it was visited thus the river was literally swarming with fish, from 40 pounders downward. In June 1906, however, when I visited it the dam was in existence, and there were comparatively few fish in the river, though still our sport would have been quite good but for continuous thunderstorms. It runs a

IX

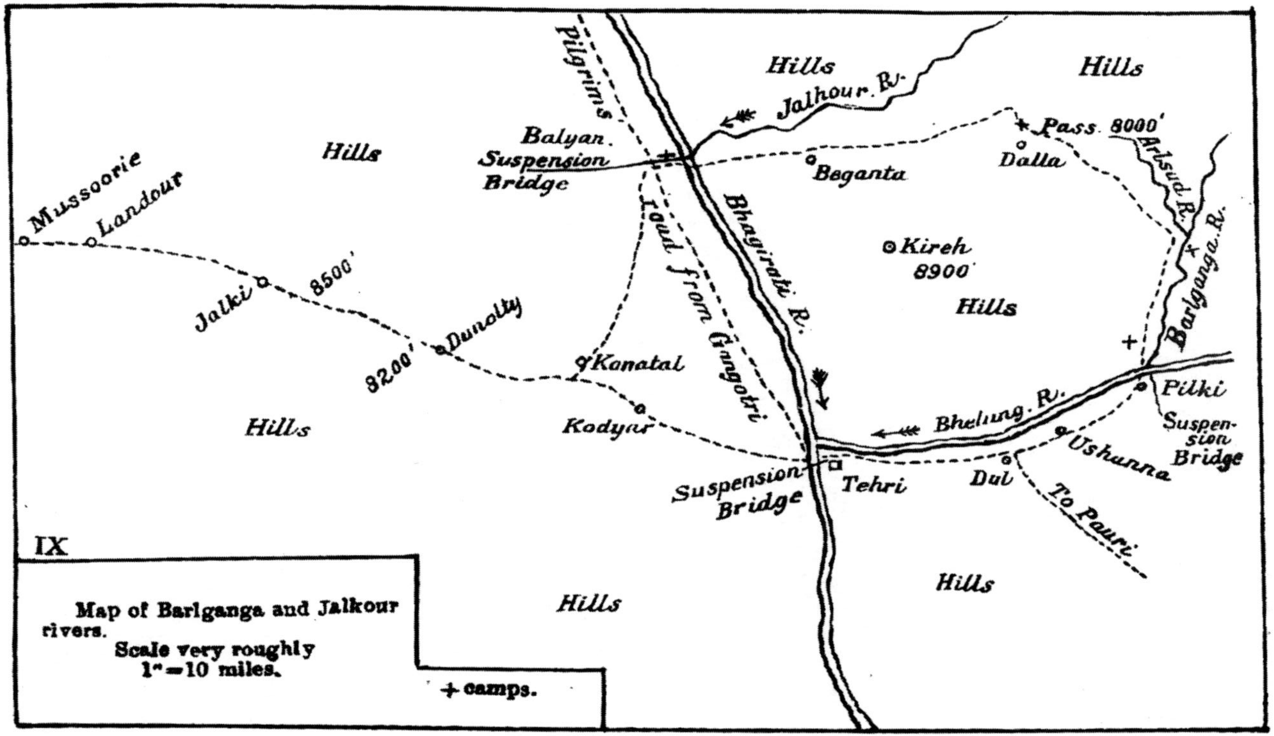

Map of Barlganga and Jalkour rivers.
Scale very roughly
1" = 10 miles.

comparatively short course, under 30 miles, but the volume of water is large and the river is a continuous string of glorious pools.

To reach it, Mussoorie to Jalki 11 miles, next stage to Dunolty 12 miles. The first stage is uninteresting, and by starting one's kit a day ahead could be missed out, since one could ride or go in a rickshaw the first half of journey next day. At Dunolty are two bungalows, furnished, but I would advise the avoidance of beds in the old one. Next stage is Kodyar, 14 miles, where also a bungalow, road up to this runs along a ridge 8,000′ high, and after leaving Dunolty glorious views of the snows are obtained. The track is fair for foot traffic and mules. The fourth march is 14 miles all down hill to Tehri, the capital of the State of that name. Bungalow just before reaching the town, the Ganges (or Bhagirati as it is here called) is crossed by a suspension bridge. The Bhelung, a very large tributary, snow fed, joins the main river here. From Tehri follow the Paohri road alongside the Bhelung as far as the 10th milestone, where a bridge crosses a big stream, then follow a track through Dul to Ushanna village, the march being altogether 14 miles. Camp here in some small fields, near a splendid mango tree, looking right down on to the Bhelung river. Next march is only 6½ miles. Pass Pilki five miles and half a mile up cross the river by a suspension bridge, 100 yards above which the Barlganga pours its crystal waters into the white flood of the Bhelung. The place to camp is about one mile up on a small bit of level ground on right bank. This junction pool is a glorious one and always holds some big fish. Next nice spot to camp is about 4 miles up on the left bank, just opposite where the Arlgud tributary runs in on other bank. There are some nice trees here and a splendid spring. The flies are rather bad in all these camps, even away from villages. There is quite good shooting on the hills round, gooral, serao, bear, etc. ; a permit required from Tehri Rajah.

Coolies can be got at Mussoorie at six annas each daily ; it is advisable to have a tindal or headman as well at Re. 1 ; also it is a good scheme to write for a State chaprassi from Tehri (to whom it is the custom to give 2 annas daily for ration money, and a tip), as his presence obviates any difficulty in procuring supplies.

The Jalkour River.—Reached from Mussoorie, first two marches same as for Barlganga river. Then from Dunolty, instead of continuing to Kodyar, leave the road about ninth mile and camp on hillock about half a mile further on above small village of Kanatal. Next day a march of 12 miles down hill takes one to a delightful camp above a suspension bridge over Bhagirati, just below some ruined huts, under shade of a huge cliff of rock, quite an ideal camping ground. Above the camp on a hill is Balyan, a stage on Tehri-Gangotri road. Opposite camp the Jalkour river flows in. Though not nearly so big as the Barlganga, it holds some very fair fish, being a direct tributary of Bhagirati and unaffected by melting snows. A camp can be made some seven or eight miles up Jalkour river on left bank, on a bluff some 300′ above the water, where the Pertabnugger stream runs in and below village of Beganta. (Pertabnugger is a high hill, on which is summer palace of Tehri Rajah). There is a good spring here, also a fine spring wells up in a pool in the river below.

A cross march can be made from the Barlganga river to the Jalkour river. Follow the Arlgud tributary up the valley, past the big village of Dalla, over the top of pass. About 12 miles and a pretty stiff pull up, only redeemed by a pretty wood one passes through near top, and by a delightful little stream that brawls for some miles by side of track. Camp Jalkour side of pass, near Kanadekal, some 8,000′ up and near a nice spring. Flies very bad in this camp. Gerao, serao, gooral and bear up here, to say nothing of pheasants. Then next day march down to Beganta camp on Jalkour, a pretty awful march about 15 miles, with what seems an unnecessary amount of climbing up and down.

N.B.—A pony could hardly be taken this route as there is a good lot of khud climbing to be done.

Notes on the Western Nayar River.

By C. Boyce, Esq., S. and T. Corps.

"This is one of the tributaries of the Ganges and flows into it, some 20 or 30 miles above Tapobun, on the left bank. The best way to reach the river is by rail to Kotdwara, the station for Lansdowne; from here the nearest point on the river is Bang-ghat, 29 miles distant. It is advisable to do this in two marches, first march to Dharamandi, four miles beyond Dogadda, where the road branches off from the Lansdowne road, and the second day to Bang-ghat; this is a long and tiring march, the first nine miles being up hill, then the road goes over a pass and one drops down six miles to Bang-ghat.

There is a bridge at Bang-ghat and from it one can see hundreds of fish lying below, but they are seldom caught here. There is a grand pool with a magnificent run into it about 200 yards above the bridge. I have not fished the river any higher up than this pool, but it must hold large fish for a considerable distance up. Then below the bridge are some very deep runs and pools, in fact the river must be fishable to its junction with the Ganges, but I have not fished it more than a mile below the bridge.

The fish here run large; the largest taken by me was 29 lbs., but I heard that very much larger fish had been taken by officers of the Gurkha regiments stationed at Lansdowne. One must fish fine and I found traces made of the finest killin wire, the most satisfactory. By the way the only good method I know of to make traces of killin wire is to make a single loop round the swivels, twist the short end round the main link and then solder the joint. At one time my wire traces were continually breaking through the joint slipping down on to the swivel, when the wire would break through being given too sharp a bend. Since I have soldered the joints I have never had a wire trace broken.

The only bait I found to be of any use for the Nayar was a spun chilwa. There used to be a man named Buchoo, who owned a cast-net at Bang-ghat; he was well known there and

XII

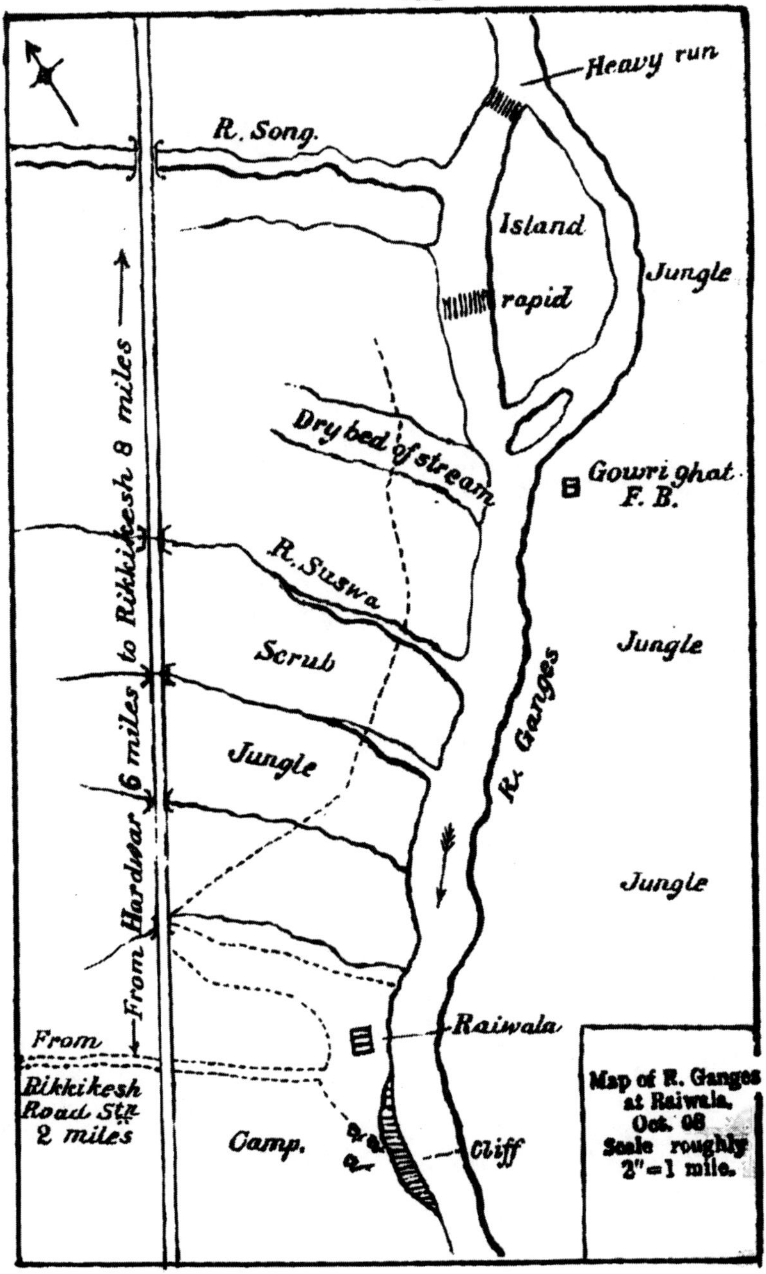

Map of R. Ganges
at Raiwala.
Oct. 08
Scale roughly
2"=1 mile.

always accompanied any one fishing ; if he is still there one could easily get hold of him by asking in the village. I believe there is a bungalow now at Bang-ghat on the left bank of the river near the bridge, and there are some good sites for camping on the right bank below the bridge on high ground.

The best times for this river are April and I hear October, but I only fished it in the Spring. A 16-foot rod is necessary to properly command the pools and runs."

Raiwala.—On the Ganges, lies about two miles from Rikkikesh Road station. This is only a small wayside station and carts and coolies are not procurable. Also it seems a matter of chance if a letter posted ever reaches the station-master, so if visiting the place it would be as well to send a man on ahead. Ekkas can be got from Hardwar 6 miles south, Rikkikesh Road station being 8 miles from Rikkikesh itself. Coolies and carts can be got with infinite difficulty from Raiwala, but it is only a small village. Road fair from the station to where it crosses the Hardwar-Rikkikesh road, then only a cart track through jungle to the river. Nice camping ground on high bank, under some shady mango trees, and there is a beautiful spring just near camp.

Monkeys are a bit of a nuisance. There is about 3 miles of good water that can be fished from here. The best way to describe the fishing is to start from furthest point up, conveniently reached—concerning fishing above this see later—and then to work back to camp.

Leave Raiwala village on your right and follow a track till you strike Hardwar-Rikkikesh road. Almost immediately you cross a small stream and pass between two shops beyond. Here take a track that branches off half right. Following this through some scrub jungle you cross another small stream, then a short half mile on you cross a branch of the Suswa stream, and soon after the main stream itself. Beyond this the going becomes sandy in places, and a sandy bed of another stream is crossed, dry in 1908, but liable at any time to become one of the channels of Song or Suswa rivers. It must not be forgotten that these two streams belong to the Dehra Dun Fishing Association, so that unless a member you should not fish in them. Another mile on and the Song is crossed. Follow this down to the Ganges. Immediately above the junction is a fine rapid in the Ganges, the river splitting into two and forming a big island. Start fishing here and work down. The Ganges is a big river here and not easily fished from the bank unless you can get out a very long line. If procurable from Raiwala it is as well to hire a surnai (raft on inflated skins), or, better still, take your own boat if you have one. The Song junction depends on year how it fishes, sometimes it is very good. Just at tail of island comes some very good water which can be fished by wading. Opposite Gaori Ghat forest bungalow (on left bank) the water is slow, but a little below comes another nice run. The Suswa junction is the next spot, indeed all the small junctions are worth trying; even if the Ganges is coloured the water from these streams generally keeps the right bank warm and more or less clear. Just under the camp water is dead and deep, and some very large fish lie here, but are not easily caught. I heard of a 51 pounder being caught here recently, and also a 72 pounder a little higher up. Down towards Hardwar at a place called Bhungoda I have heard that the fishing is good. Above Hardwar the Ganges is split up, and the best fishing is to be got in the branch furthest from the city. Best time to fish is in March before the snow water comes down, in April and May fishing also can be had, and then in September or October as soon as the small streams have cleared.

At Hardwar itself there is a certain amount of fishing to be got in the river, especially in the further branch. If passing through a visit should be paid to Hirapiries pool, to see the sacred fish, which will, if one's patience runs to it, actually feed out of your hand, and to have a 20 to 30 lb. mahseer sucking atta from between one's fingers is an uncanny sensation. Above the canal head and below the overflow sluice opposite the sacred pool, are 3 or 4 crated piers to check flow of river, all on left bank. The water swirling round these makes fair runs, but personally I have always found Hardwar itself a disappointing place.

But a short distance down the canal come four falls, all worth a visit; indeed this Ganges canal seems to be a marvellous one for fish; as far down into the plains, wherever there occur falls, mahseer are to be caught in it. A good canal road runs to—

Ranipur falls—bungalow, 5 miles from Hardwar.

Bahadarabad falls—bungalow, 6·6 miles from Hardwar.

Salempur falls—bungalow, 7·4 miles from Hardwar.

Parthri falls—bungalow, 9·5 miles from Hardwar.

To use these bungalows permission should be asked for from Executive Engineer, Ganges Canal, Hardwar.

At Roorkhi again come falls on the canal, but it is not worth making a pilgrimage there as the local fishermen levy a full toll from them.

At Bhola, about 7 miles by good road from Meerut, come more falls, but again it is no use making a pilgrimage to these, and if you are a member of the garrison there, a few questions to some brother angler will very soon put you in possession of all facts required to be known. A correspondent wrote me that he had only tried there, once, catching three fish up to 8 lbs., but adding that they were caught (mahseer) 20 and 25 lbs. there.

At Dasna, a station near Gaziabad, there is fishing below sluices in Ganges Canal 1½ miles from station. There is a canal bungalow here situated between the two branches of canal which unite about a mile lower down. Water is always dirty here. Bait to use, atta, and one can fish in either branch either below sluices and off piers, or below Panchakkies in other branch. I have known of some enormous fish being caught here, and there is a tale of one well known mahseer said to be over 3 maunds in weight, who broke one man three times one day though he was using the strongest of tackle ! ! ! You may find some difficulty in getting a cooly at station, so if going from Delhi it would be simpler to take a man with you. There is some marshy ground near station where a few couple of snipe are to be picked up in season.

Then the fishing above Raiwala. From Rikkikesh 8 miles up you can fish the whole way down, but the river is very big and strong, and only a small portion can be covered without a boat. At Rikkikesh there is a bungalow. From here up to Lachman Jula, where there is a suspension bridge and a small bungalow, is 4 miles, but the river seems to be considered sacred this portion, and one is liable to have trouble with the fakirs belonging to numerous temples along the bank if one fishes it.

To the junction of the Huil river is again four miles. At the junction and below are some very fine pools, but here the river is still so big that only a very small portion can be got at without a boat, but the fish run big, and if the right time is hit off, *i.e.*, in March or after rains, one is sure of fair sport. The Huil itself which flows in on left bank is but a small stream, and not fishable itself except perhaps in the rains. Here the road leaves the river, rejoining it some 12 or 15 miles further up, cutting off a tremendous bend in the Ganges. Some miles south of the Alaknanda junction at Deo Prayag, the Nayar river joins the Ganges from the left bank, this tributary being formed by the junction of the Eastern and Western Nayar streams, which unite a few miles north of Lansdowne. I believe the garrison there fish it and have fair sport. The junction with the Ganges is a good one. The Nayar itself is probably like the Giri, the fish only running up it at certain seasons. A correspondent tells me that he visited it at the end of October—certainly in a year of deficient monsoon—and then he saw no fish in the river except in a pool near the junction

A trip that I should say would be well worth making, for any angler who could get away early in March, would be to start at Deo Prayag, and give a fair trial to the Bhagirati and its still bigger tributary the Alaknanda above the junction before the snow water comes down.

Narora.—Headworks of Lower Ganges Canal. Station Rajghat on O. & R. Railway, *viâ* Aligarh or Chandausi. The anicut lies four miles from station, but the canal authorities will send a trolley for yourself and kit. Several bungalows here belonging to canal, to occupy which permission should be asked from the Executive Engineer, Lower Ganges Canal, Narora, *viâ* Rajghat. There is a village at Narora where such supplies as milk and eggs can be got. The bed of Ganges is broad and sandy, the length of the weir being 3,800′. It is rather hard to know when to fish here, and it is advisable to write to Executive Engineer for information *re* state of water before deciding to come and fish. The river below weir in hot weather is practically dry and empty of fish nowadays, till either rain or snow water comes down in sufficient volume to cause some of the sluice gates to be opened; as soon as this occurs and a flow commences to go down river, the fish begin to work up. In October also, before the gates are closed down and the pools in river below begin to dwindle, is a good time to come. The snow water apparently does not affect the river here till many weeks after it has ruined the fishing in the hills. In May when I visited Narora the water was clear, or at least as clear as one can ever expect to find the waters of a big river so far down in the plains. The place to fish is below the sluice gates in the Ganges itself. The gates here differ from those at Okhla and Rupar. There are a very large number of them between two strong bunds. The sluices are worked from top wall which forms a bridge across portion of river. Below comes a long passage a little above level of tops of gates when closed, and between the arches one can sit in shade and fish in the water below. But if one hooks a fish larger than one can haul up by brute force, fishing off the sluice gate barrier seems to be no use, as it would be quite impossible in lower passage and almost impossible off upper bridge, however acrobatically inclined one was, to hold on to a fish and pass one's rod round corner tower and down on to bank below. It is a curious place too. When any gates are opened the water rushes through covering a platform the whole breadth of barrier, some 4′ deep and 50 yards long, divided to a certain extent by two piers about 3′ deep and 3′ broad, that run out across platform parallel with flow of water (these piers inaccessible from above) and then the water hurls itself over a sheer 4′ drop rushing on down an inclined stony slope till it flows away in a channel of the Ganges, some 50—100 yards wide. When some of the gates are open, this platform is simply alive with fish, mulleys, mohi, rohu, kalabanse, butchwa, trout, and some mahseer, to say nothing of countless chilwa, barils and other small fry. Below the fall, when rush is heavy, are to be seen several enormous goonch, swimming calmly in the wall of white water that rises at a distance of from 5 to 20′ from the fall according to the flow of water passing over. Below too may be seen an occasional big mahseer, and also quantities of murral. Of course one can fish off either bund, but as large quantities of natives seem to flog the water off these it is hardly worth it. If rush of water not too great one can wade out below the fall and fish in broken water, where if you use a big enough bait there is no reason why you should not hook a goonch of from 80 to 150 lbs. There, too, morning and evening when the butchwa are on the feed, which will soon be apparent by the water seeming to boil as they chase and scatter the fry, very good bags may be made by using a fly-spoon or a fly (lake trout or small salmon size). If the near or far gates are shut down, and you can get along the *top* of fall, and mount on to one of the aforementioned piers, this is an excellent place to fish from, and very pretty sport may be had with the butchwa and trout, especially the latter, using a light rod and fly-spoon. Nowadays the big fish seem to refuse all lures. Why it should be so I cannot say, unless it is that they soon get shy, and as the fry are so countless their food supply is amply assured without necessity for any hustling. A lot of netting goes on too, and also the natives told me that a great many fish were speared. Below the further bund is the fish ladder, and beyond this comes over half a mile of shutters. It is difficult to work along these, and almost impossible if any were open except by walking through river bed some 50 to 100 yards below ; if any shutters were open it would probably be worth fishing in the runs so made. Also if the gates are closed it is worth trying off bridge into pool above, using a small dead fish and a float about 8 or 9′ up. This pool is full of fish, and one evening I had two runs from quite decent fish. About half a mile up a barrier marked I. R. juts out into the river, off this is a very deep pool full of big fish and muggers, but bottom fishing one is liable to get frequently hung up on the kunker bottom. There is no reason apparently why fish should not be caught in the canal head, as at Rupar (personally I moved nothing, but that is no proof that fish could not be caught), since I am told that when the canal is closed down, large numbers of mahseer are taken from the pools so left. There seems to be an idea that there are no mahseer at Narora, but this is quite erroneous ; there are a certain number which are caught in nets and on atta but never by spinning as far as I could gather. The splendid bags made in 1887 by Captain Maycock & Co. do not appear possible of repeating nowadays, I am sorry to say, excepting the butchwa and trout which can be caught in equal, if not greater, quantities. And catching butchwa and Barilius bola thus side by side, one is able to make a very fair comparison of the two fish, and there is no doubt that weight for weight the trout puts up the finer fight. But from an edible point of view he is a very bad second. Using a lake trout size fly is really the best sport, as the fish take it greedily, and thus lightly hooked make a great fight of it. Since this canal, like all others in India, is always demanding from the river more water than the latter can supply, I hear that a canal is to be taken off the Sarda river and run into the Ganges above the railway bridge, a mile or two up stream. Perhaps some of the Sarda mahseer will descend and infuse a more sporting spirit into the mahseer of the lower Ganges!

Notes on Fishing at Narora.

By Capt. R. W. Middlemass, S. and T. Corps.

Narora is one of the big gathering places in the Ganges for all kinds of fishy beasts, pleasant and unpleasant. All the most sporting kinds of fish are there, mahseer, silundia gangetica, seetul, butchwa, rohu and lanchi, and the lesser lights down to the humble yet sporting little chilwa. There are also there, bad luck to them, shoals of huge hideous goonch brutes that take anything and everything as food. Turtles, mugger and gharial are also wandering round, but as they usually fight shy of human beings they don't much matter. The fishing lasts, as in other parts, from March till the rains, the best period being from May till the water is discoloured and the river swollen by rains in July. Bait in the shape of chilwa, mugil, small butchwa, shrimps, etc., are easily got from the fish ladder. The portly tindal at Narora can work the trick of producing small meshed nets to catch bait; of course the importance of a judicious application of bakshish, for services rendered, must not be lost sight of.

You will probably find an enthusiastic crowd of youngsters ready to follow you wherever you go. Disperse them at once or they will spoil your sport by playing the fool round you, and while you are not looking snaffle hooks, traces, etc., out of your bag if left for a moment. They are keen fishermen these boys, and have to steal their tackle, and consider all Sahibs as legitimate game. Whenever possible use one of your own servants as carrier, as all the local people are prone to steal. A few days' leave spent here is something to remember, as apart from the actual sport, life in the hot weather is made more pleasant by the cool breezes off the river. The best way of fishing the place is by boat in the pool below the falls. You don't want to fish too close to the falls, because for one thing the water is very turbulent and dangerous to take a small boat into, and also because in the heavy white water lie rows of those beastly goonch, who would promptly pinch your spoon or other bait, or if you happen to hook a smallish fish, your fish as well. As they run up to a great weight, the chances are you would lose your tackle and your hair. If you spin in the main stream with a large spoon or dead bait, you may expect mahseer, silund, butchwa and the inevitable goonch. The two most likely to take are silund and butchwa, as mahseer are rarely caught, for what reason no one seems to know there. The silund, however, makes up for the lack of enterprise on the part of the mahseer. They are grand fish to catch. If you want to make a big bag of butchwa, with an occasional silund, fish with a small spoon or chilwa. The big butchwa are shy and you must fish far out or you will only get small half pounders. In the quieter water below the fish ladder you can have a go at the seetul, spinning slowly a small dead bait, deep down. Look out lest you take a firm hold of the Indian Empire. By the way, *never* forget to take with you and wear smoked glasses, or you will get a headache from the glare which you won't forget in a hurry. Fishing from the shore, the best place is in the pool off the right bank. The natives nearly always fish along here for silund, as all the big fish seem to lie along these parts. The reason I think is that there are always natives about on this bank, and the mugger and gharial don't come near in consequence. The bait used by the natives is the tail half of a fair sized butchwa, and is most effective. They cast out as far as possible across the current and let the bait swing round with the rush of water. It is usually taken when just at the end of the swing, and must appear to the fish like a stray butchwa making for the edge. Watch the natives fishing ; what they don't know about the best places, and the most effective bait, is not worth knowing. Another place is off the pier above the fish ladder. But this is a difficult place to fish, as you are perched high up on a pier and no place to land a fish, until you go round and climb down, a precarious proceeding with a big fish to deal with.

Below this is the slaughtering place for butchwa up to a pound in weight. You can kill two or three hundred if you like to stay there all day. There is no doubt that the fishing is greatly spoiled by the goonch. The size and number of these must be seen to be believed. They mess up your tackle, and the number of fish they destroy must be enormous. It would be a great thing if everyone who went to Narora helped to keep their numbers down. We tried shooting, spearing and fishing for them. The most effective method appeared to be the last named. Get a line of some 50 yards of cotton rope, about the thickness of your little finger, and tie a hook about the size of a meat hook, or a couple of very large and powerful trebles on to it. Bait with a half pound butchwa, and hand the line over to your servants or a group of small boys. If they cast into the heavy water where the goonch can be seen lying, the bait will soon be taken. This appeared the best way as it did not interfere with one's own sport. See that the end of the line is secured to something, or a big goonch will walk off with the whole show. The hooks should be very sharp and powerful, as a goodly number of the goonch must be as heavy as a man. If every angler would do something of this sort, the fishing would be greatly improved. Take a rifle to Narora with you, as you can have a pot at mugger and gharial when weary of fishing. As these *janwars* eat fish in large quantities it is as well to blaze at them.

The Kosi River rises up in the hills beyond Almora, and flows down nominally to become a tributary of the Ganges. But below Ramnugger, where it issues from the hills, its waters are carried off in several small canals, so that as a river it ceases to exist. But this does not affect the fishing, as rivers such as the Ramgunga and Kosi are probably self contained in the matter of their fish, differing in this from the Giri, Asan, Barlganga and others, since the mahseer are hardly likely to have ever dropped back to the Ganges through many miles of slow flowing river with sandy bed. There is a little fishing to be got I believe in the higher reaches of the Kosi, near Khairna bridge, a spot equidistant from Almora, Naini and Ranikhet, but the best fishing is to be got between Kumeria and Gurjiya, not a very big stretch of water but enough to give a very pleasant ten days' fishing. Station is Ramnugger, *viâ* Moradabad, thence to Gurjiya 7 miles along the Ranikhet cart road, a pukka road suitable for motors. At about five miles Dikhuli village is passed on the right. At Gurjiya are two bungalows, the one on hill to left of road is a forest bungalow, to occupy which a permit must be got from Forest Officer, Ramnugger, the other is a P. W. D. bungalow for which a fee of Re. 1 daily is charged. Both are nice bungalows, the latter being fully furnished with servants, etc. To fish in the Kosi river a permit is necessary, procurable from the D. F. O., Ramnugger, for which a small charge is made of 8 annas for less than 15 days, and one rupee if over. Below Dikhuli there is no fishing whatsoever, nor is there any really below Gurjiya except for a couple of shallow runs out of which one might take a

XI

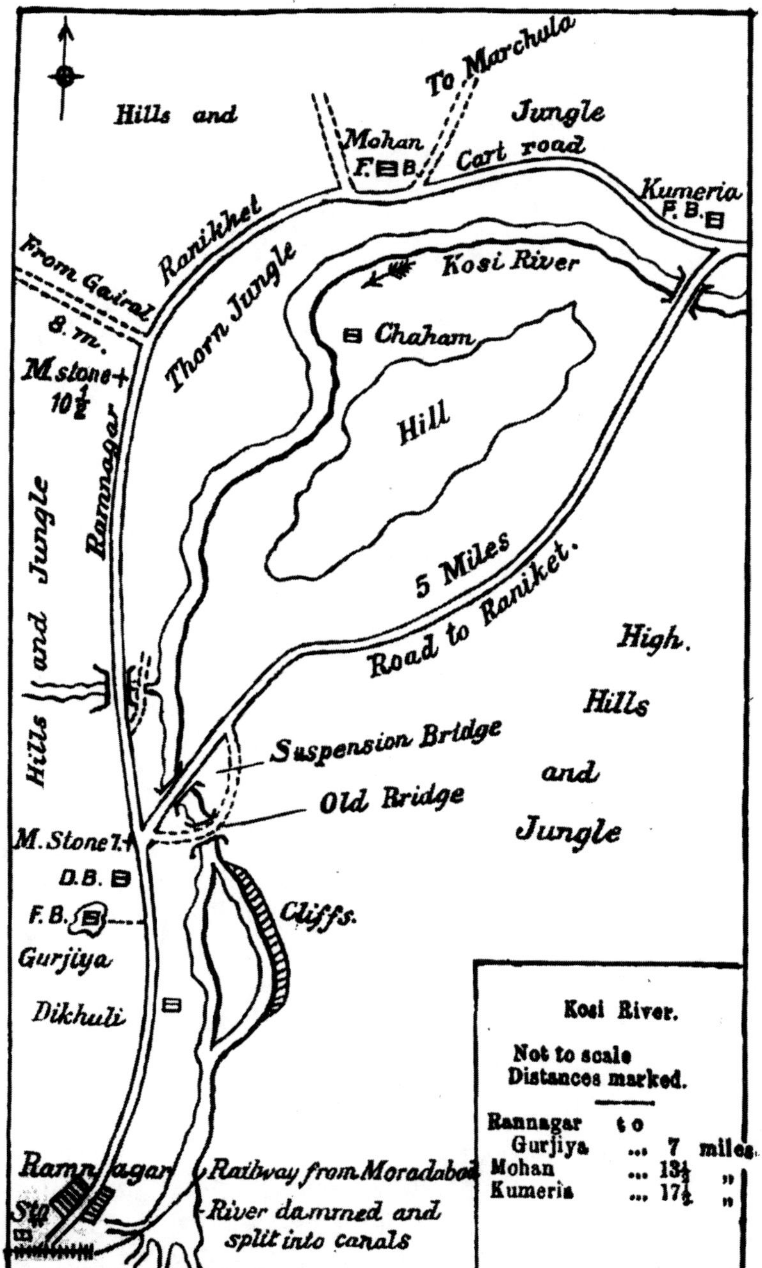
To Marchula
Hills and
Jungle
Mohan
F. B.
Cart road
Kumeria
F. B.
Ranikhet
From Gairal
8 m.
Thorn Jungle
Kosi River
Chaham
M. stone 10½
Hill
Rannagar
Hills and Jungle
5 Miles
Road to Raniket.
High.
Hills
and
Jungle
Suspension Bridge
Old Bridge
M. Stone 7.
D.B.
F. B.
Gurjiya
Cliffs.
Dikhuli
Ramnagar
Stn
Railway from Moradabad
River dammed and
split into canals
Kosi River.
Not to scale
Distances marked.
Rannagar to
Gurjiya ... 7 miles.
Mohan ... 13½ "
Kumeria ... 17½ "

small fish or two. At the seventh milestone just beyond the D. B. the road divides up, the left hand following the right bank of the river round to Kumeria, the right fork crossing the river by a large new suspension bridge cutting straight across and rejoining the other branch at Kumeria bridge, 5 miles. The best months for fishing are March, April and May, and again after the rains, but it must be remembered that May is very hot since Mohan is but 1,000′ above sea level. The fish are mahseer and run to 30 lbs., but though there are a lot of big fish they are not often caught. Usually the ones captured run between 1 and 6 lbs. The Kosi is also a great river for trout, and this last April I knew of one caught 3¾ lbs., a very nice fish. A 14′ rod, light tackle and fly-spoons are about the best outfit for this river. It is very well preserved by the Forest Department and hardly any poaching goes on. There is A-1 shooting in the forests round, but this is at present denied to the ordinary humble individual, as *all* the jungles along the Ramganga and Kosi rivers are kept as a preserve for the L. G.'s yearly shoot. Also the big pool at Gurjiya was netted while I was there to provide fish for the L. G.'s camp, which does not tend to improve the fishing. From Gurjiya to Mohan is 6½ miles by road, less by river. Here is a forest bungalow situated on a nice elevated spot on right bank of river. It is a two-storied bungalow, very old, and it is as well to keep an eye open for scorpions and such like. Mohan to Kumeria is about four miles, and here is another forest bungalow. One can either fish up, or cut across by the direct road, Gurjiya to Kumeria and then fish down. Carts and coolies can be hired at Ramnugger, by giving due notice to the Tehsildar. Supplies are not easily procured, except at Gurjiya where there are a couple of bunniahs' shops. Now to fish up. Below the bridge is a shallow pool, generally only holding small fish, but occasionally morning or evening one sees a 10 or 15 pounder from the pool higher up, who have dropped down to hunt the fry here. But the best way is to follow the left hand road up the hill, till, shortly before a new iron bridge is reached, an old track leading off to right is seen. Follow this but go canny over the old bridge! Drop down to the water's edge here, and by climbing a big rock just over river, one of the best pools lies below one. If water is clear you will see it simply full of regular ironclads and heaps of smaller fish. There is, or was, a small shallow rapid into the pool. By going up a short distance and then paying out line so that my fly-spoon was carried into pool, I have had some terrific tugs but no other result. The only time I ever hooked one of the ironclads was with live bait, my last day and last half hour! I had caught a half-pound mahseer about a mile up stream, and nursing him with infinite difficulty brought him alive to near the pool, then hastily climbing the overhanging rock I let him down. For five minutes nothing happened, then at last swinging him into rough water at head of pool a fish of about 15 lbs. seized him with a violent bang, and for one minute the pool was in terrific commotion Then—a slack line and empty hook came back,

Above this come several fair runs though not many pools, and it behoves one to keep out of sight as much as possible. Below a village, and above where a huge rock with flags on top stands in mid-stream, is quite a good run and generally is full of small fish with a chance of a 4 or 5 pounder. Also sometimes full of buffaloes. Then there is a good pool, some way up, below where the big hill on left bank comes down to river, the latter having bent in toward the hill and away from road. After this the stream takes an immense curve back to near the road and swings round to meet the hill again further up. In this bend below the hill lies Chaken village amid a lot of cultivation, the opposite bank being covered with thorn jungle not pleasant to walk through. It is best therefore to take a short cut from this pool under bluff right across to Mohan, the more especially as all the water thus missed is indifferent, the first half of curve being in 1909 shallow open runs. Just below Mohan is a ghat, and then above this is an A-1 pool quite close to bungalow, and in the next mile up there are three or four good pools and runs. The road which all this time runs back from the river and a good height above it, turns in over the river at the second milestone above Mohan. Half a mile on beyond this towards Kumeria comes one of the best pools on the river, and one full of big fish, followed by more good water, till 1½ miles from Kumeria it ends with another pool holding ironclads, after which the last bit to Kumeria is again indifferent. The above account does not pretend to be in any way exhaustive, and of course may be stultified by the river slightly changing its bed, still it gives a fair idea to work on for anyone who may wish to essay the trip. The Kosi is only a small stream and quite unaffected by snow water, it is waded easily almost anywhere in a normal year. Sometimes logs floating down may affect the fishing for a short stretch of time. Following the left hand road, just beyond 10½ milestone from Ramnugger (3½ from Gurjiya), a cart track branches off at right angles to the left, leading to Gairral on Ramganga river, 8 miles, *viâ* Sultan forest bungalow, three miles.

The Ramganga River rises in the Himalayas a long way north of Ranikhet, and leaving the hills through the Patli Dun by a gorge at Kalagarh, flows on to join the Ganges north of Cawnpore. Yet even as these notes are penned envious eyes are being cast upon its waters, and I hear that there is a talk of using the river below Kalagarh to feed small canals as has already been done with Kosi. This would effectually cut off all communication with the Ganges, if the bigger fish ever do drop down. In the lower reaches there is little fishing, the river flowing through the plains in a sandy bed often broken up into many separate streams. But above Kalagarh it becomes a typical Himalayan river with deep pools and glorious runs. The best known portion to the angler lies between this latter place and Gairral, a matter of some 23 miles. Gairral can be reached from Ramnugger, *viâ* the Kosi river, as described under the latter heading. Though the Ramganga has a fairly long course it is quite unaffected by snow water, and can be fished till

X

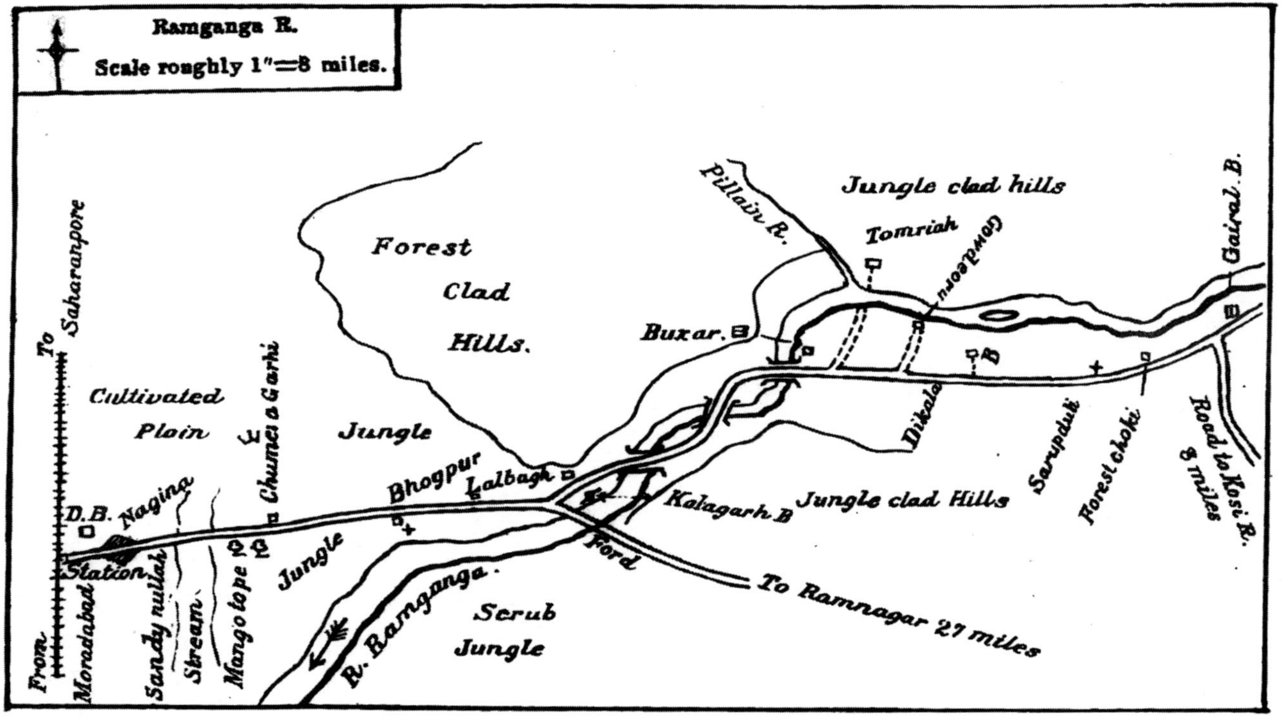
Ramganga R.
Scale roughly 1"=8 miles.
To Saharanpore
From Moradabad
Station
D.B.
Nagina
Sandy nullah
Stream
Mango tope
Chumes a Garhi
Cultivated Plain
Jungle
Forest Clad Hills.
Bhogpur
Lalbagh
Jungle
R. Ramganga.
Scrub Jungle
Ford
Kalagarh B
To Ramnagar 27 miles
Jungle clad Hills
Buxar.
Pillain R.
Tomriah
Gowdeoru
Jungle clad hills
Dikala
B
Sarupduli
Forest choki
Road to Kosi R. 8 miles
Gairal. B.

well on in June; though in May and June the runs dwindle, the pools become crystal clear and the fish very wary. Also it must not be forgotten that the heat becomes great in these two latter months. Unlike the Giri the fish are permanent inhabitants of the river, since the Ganges is too far for an annual migration. This fact, though it has great advantages, is not also without its demerits. If even in a year of deficient rainfall, the fish are to be found in the river, when in other streams they may never have run up at all from the bigger rivers, on the other hand, it means that the water will not stand the same amount of flogging and the fish soon become more cunning. As yet, however, the Ramganga is but little known, and as one is only human I must admit it rather goes to my heart penning the following notes :—To reach the lowest point where fishing commences. Station Nagina on O. and R. Railway between Saharanpore and Moradabad. Here carts and coolies can be procured by writing to the Tehsildar. The dâk bungalow is just opposite the station if one wished to halt here at all. Pass through the town and make for Chamera Garhi (called Raepur Garhi on Ordnance maps), 8 miles. Road very heavy sand, a mere cart track. One can make this the first camp, halting in a mango grove to right of road just before entering village, but it is better if one can manage it to push on another 8 miles to Bhogpur, and striking off to the right, camp on the banks of the Ramganga. But this is a stiff march owing to the heavy sand that has to be traversed; unfortunately owing to shortage of water there is nowhere to camp between these places. The country in March is beautiful with the brilliant red blooms of the dhak trees, and later the scent of the mango blossom makes the road a pleasant one. The river here is broad and shallow, and there generally are some brahminy ducks upon it. Between Chamera Garhi and Bhogpur are a fair number of partridges and jungle fowl, also peafowl and cheetal. It is all in some Rajah's territory. From Bhogpur it is 3 miles to Lalbagh, and another 3 miles on to Kalagarh, road still very heavy. About one mile above Bhogpur the river curves and one can start fishing from here up, through I have never caught anything of over 3 lbs. in this bit as there are but few runs and these shallow. The track is all through jungle and there is a lot of game about. At Kalagarh one strikes the Government jungle, which is simply crowded with tiger, panther, sambhur, cheetal, small game, and higher up wild elephants, but like the jungles on the Kosi it is all looked on as a preserve for the L. G.'s yearly shoot, and one is not even allowed to kill a hare in self-defence. At Kalagarh is a forest bungalow, and there are bungalows also at Buxar, Dikala, Surapduli (under construction) and Gairral, to occupy any of which a permit must be obtained from D. F. O. Ramnugger. Also it is necessary to get a license to fish in the Ramganga, from the same authority, annas eight being charged for under 15 days, and Re. 1 for over. The river is most strictly preserved, as there are several forest posts all the way up. Also the country is absolutely wild, and there are practically no villages in all this portion of the river. Kalagarh stands at the foot of the great gorge by which the Ramganga leaves the hills, and from here up the river is full of fish. To Buxar the next camp is eight miles, the road—still exceedingly heavy in parts, in fact this is the most difficult portion owing to the gradients, which, though slight in themselves, combined with the sand, impose a most heavy tax on one's bullock carts—runs along a track high above the river for two or three miles, then descending crosses it by a rough bridge. The pools in this portion are deep, and from above one can often see heavy fish in the clear water, but in only a few places can one climb down to the water's edge, and for some reason the fish are extraordinarily hard to catch in this lower portion of the river. Also there are large numbers of gharial and mugger, and if a rifle is taken one or two can easily be bagged, as they lie basking on the banks. They are seldom shy, being used to the continual passing of the carts and bullocks bringing down logs from the hills, and besides one is here a great height above the water. From this bridge, the first of three between Kalagarh and Buxar is the place to commence fishing. The rapid and pool just below are A-1 and the long run about 150 yards up is another very good spot. Then comes pool after pool, all glorious water, till the second bridge is reached. Here the road makes a short cut to third bridge, and the river swings away to the right. For a bit the water is indifferent, then come three or four pools, some of the finest on the river. Within sight of Buxar bungalow, if one stands on a high cliff on right bank one can see down into a great long pool simply full of fish, and above there is another fine pool with a shingly bank, through which the water percolates. The last bridge is just under the bank on which stands the bungalow; the run below this bridge, though not very deep, holds a lot of fish, and especially in the evening it is worth paying out a fly-spoon down the run and working it backwards and forwards across the river. And the pool which holds the biggest fish of all, but fish which no one seems able to catch, lies 200 yards below the bridge. To get to it leave the bungalow and follow down left bank, crossing a small tributary which plunges a waterfall into head of pool. Stand on the high bank and if the water is clear and light correct, you can anyhow have the pleasure of seeing big fish. They seem to congregate round a large rock about ¾ way up the pool; the first time I saw it there were three goonch on the rock, none of them less than 60 lbs., and four or five mahseer all over half that weight. From Buxar to Dikala is seven miles by road, though by river it is longer, as the latter sweeps away to follow under line of further hills, the next 10 miles being more or less an open plateau. The whole of this portion of river is rather disappointing (though there are one or two deep pools holding big fish below Pillain junction), since there are not really more than three or four first class runs in the whole eight miles. A little over a mile up the Pillain stream runs in on right bank, and holds fish up to 2 lbs. for a short distance up. A track, leaving main road near Buxar, leads to Tomriah where there is a forest hut situated just above junction. About half way to Dikala a side road leaves the main track and goes about a mile to Gowdara, a small wood-men's village on the river. Dikala bungalow is two-storied, and is nicely situated a short distance from, and above the river on a bluff, the Ramganga here splitting into several streams. From Dikala to Surapduli is six miles. The first three are hardly worth fishing, though there are two good spots. The best way is to follow the road till at about three miles the hills suddenly close in on the river. From here up to next camp the water is magnificent, pools and rapids alternating the whole way. The pool where you start is a grand one, the left bank is all rocky bluff, and by climbing along it one can see heaps of big fish cruising about. There is one splendid pool with a great rock on right bank. Climb on to this and cast far out into head of rapid, and then across and down. I hooked and lost a monster in this pool ; he took a mahseer of about one lb. that I was playing, and though for a short time I had him on, the hookhold gave somehow. There was no bungalow at Surapduli in 1909, though preparations for building one were under way. This is one of the wildest and most delightful camps. Just under the camp itself, which is on left bank, is a deep pool with a huge rock above it, on which one can sit and watch the fish below.

A short way above the camp is the forest chowki, and the run below this is a good one, generally holding 2 or 3 big fish. Sarupduli to Gairral is four miles, all fair water. This is another wild camp and what with sambhur belling, cheetal calling, an occasional tiger roaring, or a herd of wild elephants trumpeting as they come down to drink on the far bank, one's slumbers are liable to be disturbed. But even if you could sleep through all this, the unwearying persistence with which the night jars call will tell on your nerves at last. Just above Gairral bungalow is a run, and then for $2\frac{1}{4}$ miles up the river meanders through a great gorge, in which there is absolutely no fishing, as the water is all shallow, flowing gently over a shingly bottom. Two and a half miles up the Mendak tributary runs in, quite a big stream, and above here the Ramganga is much diminished in size. From Gairral one can cut across as before mentioned to the Kosi river. The road goes five miles to Sultan forest bungalow, and thence three miles further on it strikes the Ramnugger-Ranikhet cart road at $10\frac{1}{2}$ milestone from the former place. It is quite a fair cart track all through thick jungle intersected at intervals with streams of crystal water. Your carts could be sent back from Ramnugger to Nagina by a fair road, which is 27 miles to Kalagarh. The forest bungalows are all nice ones, provided with the necessary articles of furniture, such as beds, tables and chairs, but have no servants, the forest guard keeping the key. The country is wild and no supplies of any sort are to be got, except that at Buxar your coolies can procure a little atta, etc. Eggs, fowls and such like must all be taken from Nagina, and tinned milk and butter must be carried. There are a large number of otters in the river, also muggers, a few above Buxar and quantities below. Kalabanse abound in the river and there are a few goonch and trout. One's fishing is liable to be interfered with by bamboo rafts coming down, and in 1909 the fishing in

April was ruined by thousands of logs being floated from the higher forests, but this was exceptional and was owing to an accumulation of timber, due to sickness in the previous two years. This river as well as the Kosi badly needs two or three years of really good rainfall, to fill the springs that feed it, otherwise the fishing will continue to fall off woefully. A 14′ rod, gut casts and fly-spoons are the things to use: if natural bait is wanted a cast net must be taken with one and even then it is not always easy to procure. This river and the Kosi are two of the slipperiest rivers to wade in that I have ever struck, the boulders in the stream also producing a great crop of fresh-water shrimps. In a normal year the Ramganga can be forded fairly easily when fishing it, the kit never requiring to cross it after Buxar, the road and all camps lying on left bank. To get one's letters, arrangements must either be made with the Tehsildar at Nagina, to send out special coolies, or the Forest Officer at Ramnugger can be asked to allow the forest dâk runners to carry one's letters as they pass along the forest posts carrying official memos.

Concerning the **Gola** or **Gowla** river, I have received rather conflicting reports. One correspondent has a very high opinion of the river and certainly had good sport in it not so very long ago. For about 10 miles of its course it appears to be fishable, and very large mahseer apparently find their way into it. Certainly it should hold good fish, especially after a good monsoon, since it receives as tributaries, both the Bhim Tal overflow stream, and the Kalsa river which passes through Malwa Tal. The Gola rises in the hills east of Naini Tal, and joins the Ramganga north of Bareilly, passing close to Ranibagh D.B. on the Kathgodam Naini Tal road. Ranibagh by road is two miles from Kathgodam station, seven miles from Bhim Tal, and 28 miles from Naini Tal.

THE SARDAH RIVER AND ITS TRIBUTARIES.

The Sarju and Kali rivers join over 50 miles north of Pilibhit, at a place called Pachisar, near which I am told A-1 fishing is to be had, though it is not an accessible spot. From Pachisar these two rivers flow on under the name of the Sardah, which, lower in the plains, is called the Chauka river, and joins the Gogra, the latter uniting with the Ganges north of Dinapore. Now the Sarju is not a snow river, only in a very exceptional year could snow water find its way into it above its junction with the Ramganga, since though its actual source is in a mountain 14,500′ high, none of the other hills round exceed 12,000′. The Kali river, which is a good bit larger than the Sarju, is a snow river pure and simple (as are also its two large tributaries, the Gori and Dhauli rivers), its course for miles passing beneath mountains over 20,000′ high. Fifteen miles above the junction of the Kali and Sarju, the latter receives the Ramganga,* this stream seldom carrying snow water, even though it issues from a mountain near the Poting, one of the great glaciers (the Pindari is another) of a

* Not to be confused with the other Kumaon Ramganga that flows past Moradabad.

mountain 22,500′ high, which itself is a spur of mighty Nanda Devi (25,600′). To reach Bageswar on the Sarju, the marches from Ranikhet are, to Majkala B., 9 miles, thence road goes 16 miles to Someswar B., and from there it is about 15 miles tothe river at Bageswar. An alternative route would be north to Dwarahat B., about 10 miles, and thence due east *viâ* Lod to Someswar, 12 to 15 miles.

Notes on the Sardah River.

By Major A. R. Saunders, 29th Lancers, and Captain H. W. Kettlewell, 85th King's Light Infantry.

"The best, if not the only route to the river from the south is to Pilibhit by rail (dâk bungalow and Tehsildar), thence about 30 miles to Tanackpore,* called more generally Mundwa by the natives, by katcha road. This track is all right for ekkas, and even bicycles, provided there is no rain, otherwise it is a caution. At Tanackpore is a bazaar, and a small two-roomed bungalow, on the edge of the river. We went to a place some three miles E.-S.E. (*i.e.*, down stream) from Tanackpore; here supplies to be got were *nil*. The name of this place is not remembered; there was a ford there. The river fishes best from middle of February to beginning of April, that is, till the snow water commences to come down, when it is useless to continue. The water is very clear, rapid and shallow, and owing to the numerous channels in which the river runs, a

* Neither Tanackpore nor Mundwa appear to be marked on the Ordnance map, presumably however they lie close to Barmdeo.—S. D.

portable boat or an elephant is necessary to get from stream to stream. About nine miles down it splits up into a series of small, slow streams, no good for fishing. We tried fly, phantom (neither any use), dead bait and spoons of $1\frac{1}{2}$ to 2″, these latter seemed the thing. A man should be taken with a casting net to catch bait. The fish average 10 lbs., our biggest was 27 lbs., though one was lost, a good 10 lbs. heavier. There are numerous natural gravel weirs in the river, below which fish lie. A rifle should always be taken whilst fishing, as numerous islands densely clad with sheesham coppices harbour all sorts of animals. There is a lot of game in the jungle, from tiger to quail, and there are a tremendous lot of otters in parts, and lower down some muggers. Tanackpore is at the bend of the river, on the right (south) bank, where it comes down from the north from Almora. Permits to fish must be obtained from the Divisional Forest Officer, Kumaon Division, Haldwani, R. and K. Railway."

The following note is by Captain Kettlewell:—

"Another river in which I have fished is the Kosi, * which flows through Bageswar (Kumaon). Some three to four miles above Bageswar, a tributary joins the stream on its right bank, and the river makes a sharp turn north through a very narrow and precipitous gorge. The Pindari glacier road runs close by the right bank here. The cliffs rise some 40′

* (I think here that Captain Kettlewell must have intended to write Sarju, not Kosi, as the former river runs past Bageswar, the Kosi passing Someswar which lies 16 miles west of Bageswar.—S. D.)

above the water and overhang. Below, in a still fathomless pool, lie some of the biggest mahseer in India. I brought one, which might have weighed anything from 80 to 120 lbs. right up to the very surface, by dangling my spoon from the top of the rock, and saw every scale on his huge back. Soon after, by dangling with a live chilwa, I got one just under 30 lbs. there, and had to be let down to the water's edge by ropes made of puggaris before I could land him. I think Dopping Heppenstall got a fish of 67 lbs. out of that pool. I saw the dim shapes of other fish as big as my monster ; he haunts me still, and never will I forget his enormous proportions."

The following note was given me about the Sarda, but I do not guarantee its accuracy :—

" On the Rohilkund and Kumaon Railway is Mailani junction, and from here a line runs north to Sonarpur. Fishing is where railway crosses river ; station Sarda South Bank. The pools are big and runs heavy, as the Sarda here, nearing its junction with the Gogra, is big. Fish mahseer, and run to a fair size."

The same correspondent adds "Bharm Deo, 30 to 40 miles from Pilibhit and Kateema, shooting and fishing both good "

The Sarda being a snow river, one would have to visit it in March or after the rains.

DEHRA DUN FISHING ASSOCIATION, LIMITED.

The following paras. are taken from the Club rules and bye-laws, and also from some notes most kindly sent me by the Secretary. Should any angler be in these parts and wish to join the Association he cannot do better than write to the Secretary at Dehra Dun for the Club booklet.

The Association is a registered Limited Liability Company under section 26 of the Indian Companies Act, VI of 1882, and is called the Dehra Dun Fishing Association.

Subscriptions are payable in advance and are due on the 1st of January each year. The rate is Rs. 15 per annum, or any portion of that period. When payment is made by cheque it should include cost of commission for cashing it.

The General Committee (seven members elected by Annual General Meeting, usually held in September) shall elect three of their number to form an Executive Committee, one of whom will be elected President.

Gentlemen may be admitted members with the approval of the Committee. Whenever it may be deemed necessary to limit the admission of members the maximum strength of the Company for the ensuing year will be fixed at the previous Annual General Meeting.

Guards are employed on the Association waters. Those employed on all waters leased from Government are under the direct control of the Divisional Forest Officer.

Members must produce their fishing tickets or license on demand by the Guards and fill in particulars under specified headings in the Guards' record books. Four Guards are employed on the Rae, Song, Suswa and Asan rivers. Any member, or other person, who infringes the following rules of the Association, will render himself liable to be expelled from the Association or to a fine not exceeding Rs. 50, at the decision and option of the Committee :—

(i) Fishing without having first obtained a license.

(ii) Fishing with hand lines, or catching fish by any other means than by rod and line, except as under rule 4.

(iii) Permitting servants or attendants to fish.

(iv) Using nets for any other purpose except landing hooked fish, or catching for dead bait.

(v) Retaining mahseer less than 1 lb., and Indian trout weighing less than $\frac{1}{4}$ lb. Mahseer and trout under these weights must be returned to the water immediately after being landed, unless required for dead bait.

Association Fishing bungalows.—One on the Song river at Rikkikesh road, about $1\frac{1}{2}$ miles from Rikkikesh Road Railway Station. One on the Asan river at Kulhal, near the junction of the Asan and Jumna. This part of the Association water is only get-at-able by road, the approximate distance to Kulhal being 27 miles. The Association own the fishing rights of about the last two miles of the Asan river, to its junction with the Jumna. There is a Post and Telegraph Office at Herbertpore, about four miles from Kulhal bungalow. Both above bungalows are furnished.

No servants of any sort are employed by the Association in the fishing bungalows. Members using them are held responsible that the bungalows, cooking and bath-room utensils, etc., as used by them, are thoroughly clean, and in order before leaving. They are also responsible for any breakages or deficiencies caused by them or their servants.

Supplies.—Butter, ghee, milk, dhal, rice, gram and occasionally fowl are the only provisions obtainable in the vicinity of any of the Association waters. Sernais can be hired for fishing at the junctions of the Song, Suswa and Ganges, and Asan and Jumna, but members must make their own arrangements for the use of them. As coolies are not always available or procurable, it is advisable for members to take such attendants as they may require with them.

Railway concessions.—Members on presenting their membership tickets to the Station Master of Dehra or Rikkikesh Road, may have the train stopped for them at Luchiwalla and Khansrao between 31st March and 30th June, and again between 15th September to 31st October. It will however be necessary for them to pay full fares from Dehra to or from Doiwala, or Rikkikesh Road on the outward or return journeys.

Fishing tackle.—Direct from the leading makers at home, and specially suited to the Dun fishing, is stocked by the Secretary, and available at reasonable prices. Also Messrs. Luscombe and Co.'s spoons at his catalogue prices.

The Association holds the fishing rights under lease from Government of all the Song and Asan rivers where they run through Government lands or forests.

The former is a tributary of the Ganges, the latter of the Jumna.

The Suswa river has now broken into the Song about two miles below Khansrao, and about seven miles up from the Song and Ganges junction.

The last 1½ miles of the Song to the junction is owned by zemindars, but the Association holds the lease with right to renew it annually. Owing to the rapid strides made in irrigation in the Dun, the Association waters may now (except during the rains) be looked on more in the light of being breeding preserves, than affording good sport, in comparison to what these rivers were some years ago. Grants of these adjoining lands to retired Gurkhas, who have opened up the country and irrigated it, has been the cause of making these rivers what they are now, most of the water being taken off for irrigation purposes. However, there is always fair sport to be had in the lower reaches of the rivers with fish of up to 7 lbs. When the snow water comes down the Ganges, which it generally does before the end of April, it sends a lot of nice fish up the Association waters. Fly and mother-o'-pearl spoons are the most killing bait from April till the rains break. During the rains and until the end of October the big fish remain up the Association waters, but get back to the junctions when the rivers go down a little. During this period 2 to 2½″ and sometimes 3″ silver spoons, or natural dead bait kill equally well.

The junctions are fishable all the year round, except during flood and dirty water."

Just as this goes to press I am told of a 23-lb. mahseer, caught lately on fly, in the Song.

Notes on Angling in the Kumaon Lakes.

By Captain M. Trench, Duke of Wellington's Regiment.

Although the fishing on the Kumaon lakes has deteriorated steadily since Dr. Walker wrote his well known book, "Angling in the Kumaon Lakes," still a good deal of amusement is to be obtained by the lover of fly fishing, beautiful scenery and a genial climate. The grandeur of Malwa Tal, and the quiet beauty of Naukatchia are full of recompense for any shortcomings of the wily mahseer. Dr. Walker in his book gives full details and descriptions of the lakes and their scenery, though the fishing and accommodation are out of date. The lakes worth fishing now are Bhim Tal, Sath Tal, Naukatchia Tal, and Malwa Tal. Naini Tal can be put out of the question altogether. The growth of that place and the boating have quite spoilt whatever fishing there may have been there in the past. The four lakes mentioned above are all fairly close together, and are within convenient reach of both Naini Tal and Kathgodam, which latter is the railhead of the Kumaon and Rohilkund Railway. Bhim Tal is the most central and popular of the lakes, and the accommodation there consists of a Hotel "The Lake View"—* Mr. Jones; a Boarding House "Kilmorah House"—Mr. Ruxton; and a dâk bungalow.

* Mr. Jones has got a very good dairy, and also excellent apples and pears can be got in season.

XIII

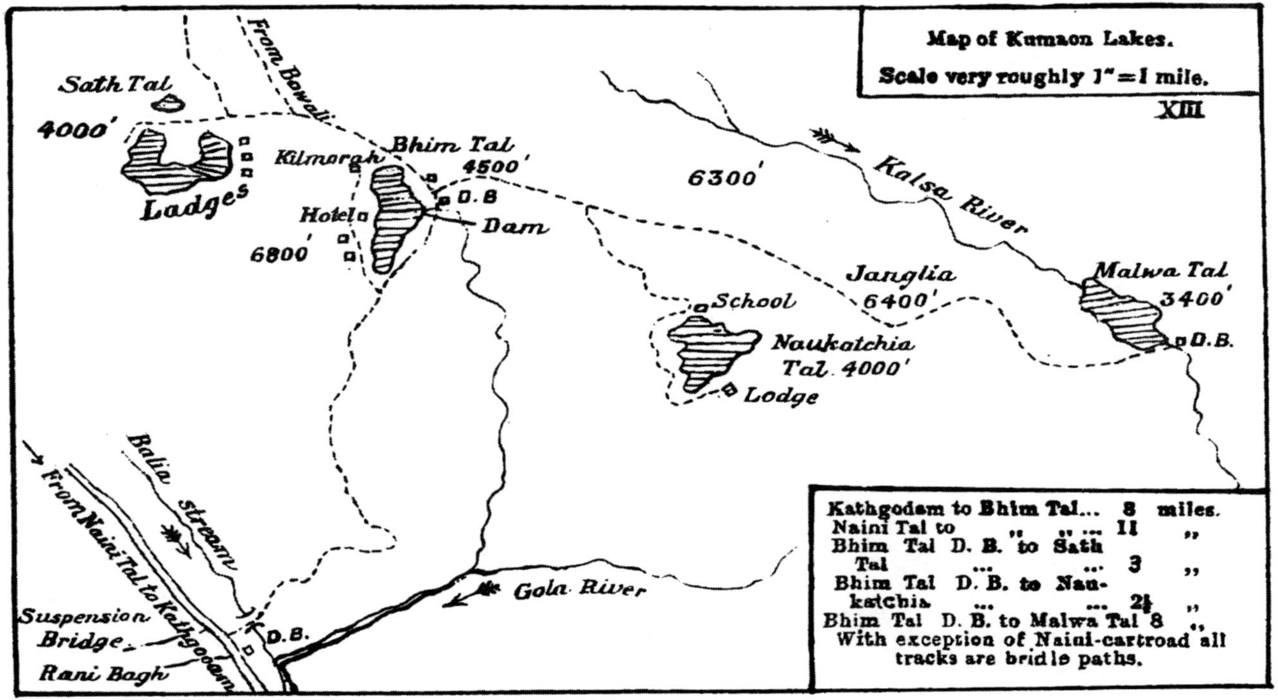

Map of Kumaon Lakes.
Scale very roughly 1" = 1 mile.
XIII
Sath Tal
4000'
From Bowali
Ladges
Kilmargh
Bhim Tal
4500'
D.B
Hotel
Dam
6800'
6300'
Kalsa River
Janglia
6400'
Malwa Tal
3400'
D.B.
School
Naukatchia
Tal 4000'
Lodge
From Naini Tal to Kathgodam
Balia stream
Gola River
Suspension
Bridge
Rani Bagh
D.B.
Kathgodam to Bhim Tal... 8 miles.
Naini Tal to " " ... 11 "
Bhim Tal D. B. to Sath
Tal ... ... 3 "
Bhim Tal D. B. to Nau-
katchia ... ... 2½ "
Bhim Tal D. B. to Malwa Tal 8 "
With exception of Naini-cartroad all
tracks are bridle paths.

Besides these there are a few private houses, some of which can be rented for the season, and most of them belong to Mr. Jones, I believe. A bachelor to my mind cannot do better than put up at the dâk bungalow, where, if he pitches his tent, he has no fear of being turned out when an influx of travellers claim the accommodation. Arriving at Kathgodam one can get coolies or baggage ponies to take one's kit the eight miles to Bhim Tal, and a riding pony for oneself, the first two miles are along the Naini Tal cart road till it reaches Ranibagh, here one leaves the cart track and proceeds past the spacious dâk bungalow to the suspension bridge over the Balia stream, which a few hundred yards further down flows into the Gola river. In earlier days the latter was worth fishing between Ranibagh and Kathgodam, but now it is hardly worth wasting time over, and the heat is considerable from May to September.

After crossing over the suspension bridge the road starts to climb steadily the six miles to Bhim Tal. The first two miles are very steep and the road, or path as it really is, zigzags up the khud through fine jungle. On reaching the lake the road divides and goes round both sides of it, that on the right or east side goes past the dâk bungalow which is situated on a slight rise. The left road passes Lake View Hotel and Kilmora House which are both up the hill side above it, and on reaching the far end of the lake it turns sharp to the right crossing a small stone bridge, which, by the way, was partially washed away last year (1908), and joins the right hand road again. The continuation of this road passes through the baazar, and for about a mile goes through a flat open valley, then climbs the ridge steadily to Bowali where it joins the Ranikhet Cart road.

If the traveller is coming from Naini Tal he comes along a narrow path running along the precipitous flank of the Lyriakanta, keeping fairly level till it dips down to the cart road and rising slightly again before it reaches Bowali. The distance from Naini Tal to Bowali being 7 miles and from Bowali on to Bhim Tal, four miles.

Bhim Tal.—At Bhim Tal there are a considerable number of boats of varying quality. They can be hired at Re. 1 per day, or if taken for a whole month, Rs. 20. Boatmen who will also act as shikaris when necessary are Rs. 15 a month. Many of them understand the anglers' requirements and are skilful in handling their boats; the tackle they try to pass off on you is to be avoided. Mr. Ruxton of Kilmorah House keeps a stock of good fine casts and flies for his guests; and good tackle can be got from Murray's in Naini Tal. The boatmen make very good light ringalls and I have fished for three weeks with one of these when my rod was out of order and found it very nice to cast with; and some men even prefer the ringall.

Some anglers prefer a single-handed trout rod, but I think the majority find a light two-handed rod about 14 ft. preferable. A fine cast is essential as the fish are very wary, and one must cast deftly and lightly under the overhanging trees at the very edge of the shore keeping the boat parallel to it.

The flies used here on all the lakes are

those recommended by Dr. Walker in his book, and are known to most tackle-makers out here as Dr. Walker's flies. They are Silver Doctor; Jock Scott; Yellow Spider; Claret, and Alexandra lake trout size, and my experience of these has been that the Claret is about the best at mid-day, while in the mornings and evenings the Yellow Spider is often successful. From twilight till after dusk a white moth or Tag O Towel fly will take, though it is not such good sport; but my advice is to try every fly you have in your book, sometimes a big gaudy salmon fly will take, at others a tiny olive dun. There is an irrigation dam just below the dâk bungalow that controls the flow of the water to the Gola river, and after the rains the lake is allowed to fill up till the water is required in the plains.

This, I think, is inclined to spoil the fishing in August and September, as the fish seem to lose their bearings. At this time the best part of the lake to fish is in the reeds at the north end which become submerged, and in the nullah north of the stone bridge where the stream comes in. The last few years Bhim Tal was open for ground bait fishing, and the natives and soldiers camping there caught not a few that way; but last year it was stopped and Naukatchia Tal, which had been closed to ground baiting, was opened; the few natives that tried it, however, gave it up as it was apparently not lucrative enough. At the end of the rains when the lake water gets really muddy, and the fly seems to be useless, I have found a small silvered $\frac{3}{4}''$ fly-spoon take. One can fish from March till the end of September or middle of October, but I think the best time is May and June, though it is a trifle hot, and the house flies, a pest here, are bad.

Sath Tal.—This is really two lakes joined by a cut; there is another small lake about 150′ above the larger ones, but it is of no use for fishing For accommodation, there were four bungalows, now I believe increased to six, all fully furnished, and they can be rented from Mr. Evans, who has a house and resides there. There is also a camping ground. Coming down from Bowali towards Bhim Tal, about one mile out of the former place, there is a bridle path which branches off to the right, marked by a sign post to Sath Tal, 2½ miles; this path crosses the valley, and passing through a cut in the hills descends steeply to the lakes. From Bhim Tal a path from the west side of the lake ascends the ridge, and passing at the back and above Kilmorah House joins the path from Bowali where it enters the cut in the hills. Sath Tal is a pretty lake but not so grand as the others, as it is shut in by low hills which obscure the more distant heights. The evenings on the lake are very beautiful and still, and the setting sun tinting the back of the fir-trees, and the clear dark reflections are exquisite. The fishing is rather difficult as the water is so often calm and the wind comes in gusts and varies in direction; the water is very clear, and at mid-day, when it is very hot, the fish can be seen basking near the surface lazily turning with a single flick of the tail. They may be tempted then with a red dragon fly or grasshopper dangled on the surface from an overhanging tree, but it is no easy matter to land one from such a precarious position as it often is. The night shere turn very cold after the hot mid-day sun and there is a heavy dew, and if fishing late it is advisable to take a sweater or over-coat to put on. There is a Government boat here as there is at all the lakes which can be had at one rupee a day, and Mr. Evans also has some boats to let to his guests, but it is safer always to take one's own boat from lake to lake as the Government one may be in use. Eight coolies are required and I think the charge is about 6 annas a man, to Malwa Tal it is a bit more.

A fishing license is required for each lake, they are four annas for one day, one rupee for any time over two days and up to fifteen days and two rupees over that and up to one month. They are to be obtained from Mr. Ruxton.

Naukatchia Tal.—This is the most beautiful lake of all, and I can only refer the reader to Dr. Walker's book for an adequate description of its beauties of view and sound. Perhaps it is enough to say that even a blank day with the mahseer has not seemed a wasted one by any means. The fish here are, I think, inclined to run a little smaller than the other lakes, and one is more likely to catch them about a pound or less than over, and an occasional two pounder is a great catch. Then there was a little camping ground, dear to memory, which has since been desecrated by an ugly stone building, built by a babu as a school for the village children, one would almost think that he had planted it there to spite the humble angler. The road from Bhim Tal branches off by the dâk bungalow, and runs along the slopes almost due east bending to the right as it nears Naukatchia

Lodge, that charming angler's haven. It can be rented from Mr. Ruxton furnished (and has a small kitchen garden and two boats), from April to August it is Rs. 100 a month, but September and October it is Rs. 210, or Rs. 7 a day on account of the chikor and pheasant shooting. Of all the lakes Naukatchia seems to favour the Claret fly most. The water is a beautiful limpid blue, and so clear that one sees one's fish before he is at you, and it must be fine and far off and no bungling.

There is always a nice breeze at mid-day, as there is too at Bhim Tal, blowing more or less from the west or south-west, and this is the time to fish. In the evenings the wind drops and the water becomes like glass, then it is that all the beauties of the place are at their best, and the deep dark reflections most clear. At this time too the fish for about half an hour rise at a small light fly, and I have found a small yellow spider or an olive dun take them.

There is some fairly good chikor shooting round here, and on the hill at the back of the house ; also over the far side one can get gooral, khakur, pheasant and an occasional leopard. Supplies must be got out from Bhim Tal, as one cannot even get milk here at times.

Malwa Tal.—This lake lies deep down in a ravine between hills, which rise up sheer 3,000′ ; it is east of Bhim Tal, and the road to it branches off to the left from the Naukatchia Tal road about two miles from Bhim Tal ; from here for 4 miles it gradually rises to the village of Langlia 6,400′ which is on the crest of the ridge. The views are magnificent overlooking Naukatchia, and the plains beyond and on one's right hand the jungle clad precipices sheer down 3,000′ or more. At Langlia there is a good camping ground for the shikari, and the slopes covered with grand oak tres to the north hold khakur, gerow, serow and gooral, bear and leopard, then for a mile the road winds along the north side of the ridge and descends the last three miles 3,000′ to Malwa Tal, a steep and stony path, which after the rains is in very bad condition and unfit to ride along. As one descends one looks sheer down on to the dark mysterious looking lake below one, and the temperature gets hotter and hotter. The path emerges by the dâk bungalow which is on a rise at the east end of the lake, with the Kalsa stream flowing on the right as you face the lake. The bungalow is furnished with beds, tables, etc., and there is a chowkidar there who lives in the village on the far side of the stream close by. The heat in this valley is intense till mid-September and the mosquitoes are very bad. A cold wind blows down the valley at night and one must be careful to put on a coat or sweater if one wishes to avoid fever. The last time I was there, there were two boats, but one leaked so badly it was impossible to use it. The jungle comes down to the edge of the lake on the north and south banks, and in the evenings you may see a gerow or khakur come to the water's edge to slake his thirst. At the west end of the lake there is a sandy stretch where the Kalsa flows into the lake, this is where the biggest fish are caught and a small fly-spoon takes well. Mr. Wright caught his

50 pounder here some 15 years or so ago on a white fly in the early hours of the morning and a tracing of this fine fish is cut on the table in the dâk bungalow. All supplies must be got out from Bhim Tal, a coolie can go in and back in a day for bread and daily requirements. You must take your own cooking pots and crockery, and a cook, as there is no khansamah there now. The flies here are the same as for the other lakes. A yellow spider takes well at times, no doubt the fish take it for a yellow blossom which falls in the water and which they eat. The water is very clear, and as at Naukatchia use a fine cast and long line and cast well under the overhanging bushes, but hold your fish hard till you have him clear, as there are treacherous sunken trees near the edge. Trolling with spoon or natural bait is successful I believe, as also at Bhim Tal, but to my mind poor sport, and though larger fish may be caught this way they do not show the fight of a fly hooked one. Here again in the heat of the day the fish lie near the surface and you must use your cunning and cast deftly to avoid frightening them. For the angler who likes to shoot as well, Malwa is the best spot of all the lakes; the jungles abound with game and better shooting ground can be got to easily within 10 or 15 miles east, though one will have to rough it more than the other lakes.

The average fish caught on the fly in these lakes run about 1 lb. to 1¼ lb. anything over 2 lbs. is rather exceptional, but they are good fighters and with fine tackle and a light rod give you plenty of sport. Last year the average weight of 60 odd fish I caught was 1·2 lbs., no fish of which was over 2½ lbs. and there were a good few 1½ pounders. This year in June (1909) during 10 days' fishing, they averaged about a pound, and I was fortunate to land a 3 pounder in Bhim Tal on a yellow spider. There was a good deal of rain about, the lake was very low and I found fishing in the middle of the lake better than the shore. The following are charges for coolies and ponies from Kathgodam to Bhim Tal :—

Cooly—5 annas.
Riding pony—Rs. 1-8-0.

Notes on Fishing in the Kumaon Lakes.

By C. Boyce, Esq., S. and T.

" The five lakes that hold mahseer are Naini Tal, Bhim Tal, Sath Tal, Naukatchia and Malwa Tal. From a fishing point of view the first named is practically useless. I have fished it occasionally for the last six years and hardly got a fish with the fly and only a few trolling with a small natural bait during the monsoon in dirty water, which is the only time the fish here appear to take a spoon bait.

Bhim Tal is sadly overfished, but there is no doubt a very pleasant holiday can be spent here, as one can get very comfortable quarters either at Mr. Ruxton's establishment or the Lake View Hotel, and sometimes the fish take very well; moreover the other lakes are within easy reach and one can ride over in the morning, fish all day and return to one's quarters at night. Bhim Tal fished very well in 1908 when some very good bags were made, and whilst I was there in June one angler took a nice fish of 9 lbs.

Bhim Tal is 12 miles by road from Naini Tal and 7 miles from Kathgodam, the terminus of the R.-K. Railway.

Sath Tal is about 5 miles from Bhim Tal and 10 miles from Naini Tal. By many it is considered to be the best of the Kumaon lakes from a fishing point of view. There are two furnished bungalows here which can be hired by the month or the week, but I prefer to camp down by the lake, there are two or three good sites. The best lies for fish appear to be along the rocky hedges opposite the sluice gates in the small lake and then along the left bank of the larger lake as one enters it from the smaller. Then the top end of the large lake generally holds some good sized fish, and they seem to lie just under the half-submerged willows.

Naukatchia is about 4 miles by road from Bhim Tal. It is a most lovely lake, but from my own experience of it and from what I have heard from others, to the fisherman it is a snare and a delusion. In 1908 hardly a fish was killed in it with the fly. The waters of Naukatchia are as a rule most beautifully clear, possibly too clear for catching the educated fish of the Kumaon lakes. However, this lake has a great reputation and possibly the present humour of the fish is only temporary. I have heard it is fishing a lot better this year than last.

Malwa Tal is 9 miles from Bhim Tal. The lake is really a very large and deep pool of the Kalsa river; it is filling up rapidly and possibly before very many years may cease to exist as a lake. When the fish in Malwa Tal are on the feed they take better than the fish of the other lakes, and I have found the best time of all is just before and during the first few days of the monsoon. The Kalsa stream then makes a dirty streak across the lake and all along this good fish are lying ready and keen to take the fly.

Malwa Tal holds enormous fish, and I believe fish of over 40 lbs. have been killed in it. I have myself taken a fish of 12½ lbs. from it spinning a small fish at the mouth of the Kalsa when it was coming down in flood. I believe this was the first fish killed on this lake in 1905.

Malwa Tal is only some 3,500′ above sea-level and consequently very hot during the day lying as it does in a deep valley, but the nights are cool although mosquitoes abound and it is as well to include a mosquito curtain in one's kit.

The best gear for fishing the Kumaon lakes is a good 12′ fly rod, a 3″ reel with 80 yards line, 35 yards of which should be a good dressed double tapered line, the remainder Backing, and fine trout casts. I have only used the flies recommended by Dr. Walker for these lakes, *i.e.*, Jock Scott, Silver Doctor, Yellow Spider and Claret fly. I have seen other flies used, but when the fish were feeding I used to catch as many fish as any one else, and I am inclined to think these flies just as good as, if not better than, any others.

It has become the fashion to fish these lakes after dark with an abortion of a fly, known locally I believe as the "tag of towel" fly, it is made by tying the tag of a white towel to a hook and looks like nothing in particular. This after dark fishing is a semi-poaching dodge and cannot but scare the fish, and in my humble opinion is doing more harm than anything else to the fishing on the Kumaon lakes, which is deteriorating yearly; it would be a good thing if an order could be brought in prohibiting fishing after dark as is done in Kashmir.

NOTES ON FISHING LOCALITIES IN KUMAON.

By Capt. W. H. Lane, 94th Russell's Infantry.

This district is mainly renowned, so far as fishing is concerned, by reason of its lakes. Dr. Walker's book is well known, and a description of the sport to be obtained in Bhim Tal and its sister lochs is also given in an extract from the *Pioneer*, dated 7th December 1903, by "Juba Bill," which is reproduced in *The Angler's Handbook for India*. In the same volume Captain W. T. Fairbrother deals with the Kosi river below Khairna and the Sarju rivers, south of Bageswar. In the following few notes any further mention of these localities will be omitted. To traverse old and previously well trodden ground will be of no benefit to the prospective angler in Kumaon.

In 1896 the writer made an expedition to the borderlands of Tibet, and in the following year a similar trip was executed, the furthest point reached being the banks of the Sutlej. On each occasion the Sarju above Bageswar and the Ramgunga * at Tejam were touched. Both rivers contained good sized mahseer. The following description of the route is culled from

(* *N.B.*—This river must not be confused with the other Ramganga, also in Kumaon.—S. D.)

the diary of 1896. At this date it is impossible to state with any degree of certainty whence the information was extracted, presumably it was derived from a Government route book, but in the event of its emanating from the pen of a private author, the present writer's apologies are herewith tendered for its reproduction.

Majhkali.—Khansama's dâk bungalow, nine miles from Ranikhet.

Someswar.—A village and temple, and traveller's rest-house. Height 4,572 ft.; from Majhkali 13½ miles.

Bageswar is situated at the junction of the Sarju and Gomati rivers The name is derived from the temple which is dedicated to "Vakiswar," the lord of speech. It is a great mart for the exchange of Thibetan produce between the Bhotiyas and the Almora merchants. The road from Someswar passes up the valley of a small feeder of the Kosi, half way is the Papi ridge. Someswar is about 12 miles from Bageswar.

From Bageswar upwards the bed of the river Sarju narrows and forms more a gigantic ravine than a valley, the entire floor being frequently occupied by its bed. This channel is exceedingly deep and in many places forms dark pools abounding in fish. At times the mountains rise precipitously on either side, so that the road to avoid the cliffs has sometimes to make a considerable rise, where it cannot be carried along the face of the cliff. On the right bank large torrent feeders of the Sarju are crossed. Within two or three miles of Kapkot the valley opens considerably and gives place to several stony and uncultivated dells covered with dwarf Zizyphus. The glen around Kapkot itself is highly cultivated, yielding fair crops of rice. It is about 1½ to 2 miles long, and ½ mile wide, and about 4,000 ft. to 4,500 ft high, enclosed by a belt of gently swelling and diversified mountains, covered with a beautiful vegetation, the "chir" pine predominant. The village is on its western edge, close under the slopes of Dioli (5,471 ft.). On the right bank the Chirpat Kot peak appears (6,637 ft.), and up the glen the snowy range, conspicuous among which is the peak of Nanda Kot (22,538 ft.). The picturesqueness of the scenery is no doubt in a measure due to the limestone which from Bageswar to Kapkot forms the most important rock. At Bageswar the Sarju is crossed by a new iron wire suspension bridge of 147 ft. span and the Gomati by a similar one of 60 ft., elevation 3,143 ft.

Kapkot, 14 miles from Bageswar, on the main road to the Pindari glacier, which turns north at Kharbugr, four miles from Kapkot. The road to Kharbugr crosses the Sarju by a suspension bridge, and again a stream coming down from Lamcholi by a bad ford.

Shama.—12 miles.

Tejam.—8 miles.

Some personal observations relative to the last two stages have also been recorded.

Shama.—The last two miles of the road from Kapkot ascend abruptly. There is a dharmsala, and a small camping ground at an elevation of about 6,000 ft. near the watershed.

Tejam.—The road from Shama soon crosses the watershed and descends steadily to Tejam, about 4,000 ft. Camp was pitched close to the left bank of the Ramgunga river, with "dharmsala" near at hand. In order to furnish the reader with an idea of the value of these two rivers from a piscatorial point of view, excerpts from diaries will first be quoted, and subsequently comments and suggestions will be offered.

31*st July* 1896.—River Sarju at Bageswar—went fishing in the morning but the river was muddy. About noon a native brought in to the dâk bungalow a mahseer which he had just caught. The spring balance registered its weight as 12 lbs. I tried with live bait in the evening but did not get a run.

10*th October* 1896.—Marched into Tejam [on the return journey to Ranikhet] in the morning and started out fishing at 3 P.M. Fished one small pool without result. At the next pool hooked a good fish, but the split ring parted, and I lost both fish and spoon. Put on a fresh spoon (No. 7 narrow hogged) and a few casts later distinctly saw a mahseer of some size make three separate attempts to seize the spoon, but he failed to get hooked. Towards the tail of this pool at another time three mahseer were seen following the spoon, but they refused to take the bait. I then went down to the next pool. At the head a fish came for the spoon but did not get securely hooked. About half way down the pool got into a mahseer, which was successfully landed, and scaled 9 lbs. The next pool was about a mile down, so stopped for the day as it was getting late.

21*st May* 1897.—Left Someswar early, and rode into Bageswar arriving there about 10 A.M. and started off fishing about 1 P.M. I fished till

5 P.M., but did not stir a fish although I tried with both spoon and chilwa. Rained pretty heavily about 6 P.M. which I hope will make it cooler in the night, for this is a terribly hot place.

22nd May 1897.—The coolies left Bageswar early and I followed fishing. I fished about four miles of river carefully with spoon but did not stir a fish. I then mounted my pony and rode three miles to breakfast. After breakfast I again fished till about 5 P.M. covering another four miles of river. I tried both with chilwa and spoon and two fish took the spoon, a narrow hogged No. 5, but they both got off. I then rode into Kapkot and had dinner.

23rd May 1897.—I tried fishing again in the morning but did not move a fin, although I fished two pools most carefully with spoon. After breakfast I started off to Shama.

24th May 1897.—Left Shama early. Had some fried bully mutton for breakfast, nothing else to be obtained here (Tejam). After breakfast I went fishing. In the first pool I had not had many casts before I felt a fish, which was successfully landed and scaled exactly 7¾ lbs. I then tried the next pool, and a fish missed my spoon. I saw the swirl on the top of the water. I saw several others following the spoon now and again, but I got nothing in that pool, and as it had begun to rain I stopped fishing and returned to camp, time about 12-30 P.M. I then had a cup of tea and as it cleared up I started out fishing again, and continued till 5 P.M., but did not get another run. Fish several times followed my spoon and chilwa, but they did not get any further.

25th May 1897.—Tried for mahseer before marching, but as it had rained very heavily during the night, the river was very much swollen; so after fishing two pools without result I put on a smaller spoon and tried in the tributary river but caught nothing.

Comments, suggestions, etc.—The reader will probably remark that the results as tabulated above are barely sufficient to warrant a trip to the Sarju above Bageswar, or to the Ram-gunga at Tejam. There are certain other facts also that must be taken into consideration. When the writer set out on his expedition in 1896, he had attained the vast age of 21 years. The mahseer recorded on 10th October was the first one that had ever been creeled! Hence it may reasonably be supposed that extreme youth and inexperience tended very consider-ably to the want of success. In the autumn of 1908 three months' privilege leave fell due. Negotiations were opened with the Collector of Almora for a third pilgrimage to these regions. The plan formulated was first to camp half way between Bageswar and Kapkot, and to give the waters in both directions a thorough trial. Thence to move to Tejam and finally to fish down the Ramgunga to its junction with the Sarju and gradually to work up the Sarju to Bageswar. In reply that official forwarded a circular order, over the signature of the Com-missioner, at Naini Tal, stating that owing to scarcity passes at that season could not be granted for a tour north of the Inner Line. A second letter was thereupon indited to the Collector of Almora pointing out that special arrangements would be made to procure all supplies at regular intervals from Ranikhet; that thereby no extra burden would be forced on the shoulders of the villagers, in fact under such circumstances a distinct advantage must accrue; for employment, within reasonable bounds, would be forthcoming, and money would be exchanged for manual labour. An answer was received that after the 1st September a limited number of passes would be issued for travel beyond the Inner Line, and that early application was advisable. Whilst this correspondence was in progress an agreement with the head of another circle had been drawn up; in consequence the visit to Kumaon fell through.

There should be little hesitation in assuming that the gorge between Kapkot and Bageswar must hold mahseer of considerable size. The numerous tributaries in this stretch must furnish food in abundance. Some magnificent pools exist, but owing to the precipitousness of the cliffs in many places approach is a matter of very great difficulty. The question as to whether a light boat could be manipulated on this portion is a matter for surmise. It would prove, if found practicable, an important adjunct, more especially to enable the fisherman to move from one point of vantage to another. Whether such an experiment has ever been attempted the author of these notes is not in a position to aver or deny.

As regards the Ramgunga at Tejam—12 years ago in its holts lurked mahseer innumerable.

Whether their numbers have since been thinned down is unknown to the writer. This stream is distinctly off the beaten track, and there is no adequate reason to suppose that such should be the case.

The intending visitor to these parts should place no reliance on local resources. Weekly supplies could easily be forwarded by a runner from Bageswar or Ranikhet. Rates are comparatively cheap, and for the angler, who is not impartial to enduring some slight discomforts, a very pleasant holiday should be enjoyed say in October and November in these regions. In addition to mahseer fishing in the rivers, by dint of perseverance both large and small game should be obtained in the wooded slopes of the surrounding hills. A 14 ft. rod should suffice for the Sarju above Bageswar, and for the Ramgunga at Tejam ; spoon bait is the most killing lure and the sizes should range from No. 3 to No. 7, but split rings, except of special manufacture, should be avoided.

Notes on Fishing in Assam.

By Capt. W. H. Lane, 94th Russell's Infantry.

" To the angler this Province is a paradise. To attempt to state with any degree of accuracy what particular river is the best would seem a practical impossibility.

The Angler's Hand-book for India contains liberal notes on many fishing localities in Assam. It was a perusal of these notes that led the writer's footsteps in the autumn of 1908 from Baluchistan to the fairy tea-gardens of India. Being an utter stranger to the land it was a matter of difficulty to definitely settle upon a locality. The following few words from Phoonghee's description eventually decided the question :—

"In the waters of the Upper Burhampootra—especially near Suddyah—mahseer are very plentiful and run to a very large size."

On the strength of the above quotation, it seemed that by making one's base of operations at Sadiya, good sport would be assured. This plan was adopted, but from the very outset it must be acknowledged, from an angling point of view, that the expedition proved a failure. Perhaps somebody who has captured the monsters referred to by Phoongee will be magnanimous enough to come forward with the requisite information, as to where they lurk. A few miles below Sadiya three rivers unite to form the Brahmaputra. From the east flows the Lohit, from the north the Dibong, and from the north-west the Dihang. Sadiya is situated on the Lohit. This military outpost was reached at the beginning of October, the Lohit was then in flood, and when this vicinity was quitted on 1st December, that branch had not sufficiently cleared to warrant spinning a success. Between the 11th and 16th November, the Dihang was visited, and it likewise was perfectly useless for trolling. A good spot, or rather what is supposed to be a good spot, is Sibiyamukh. Fish up to 40lbs., so rumour has it, have been captured at the mouth of the Sibiya stream. When this locality was visited the extent of fishable water cannot have exceeded 75 yards. The neighbourhood was abandoned without delay. The only fishable affluent near Sadiya was the Dibong, and as this river lies within the inner line, a permit from the Collector, Dibrugarh, has to be obtained. The local Miris are not overkeen on helping the visitor, and the prices demanded as wages are exorbitant. When camping out five men are necessary, four to manage the boat and one to remain in camp. Five boatmen at 12 annas per diem each and 4 annas for the hire of the boat will amount to Rs. 4 per day. Servants' wages have also to be reckoned upon, and extra boatmen and boats when camp has to be moved. The total expenditure leaps up at a truly alarming rate. The charge for hiring an ordinary country cart even to go three miles is Rs. 2. From Sadiya a start was effected on 7th October, but three days' rain without a break produced a 10 feet rise, which rendered the stream unfishable for 12 days. Below is an extract from a diary. It should be remarked here that to tabulate the actual spots where each day's basket was secured would be of no practical use. When the Dibong river is sufficiently clear for angling, from Deopanimukh to Keringpanimukh, a distance of about four miles, which was the furthest limit of the passport, the pools vary with the height of the water, and after every rains fresh channels are excavated, and new pools formed. Mahseer are to be found in every favourable run. The angler must utilise his own judgment and experience as to where the best holts lie.

Date.	Description.	Weight.	How caught.	Remarks.
19-10-08 ...	1 Murral ...	7 lbs.	Trolling with S. & G. 3″ broad hogged spoon.	Cloudy day with occasional showers of rain.
20-10-08 ...	1 Mahseer ...	$1\frac{1}{2}$ lbs.... ...	Ditto ...	Cloudy day, lost one and had one other touch.
21-10-08 ...	2 Murral ...	{ $3\frac{1}{2}$ lbs. / 3 lbs. ...	Trolling with all silver $2\frac{1}{2}$″ broad hogged spoon.	Cloudy and showery day, had one other touch.
	2 Mahseer ...	{ 7 lbs. / 2 lbs.		
22-10-08 ...	Water coloured, unable to fish.			
23-10-08 ...	Water still coloured			
24-10-08 ...	1 Mahseer ...	$2\frac{3}{4}$ lbs. ...	Ditto ...	Water slightly clearing.
25-10-08 ...	1 Murral	5 lbs. ...	Trolling with $2\frac{1}{2}$″ and 3″ S. & G. spoons.	Cloudless sky, water rapidly clearing, fishing from 9-30 A.M. till noon, catching first five, lost three others, and one fish broke mount. Fishing again from 2-30 P.M. till 5 P.M., lost one other, and got broken by a turtle.
	5 Mahseer ...	{ $1\frac{1}{2}$ lbs. / $2\frac{3}{4}$ lbs. / 6 lbs. / 8 lbs. / $4\frac{1}{2}$ lbs.		

26-10-08 ...	3 Mahseer ...	6 lbs 3 lbs. 19 lbs. ...	Trolling 1st fish on 2½" S. & G, 2nd and 3rd on 3" S. & G. spoon.	Fishing only from 7-30 A.M. to 11-30 A.M., cloudless sky, water dropping and clearing.
27-10-08 ...	—	—	—	Did not fish all day.
28-10-08 ...	1 Mahseer ...	3 lbs. ...	Casting from bank with 3" S. & G. spoon.	Fished for half an hour before sunset.
29-10-08 ...	—	—	—	Fished for an hour in the morning after breakfast, did not get a touch, sky cloudy, heavy rain during night.
30-10-08 ...	1 Mahseer ...	3 lbs. ...	Trolling with 2½" S. & G.	Fished for 1½ hours in evening, one other run on 3" S. & G., bright sun, fish began to take just before sun-down.
31-10-08 ...	3 Mahseer ... 1 Murral ...	3 lbs 8½ lbs. 4½ lbs. ... 5 lbs.	First two fish on all silver 2½", other two on 3" S & G. trolling.	Fished for 1½ hours in evening, one touch on 3" S. & G., cloudy evening, no sun. The 4½ lb. was snub-nosed variety, a much shorter head and darker body all through.

Date.	Description.	Weight.	How caught.	Remarks.
1-11-08 ...	1 Mahseer ...	5½ lbs. ...	Trolling—2½″ S. & G. spoon.	Fished morning and evening, caught as I was reeling up to come home to breakfast, water slightly coloured, bright sky, no other touch.
2-11-08 ...	—	—	—	Did not fish.
3-11-08 ...	3 Mahseer ...	2 lbs 2½ lbs. 2 lbs. ...	1st fish from bank, other two trolling on 3″ S. & G.	Fished from 7-45 A.M. till 12-30 P.M., cloudless sky, water clear, fish not taking freely, got broken by one fish.
4-11-08 ...	3 Mahseer ...	9 lbs 5 lbs. 9 lbs. ...	Trolling—3″ S. & G. spoon.	Light clouds, water clear, showery, fished from 8 A.M. till 1-30 P.M., and in evening for half an hour. Fish did not start taking till 10-30 A.M. In evening got broken by a good sized fish owing to the reel jambing.

5-11-08 ...	4 Mahseer ...	6 lbs 5½ lbs. 3½ lbs. 17 lbs. ...	Trolling— On 3″ S. & G. ... On 2½″ S. & G. On 2½″ all silver. On 2½″ S. & G.	Morning bright sky, 6 lbs. and 5½ lbs no other touch. Evening cloudy, 3½ lbs. and 17 lbs. Owing to a weak mount I lost another mahseer of 8 or 9 lbs. as it was being landed. Fish took for about ¾ before sunset.
6-11-08 ...	1 Mahseer ...	12½ lbs. ...	Trolling 2½″ S. & G.	Fished for about an hour in the evening, had one other touch.
7-11-08 ...	1 Mahseer ...	6 lbs. ...	Trolling—3″ S. & G.	Did not fish in the morning, had one other run. Fish began to take at sunset.
8-11-08 ...	—	—	—	Did not fish, moved into Sadiya.
9-11-08 ...	3 Mahseer ...	4 lbs 2½ lbs. 6½ lbs. ...	Trolling on 3″ S. & G.	Cloudy day, no sun, occasional spots of rain, fish not taking well, got broken twice, once by fish on account of weak mount, the other time by a turtle.
10-11-08 ...	3 Mahseer ...	9 lbs. 3½ lbs. 1½ lbs. ...	Trolling on 2½″ S. G.	Clear sky, bright sun, had one other touch.

Date.	Description.	Weight.	How caught.	Remarks.
11-11-08 ...	—	—	—	Did not fish moving to Sibiya.
12-11-08 ...	—	—	—	Do. do.
13-11-08 ...	*Nil.*	*Nil.*	—	Fished morning and evening. The place seems useless.
14, 15, 16 11-08 ...	—	—	—	Did not fish, moving back to Sadiya.
17-11-08 ...	1 Mahseer ...	14½ lbs. ...	Trolling on 2½" all silver.	Fished for ½ an hour in the evening.
18-11-08 ...	3 Mahseer ...	7½ lbs. ... 1 lb. 2 lbs.	Trolling—first two fish on 2½ S. & G. last on 3" S. & G.	All three caught in the morning from 10 A.M. to 11-45 A.M., had another small one on, had two touches in the evening, one a very powerful one.
19-11-08 ...	*Nil.*	*Nil.*	—	Fished morning and evening. In the morning I had two touches, in the evening *nil*; fish were not taking, cloudy, cold, sunless day.
20-11-08 ...	1 Mahseer ...	4¾ lbs. ...	Trolling on 3" S. & G.	Moving camp, fished for ¾ hour in evening, no other touch.

21-11-08 ...	*Nil* ...	*Nil.*	—	Fished for about ½ hour, no touch.
22-11-08 ...	—	—	—	Did not fish.
23-11-08 ...	1 Mahseer ...	3¾ lbs. ...	Trolling on 3″ S. & G.	Fished from 8 A.M. to 10 A.M., no other touch.
24-11-08 ...	4 Mahseer ...	4¼ lbs 14½ lbs. 8½ lbs. 1 lb. ...	Trolling all on 2½″ S. & G.	First three caught in morning, last in evening, fish were not taking in evening.
25-11-08 ...	2 Mahseer ...	19 lbs 10 lbs. ...	Trolling on 3″ S. & G.	19 pounder caught in morning, 10 pounder in evening, no other touch.
26-11-08 ...	1 Mahseer ...	2½ lbs. ...	Ditto ...	Caught in morning, fished for 1½ hours in evening, no touch.
27-11-08 ...	2 Mahseer ...	6¼ lbs 6½ lbs. ...	Ditto ...	Fished morning and evening, caught nothing in morning, the two caught in evening; in evening also had 4 other touches including two very good ones, fish were coming short.
28-11-08 ...	3 Mahseer ...	17½ lbs 15½ lbs. 1½ lbs. ...	Trolling all on 3″ S. & G.	First two caught in morning, the small one in evening, also had one other touch in evening.

The question will probably be asked—Was a big fish ever hooked and lost? The answer is in the negative as the Parliamentary saying goes. The present writer is still wondering where in the waters of the "Upper Burhamputra" those 60 lb. and 70 lb. fish are to be caught. Enlightenment may perhaps come at some future date.

A correspondent sends me the following brief note re *Assam.*

"The best fishing that I ever had in this country was at Sadiya, by rail from Dibrugarh, on the Brahmaputra. A very short visit. My two best fish were 37 and 26 lbs., but the planters there think nothing of a 50 lb. fish. Trolling tackle, *viz.*, spoon and wire trace."

Re the Teesta and other rivers round Darjeeling, I was promised notes, though unfortunately these have not come to hand at the time of going to press.

Udaipur.—Quite one of the most delightful spots in India, where both the sightseer and angler meet on common ground. And most anglers are lovers of Nature, and fishing in the beautiful Pichola Lake, the surroundings leave little to be desired. These notes are necessarily rather meagre, as the author spent less than a week in Udaipur, and part of that time the weather was inclement, and to know the lakes thoroughly a good many visits at different seasons of the year would be necessary. To reach the place, R. M. Ry., either from Khandwa on G. I. P., or from Ajmere on B. B. and C. I. change at Chitorgarh, and if some few hours have to be spent here the fort is well worth a visit. Possibly, therefore, I may be forgiven a few lines of digression on this subject. Go or send to the Hakim's house, and get the loan of the State elephant, kept for the use of

XIV

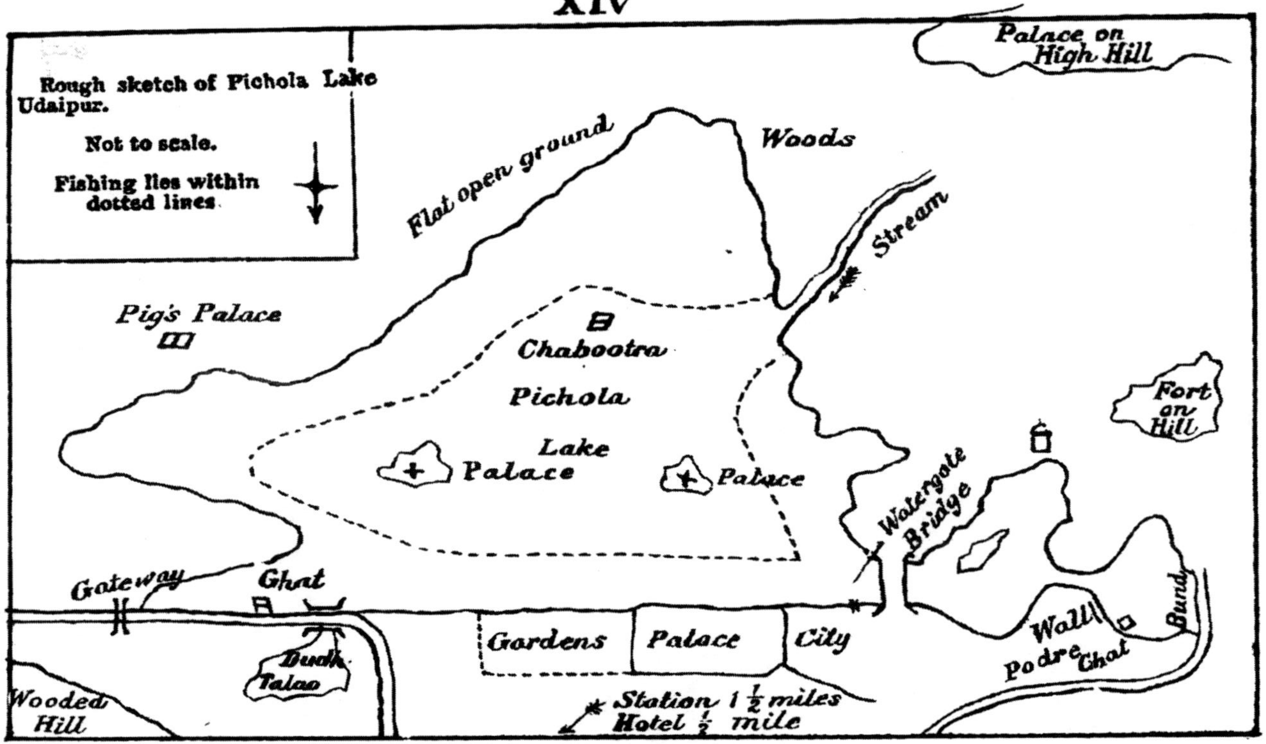

Rough sketch of Pichola Lake Udaipur.
Not to scale.
Fishing lies within dotted lines.
Palace on High Hill
Flat open ground
Woods
Stream
Pig's Palace
Chabootra
Pichola
Lake
Palace
Palace
Fort on Hill
Watergate Bridge
Gateway
Ghat
Gardens
Palace
City
Wall
Podre Ghat
Bund
Duck Talao
Wooded Hill
Station 1 1/2 miles
Hotel 1/2 mile

visitors to the fort. It is a most wonderful old place, the most striking points of interest being the two Jain towers of Fame and Victory both over 500 years old, but still in perfect preservation. Also do not miss the Gaomukh waterfall.

The train used to leave Chitorgarh at 6-30 A.M., and arrived Udaipur at 11-20. The old dâk bungalow 1½ miles distant from the station, has now been turned into a hotel, quite comfortable and charges reasonable. When driving from the station it is worth stopping to see the cenotaphs of the Udaipur Ranas, one or two of which are beautiful works of art. Also while in Udaipur a visit should be paid to the zoological gardens, which are fine ones for so small a State. The museum too is quaint and worth seeing. To fish, a boat is necessary, and for this a permit has to be asked for from the Prime Minister, and this we had to do both morning and afternoon or boat was not forthcoming. If this is still necessary it would be better to take a tiffin basket and, warning boatmen you meant to stop out all day, land somewhere in the woods the far end of the lake and make a couple of hours' halt there. The usual lake to fish in is the Pichola. Drive to Padre Ghat, on a small lake ; embarking here you pass through a narrow channel into another small lake, and thence under a bridge into the big lake. Both the small lakes hold fish, but one cannot get out a very long line. The entrance to the Pichola lake is narrow, and past rows of steps, then under palace, one sees some big fish rising here, but if not careful is liable to hook some fair maiden taking her morning bath.

The boatmen will know where to take you; some of the best ground is between the two palaces on islands,* and from each palace up to and round a chabootra you will see away at further end. Then a good lie is from the further palace up an arm towards the Pig palace (a kind of hunting lodge round which the wild pig are fed daily). Trolling is the general practice. Parts of the lake are deep, but you do not require to fish very deep, as one is liable to get hung up rather often whenever the water shoals. A 14 ft. rod with a short top, 150 yards of line and wire traces are tackle required. We found a 3″ spoon, either all silver, or silver and gold, was most successful, used without a lead. The fish usually caught are singhala or tengra and mulleys, running from 3 to 20 lbs. There are mahseer, murral and other fish, also turtles. Working along the right bank on entering Pichola lake, about three-fourth way up towards a palace that can be seen perched on a high hill, will be found a small stream entering the lake. Here in the rains the mahseer congregate, previous to running up to spawn, and at any time it is worth landing and trying a fly-spoon at mouth and a little way up stream.

N. B.—The big lake can be quite rough, and if you are not a good sailor you may appreciate this landing!

When done fishing it is best to land at the Dudh Talao Ghat, having previously ordered ghari to meet you there, and thence home to hotel. Another thing that is quite good fun, if you do not want a boat for any reason

* On one of these islands, it may be interesting to note, that the English ladies from Neemuch were given refuge in the Mutiny.

is bottom fishing off the Padre Ghat. One morning through some misunderstanding our boat was very late, and as we waited at the ghat, the fish were rising in shoals all over the small lake. Hastily sending to the Padre's house, not far distant, we got a small piece of raw meat, and mounting a gut cast, float, etc., we set to work. In the half hour before our boat arrived we caught a 17 lb. mulley, a 1½ lb. mahseer, beside smaller singhala, Notopterus kapirat and two turtles of 10 lbs. each. Also we hooked an enormous murral who got off, and were broken by another big fish.

The Fatteh Sagar lake lies half a mile away from Padre Ghat, but I am told it is not nearly so good as the Pichola lake.

Then the Udai Sagar lake, seven miles from Udaipur by road, holds big fish and a large number of mugger. A boat thereon might be arranged for by the courtesy of the authorities, if one was staying any length of time at Udaipur and had leisure to fix up matters.

The Dhibar (or Jaisamund) lake is 25 miles south-east of Udaipur, and 70 miles from Neemuch. There is no proper road from the latter place, and from the former, the track is, or was, most indifferent.

This is a splendid lake and holds enormous fish. It is a favourite resort of the Rana when he goes tiger shooting, at least so I was told. There are boats on the lake to use which I presume permission would have to be asked from the Prime Minister. There are plenty of duck, snipe, etc., here in the cold weather and excellent shooting can be got. This lake is one of the most beautiful spots in India, lying as it does amidst wild and desolate scenery. The dam is 1,000′ in length, and 98′ high. The overflow of the tank is into the Mahi river, and after the rains when a good volume of water is passing down, I have heard of mahseer up to 40 lbs. being caught here. This lake might well be worth a visit from Neemuch on ten days' leave, if one could travel light and go out on camels.

All the lakes can be fished any time during the year, except perhaps the first two months of monsoon, when water becomes too muddy. The best months are perhaps the hot weather ones, and again September.

What is now more necessary than anything to Udaipur fishing is that we should have a couple of years of really sufficient rainfall,* since it is I believe about eight years now since the Pichola lake has overflowed, and it is becoming imperative that a good volume of water should pass down the overflow to allow fish to run up from the lower reaches and restock the lake.

Thirty-five miles N. of Udaipur lies the great Kankroli or Rajsamandra lake, built nearly 50 years ago as a famine work. The bund is over 1,000′ long 49′ high in places. The town of Kankroli lies S.-E. of the lake, and the big temple here is worth seeing. There is a fair cart track out from Udaipur. I do not know whether this lake is fishable or not, but it must contain fish I should say.

Fourteen miles N. of Udaipur is the Eklingi lake, with its beautiful white marble temple,

* This year, 1909, appears to have been thoroughly satisfactory in this respect.

sacred to the family deity of the Udaipur Ranas.

Just as this book goes to press, a correspondent writing to me gives me the following information :—" *Re* Udaipur lakes, do you know that now they have restricted fishing to certain portions of the lake ?" This only shows how changes occur nowadays, and a book on localities should be re-written every year to be anything like up to date.

Although the above information may stultify to a certain extent the foregoing notes, it does not affect them in the main.

The Gambheri River.—Chitorgarh railway station, dâk bungalow near by. There used to be good fishing in this river here, some years back, and certainly it is a nice looking stream with some excellent water. While I stopped at Chitorgarh however the river was in full flood and quite unfishable. I extracted the following information though, from a source which I believe to be perfectly reliable, and this may help any brother anglers who may be visiting those parts.

"The dye works at Chitorgarh have now driven all the fish away from here, aided no doubt by poaching, but lower down the Biluch river joins the Gambheri and seven miles from Chitorgarh at Nagri, good trout (B. bola) and mahseer fishing is to be had."

"Station Hamirgarh, the third from Chitorgarh towards Ajmere, here the Gambheri river sweeps round in a bend towards hills, and below the junction of the Banas is excellent trout and mahseer fishing."

I should imagine that after the rains would be the time to visit the Gambheri river, or during any prolonged break in the monsoon; though possibly the hot weather would be all right as many of these C. I. streams are fed by excellent springs.

Notes on Fishing near Erinpura.

By Mr. G. N. Thompson.

The fishing round Erinpura itself is poor. However, one can get plenty of fun with chilwa, and other small fly takers. The following places are within easy reach of cantonments.

Jowai River.—Best place from one to two miles up stream from the railway bridge. Here the river does not dry up and there are a few small pools that always have a little water. The Jowai is only a river in the rains, and by November a mere trickle, and as a rule quite dry by February, with the exception of the above-mentioned pools which are eight miles from cantonments and two miles from Erinpura Road Railway Station. Fish obtainable: Mulley locally called Lansi (Wallago attu) up to 5 lbs. Small murral up to 2 lbs. Small labeo up to 1½ lbs. Crowds of chilwa and small fly takers. During the rains the river is crowded with Wallago attu, where they all come up from I cannot make out, unless they come up from the Luni which the Jowai joins after its junction with the Sukri. When the river begins to run low in September the whole population turn out with tulwars, round the fish up and massacre them. The pools above the railway bridge are very much poached, a favourite trick being to poison the water with cactus bushes.

Kolar Tank.— A very pretty spot situated among small hills. Fish obtainable : small murral up to 2 lbs., heaps of chilwa and giri (Barilius modestus), a small fish about the size of a chilwa that takes the fly well. Kolar also contains Lansi though I have not caught any. The lake is about six miles south of cantonments.

Dudni.—On the Jowai about five miles up stream from the railway bridge, contains a few small pools holding numerous fly takers.

The following fish are also found in the Jowai: Singhi (Pseudotripus sykesii, family Siluridæ). This is a little beast that requires careful handling, since his dorsal and pectoral fins are sharp as needles and give a poisonous wound. He is only taken bottom fishing and lives under rocks in still water. The Derai (Barilius barila ?) will take a fly and fights well for his size.

I hear that the Western Banass, a river that rises in the hills between here and Abu, and flows in a westerly direction towards Abu road and Deesa, contains some decent sized murral, rohu and lansi. I have not tried it yet, but intend to do so if I can get 10 days' leave after the rains.

" There are probably, I think, several places off the beaten track that remain to be discovered, where one could get quite good sport with murral, lansi and small fry."

(*N.B.*—I have fished the Banass at Deesa, in a very dry year certainly, and never had much sport out of it.—S. D.)

The Sabermati River flows past Ahmedabad and runs into the Gulf of Cambay. The only place that I ever fished it was near Ahmedabad, and here I had one day's quite good sport. Fourteen miles up the river lies the village of Rayasan, the road is bad, being an indifferent cart track. The best way to go out is to hire camels in Ahmedabad. At the station, too, are excellent sleeping and refreshment rooms. Below Rayasan village there is a ford. Above this is a tobacco field which runs down to a large and almost still pool in the river. This pool—from a well in field to where two rocks jut out into the water—is simply crammed with fish, mahseer, murral, rohu, paran and numerous other species. When first I saw it my heart sank, but the local ruffian who had lured me there was moved almost to tears, and swore by all his gods that the pool held lots of fish. For the current through it was very slight, and the water was distinctly dirty, and almost I was in a mind to pack up and go off home again. This was in the middle of December; but having come so far I determined to have a try, so started with a fly-spoon, and in one hour had on the bank 10 fish weighing 28 lbs., the largest being a 10-pounder. These included mahseer, murral and rohu. The pool is best fished by crossing the ford, and wading in opposite the tobacco field, though off the two rocks is also a good place. The villagers told me that further up by Indroli village was another good place, but the river-bed was sandy and tiring to walk over, so that I tried nowhere else. For some reason the villagers themselves are not allowed to net about here. I only hope this wise prohibition still remains in force.

The Mahi River.—This river, as mentioned elsewhere, is swelled by the overflow of the Jaisamund Lake, close up to which, after good rain has fallen, I have heard of a 40-pounder (mahseer) being caught. At Sevalia on the B. B. and C. I. are two bungalows, and good fishing could be had here some years ago, but the place was then badly poached, and it is impossible to say what the fishing is like there now.

Also at Bhairongarh, a station on the Rutlam-Godra section of B. B. & C. I. Ry., the Mahi is crossed by a bridge, there is some nice water, and though I caught nothing the few hours I fished here, I have heard of others catching fish in this portion of the river.

The Banass River, a tributary of the Chambal which runs into the Jumna south of Etawah, holds mahseer, paran, Barilius bola, etc.

FISHING ROUND JHANSI.

The following notes have been kindly sent me by correspondents, and are up to date as regards these parts.

"There is some very good fishing near Jhansi.

The Betwa River, about 7½ miles along the Nowgong road, teems with fish of all sorts. The mahseer run between 5 and 10 lbs. here, and may be caught with a spoon by spinning from the banks or trolling, but one will generally be disappointed to find a fresh water shark or other obnoxious fish attempting to satisfy his hunger at the expense of one's temper.

Further down stream and about 15 miles down the Cawnpore road is Paricha, and here perhaps is the best fishing in the river. Near the bund and about half a mile further down there are swarms of fish which can be seen from the banks. They run up to about 30 lbs., but I doubt if anyone has caught fish of over 10 lbs. lately. They are mostly 5 lbs. and a spoon is as effective as anything else.

Up stream towards Orchha there are some good places, but fish over 5 lbs. are rarely caught. About 22 miles down the Lalitpur road, where this crosses the river, there is good mahseer fishing, and there are trout here too.

The Barberi Nullah, six miles along the Nowgong road, holds lots of fish during the rains, but the best places are now regularly netted by natives, and sport is poor. For about two miles from where the Barberi runs into the Betwa, during the first two months after the rains, the Barberi is alive with fish, and large mixed bags can be made.

The Pahuj Nullah, about 3½ miles down the Sipri Road, holds trout, but this nullah too is netted, and it is difficult to make a good bag.

The Dhurari Nullah is about 11½ miles along the Lalitpur road. About a mile from the bridge up stream is a splendid pool which contains mahseer up to 8 or 10 lbs., and trout. It is scarcely known and hardly ever fished, though it is probable that the natives do so as the fish are very shy.

Burwa Sagar Tank, about 13 miles along the Nowgong road, holds many fish which may be caught with atta.

The above are the chief places of interest near Jhansi, and with a little trouble, a keen angler should have good sport."

"**The Betwa River.**—Start fishing from Paricha, headworks of Betwa Canal, 16 miles from Jhansi and fish up. A large pool below the masonry dam (below rocks) holds lots of fish, but the water is light and fine tackle is necessary, a boat also is necessary and above all skill.

From Paricha to the road crossing at Nohat Ghat, on the Jhansi-Nowgong road, about 15 miles in length, river is a deep pool. Lots of mahseer and goonch ; fine tackle and a boat necessary.

Further up stream and about 20 miles from Jhansi, is the Dukwa weir. The water held up is deep and about 13 miles long. Mahseer fishing to be had ; fine tackle and boat necessary.

Further up beyond Dukwa weir, all the pools hold mahseer, but the water is light, and fine tackle, a boat and skill are necessary to be successful. Mahseer above 10 lbs. seldom caught. Goonch can be had from 3 to 40 lbs.; trolling with fine tackle is the best method.

All the other streams running into the Betwa hold fish only in the deep pools, the mahseer are smaller in these streams.

For a skilful fisherman there is ample sport to be had in the Betwa from October to June. For goonch (some people call this fish the freshwater shark) the warm months are the best, commencing from March to the setting in of the rains."

My own experience of fishing round Jhansi being but of the slightest, I will not attempt to add much to the foregoing. But the following few notes may contain one or two details not enumerated above. For any keen angler who has some few hours to wait at Jhansi station, it may avail him to know that there is an excellent waiting room with bathrooms here and a good refreshment room. Also tum-tums can be hired at station at a rate not exceeding 6 annas an hour, to take one out to any of the three following places :—

The Betwa river is crossed seven miles along the Nowgong road by a ferry. It forms a large expanse of water here, being held up some miles lower down by a bund. I heard of a 50 lb. goonch, and a 32 lb. mahseer being caught here lately, the latter on a spinning bait cast from the bank.

At about six miles along the same road from Jhansi, the Barbari Nullah is crossed by a bridge under which is a good run. Then there are two or three good runs in the next mile down, the last half mile or so to the junction with the Betwa being broad and still. In the runs trout to 1 lb. and mahseer to 3 and 4 lbs. are to be caught. In the lower reaches there are a lot of big mullet, and good fun is to be had I believe shooting these with a rook rifle, an attendant being ready to dive in and retrieve.

The Pahuj Nullah lies 3½ miles from Jhansi along the Sipri road (distance is less than this from the railway station), and there are some quite good little runs in the ¼ mile just above and below bridge. The fish seem to run smaller than in the Barbari Nullah, and there are a lot of olive carp that will take a fly-spoon. Everywhere along the banks are all the signs of systematic poaching. I was told that there were two bunds, one some way up stream and another a mile or two down, and where the water is held up the fish run larger. But both the Barbari and the Pahuj Nullahs are terribly poached, and openly too ; it does seem a pity that some action cannot be taken to check this, as both streams are being ruined for sport. The time to fish them is during a break in the rains and then in September and beginning of October.

CHARKARI.

Now concerning the fishing to be had in the lakes at the capital of this most delightful State, it is not perhaps worth while giving much informatiom for the general public, since all fishing in the lakes is strictly forbidden, except to His Highness the Maharaja's guests, and as an invitation is necessary to visit the State, the casual angler may eliminate these lakes from the list of available fishing localities. But for those fortunate enough to be favoured with an invitation from the Maharaja of Charkari, to stop at the State Guest House, the following information may be of use :—Charkari is the capital of the State of same name in Bundelkhand, and lies nine miles by good road from Mahoba station (on the Jhansi-Manickpur section of G. I. P. Ry.). The State send a carriage to meet the train, and the drive out is a pleasant one through varied scenery. The Guest House is a most picturesque structure, built out into the Bija Sager Lake, it is two-storied, and very roomy and comfortable. Visitors are treated with the greatest possible courtesy, and no trouble seems too great to make their stay as pleasant as could be desired.

The Guest House is fully furnished down to the smallest details, bedding, towels, mosquito nets, library, writing tables, etc., etc., and all meals are provided by a staff of most obliging servants. In fact the guest need bring nothing except personal belongings, even fishing gear is provided, though perhaps anglers would do well to bring their own pet tackle. Men are told off to accompany those wishing to fish, and paste, livebait or any other fancied lure, is produced on demand. Of the various lakes, the three most important are— the Jai Sagar (the first to be noticed as one approaches the town), the Bija Sagar on which stands the Guest House and the Rattam Sagar lying about a mile away behind the Fort. This last is on a rocky hill overlooking the Palace, which stands near the Guest House. Probably good fishing could be got in either of the other two lakes, but the attendants do not recommend this, as though there are plenty of fish in them they do not come to bait readily, since there are but few bathing ghats along their banks. And it is near these latter that the fish congregate, since the villagers wash both themselves and their cooking pots here. Therefore the Bija Sagar may be considered as *the* lake for sport. The following spots seemed the most favoured, though with a little ground baiting probably many other sites would be discovered to be equally good. The lake is divided by a bund, a bridge crossing the waterway between the two portions.

First place recommended is under the large peepul tree, which gives grand shade, just outside and to left (*i.e.*, west) of the bungalow. Here however the water lilies, which cover parts of the lake, had encroached a lot in 1909, and the first day I fished here, three good rohu defeated me among the stalks. However a polite request, and a large space is cleared for one to angle in. Then in the further lake, off the wall just this side of ghat in middle of north face, this being an A-1 spot for live-baiting for paran. Other good spots are off the small ghat at N.-E. corner of this lake, and of the several ghats along north face to east of Guest House, the one under small temple at N.-E. corner being especially good. The best fishing months are probably July, August and September, the last being a delightful month, especially latter half. However March to June and October are all months that would yield sport. The fish are paran (Wallago attu), rohu, labeo, white carp, olive carp, tengra, murral, Notopterus kapirat, turtles, eels and innumerable small fry. The paran run enormous. I hooked and lost one that must have been nearer 40 than 30 lbs., twice we saw him, and as I had just landed a 21-lb. paran, comparisons were fairly easy to make. He fought magnificently, taking out over 150 yards of line at a great rate. After 10 minutes—during which I could do nothing with him—he got off, having bitten clean through the shank of one of Hardy's stoutest oval wire hooks (the loop-eyed spoon mounts), one hook of which was left embedded in live bait and the eye was still on wire mount, the bait coming back attached to second flight. The live bait I usually harnessed thus, *i.e.*, two separate mounts both fastened to tail swivel on trace, one flight hooked through bait just in front of dorsal fin, the second through his tail. Even with this arrangement many paran seemed to get off. The best bait is a rohu or white carp of about 1 lb. That the paran are voracious, a note by R. B. in Visitors' Shikar Book testifies, one taking a 7 lb. rohu that was being played. The rohu run to 12 lbs. and over, indeed the book chronicles two of 27 and 22 lbs., though during the last few years none over 12 lbs. seem to have been caught. The labeo probably run slightly smaller, the murral to 10 lbs. or so. The bait for the rohu, etc., is undoubtedly paste, while for the paran live bait is the thing. The best plan is to mount one of latter, and set him adrift, giving the rod to an attendant to hold, while you yourself settle down to paste fishing. At times the innumerable small fry will drive you almost crazy, dashing for your bait, and worrying it to pieces before it can reach bottom. One morning however the rohu joined the fry in this game, and in two hours I landed 10 rohu between 1 and 5 lbs. dangling the bait just below the surface. An occasional turtle too will sometimes nearly reduce you to frenzy, giving you continuous bites and fruitless strikes; on his removal, however, more peaceful times will again set in. In the season duck and snipe are to be had here; and there is also some jungle three miles off, where black buck, cheetal, nilghai and an occasional panther can be had. It might be worth trolling in the lake opposite the bungalow—both boats were undergoing repairs during my visit, so I could not try it—it has been done once or twice, *vide* the Shikar book.

Near Mahoba, a station on the Jhansi-Manickpur section of the G. I. P. Ry., there are some fine lakes, which hold large numbers of fish. There is a small but nice waiting room at the station, and a dâk bungalow three miles away. The Madan Sagar lake lies near this bungalow. The Tirwa Sagar lies one mile from station, and the Bija Sagar six miles away. There is, I am told, a bungalow near this latter also. The fish are rohu, labeo, etc., and I was told on good authority that the lake also held mahseer.

THE FOLLOWING NOTES ARE BY "R.B."

The Dhasan River.—Fishing is disappointing. Best places within easy reach from Nowgong are—Macha village 6½ miles, where there is excellent water from opposite the village to one mile below. Mahseer and Barilius Bola, the former up to 6 lbs.

Garauli village, junction of Seelap Nullah with Dhasan, is good for mahseer up to 6 lbs. and can now be got at by a metalled road, distance from Nowgong Cantonment six miles. Opposite and below Garauli is also good water. Best months are February and early March, also September and early in October.

Junction of Barar Nullah with Dhasan ¾ mile below Garauli is now readily accessible in rains, and good coarse fishing can be had. Various kinds of carp, tengra, murral and also mahseer. State of Barar Nullah has to be watched, and a drive out when the flood water has run off is well rewarded.

Jagat Sagar Tank.—A large sheet of water, excellent sport with chilwa, also with olive carp using bored gram fished as with a fly, for bait. Bottom fishing very disappointing. Usual seasons for tank fishing apply.

Gora Tal.—Now accessible by a driving road. Bottom fishing disappointing. Good sport with tengra can be had by trolling round the lake—which is a very fine sheet of water—in a dug out. No. 7 heavy pattern silver and gold spoon, with no lead, and keep 50 yards or so from the edge of the weeds.

Ken River.—Holds mahseer; 44 miles from Nowgong by road. Also to be got at by road (19 miles) to Harpalpur and thence by rail to Banda. A very fine pool above and below the railway bridge, holds large mahseer and many other varieties of fish, excellent Barilius Bola fishing at head of pool and higher up. The natives catch astonishing quantities of butchwa by using a stiff bamboo and baiting with "kullee." The bait only and not the shank of the hook must be in the water, and the strike has to be made by hand and eye and not by touch. The fish is flung out over head to hit the stone piers of the bridge 30 ft. up. As many as 60 or 70 fish are secured in this way by one man in an evening. The fish run to $1\frac{1}{2}$ lbs."

The Beylun and Sone Rivers in the Mirzapur district. Concerning these, a correspondent tells me that the fishing at Burroundah, in the former, has fallen off sadly; only after the rains for a few weeks is there much water below the Irish bridge. In the Sone, a river of large sandy pools, are lots of fish he adds, though he never caught many. But in all these Central Indian rivers there must be good fishing to be had, if only anglers who had tried them would give the results of their experiences.

The Nerbudda River.

The Nerbudda River, great rival in sanctity to Mother Ganga, is a river the charms of which have never been sufficiently realised from an angling point of view. Rising in Rewa territory near Amarkantak, a huge flat topped hill 3,500 ft. high, it runs a course of some 800 miles to debouch into the sea below Broach. All round the source is wild and desolate country, but a small body of priests have raised temples to guard the sacred spot. The Nerbudda bubbles up gently in the centre of a small tank on hillside. From here for about three miles it gathers in waters of countless springs and then leaps off Amarkantak plateau in a fall 70 ft. high. After this it continues to descend hundreds of feet by falls and rapids till it enters the Central Provinces. Here it runs in several channels broken by ledges of black trap. Dense foliage stretches up from the water's edge, and hills shut in the horizon on every side. At about 100 miles from its source it passes under the walls of the ruined place of Ramnagar and thence it flows down to Mandla an unbroken expanse of blue water, the banks clothed with verdure, one of the loveliest doks (reaches) on any Central Indian river. Then comes Gaurighat where the Grand Trunk road from Jubbulpore to Nagpur crosses the river. Nine miles south-west of the former place the Nerbudda falls 30 feet and narrows from 100 yards to 20 flowing for nearly two miles through the Marble Rocks gorge. From here onwards to the sea the river flows through wide alluvial plains, alternating with wild rocky gorges. It has three big falls in the C. P.—at Umaria in Nursingpur district, 10 feet; at Mandhar, 25 miles below Handia, 40 feet; and at Dadri near Ponasa 40 feet.

Even in the dry season the Nerbudda is never a small river, and its deep pools offer safe retreat for thousands of its finny population. And the numerous ghat streams that form its tributaries are ideal spawning grounds for the fish of the great river. Its mahseer too, mostly of the pale blue variety, seem to have taken some of their colour from the glorious blue of the waters. And what handsome fish they are—a 10 lb. mahseer freshly caught in the Nerbudda could, I think, hold its own with any other fish in the world. That almost everywhere the fish will take gram in preference to any other bait is to be accounted for perhaps by the innumerable sacred ghats that line the banks of the river, and that this is so should give no cause for complaint, as it would be hard to find any prettier form of fishing or one requiring more skill, than is called for from the successful angler with gram on the Nerbudda.

But it certainly is extraordinary this passion for *chenna*, as there can hardly be sufficient gram poured into the Nerbudda to feed the thousands of fish in all its reaches; but no matter where you fish in the Nerbudda or its tributaries (and even in tanks miles away, and unconnected entirely with the river), the fish always expect gram, and failing to get it, sulk, and refuse to associate themselves with your hook. And verily I believe, if one took a 2 lb. mahseer from Jubbulpore, and dumped him alive and kicking into Jungoo pool, he would go mooning about looking for gram and making himself a general nuisance to all the other fish, till a 40 pounder ate him, or he died of starvation. But after all, as I said before, it *is* a matter to be thankful for that the fish do like gram, for it is a method of fishing that takes a fairly high place in artistic angling, and certainly the fascination of it grows upon one.

And one other fact about the Nerbudda mahseer, they appear to have distinctly smaller mouths than the mahseer of other rivers. This may be a feature peculiar to the gram-fed fish one catches, or it may possibly be only imagination that their mouths are smaller. But it is not only that I myself have thought so, but I have several times heard others comment on the same subject.

Jubbulpore.—This is about the highest spot up the river, concerning which I have khabar, and a correspondent most kindly favours me with the following notes. But he prefaces them with this remark (a preference I may add that one learns to know and dread more and more in connection with Indian fishing).

"I do not advise anyone to go to Jubbulpore especially for the fishing. Of late years it has fallen off shockingly. The fish are much shyer than they were ; touch or bag a fish from a run, and all the other fish clear out into the pool below and there is no getting at them. One does best with very fine tackle. I have never caught fish with anything but gram, but W. who was at Jub. with me was successful I know in catching several mahseer on spoon." Then the notes.

"**The Gour River.**—Drive from Jubbulpore to Kuteaghat on the road to Mundala, and fish for a mile or two up and down the river. Also down the river from the crossing at Kuteaghat to Khiraneeghat, the junction of the Gour and Nerbudda rivers, distance about seven miles. The best time to fish this river is just after the rains, when the water is commencing to clear, and during a long break in the rains."

"**The Nerbudda River.**—Khiraneeghat, six miles from Jubbulpore, bad road, ride to junction of Gour and Nerbudda and fish down to the railway bridge."

"**Gouree Ghat.**—Six miles from Jubbulpore, good road for driving. Runs above and below the ghat."

"**Tilwara Ghat.**—Ten miles, good driving road. Runs above and below the Ghat."

"**Lumheta Ghat.**—Twelve miles, can drive, road bad for the last six miles. Very good fishing from about two miles above the ghat right down to the Marble Rocks about seven miles, the left bank going down is the best."

XV

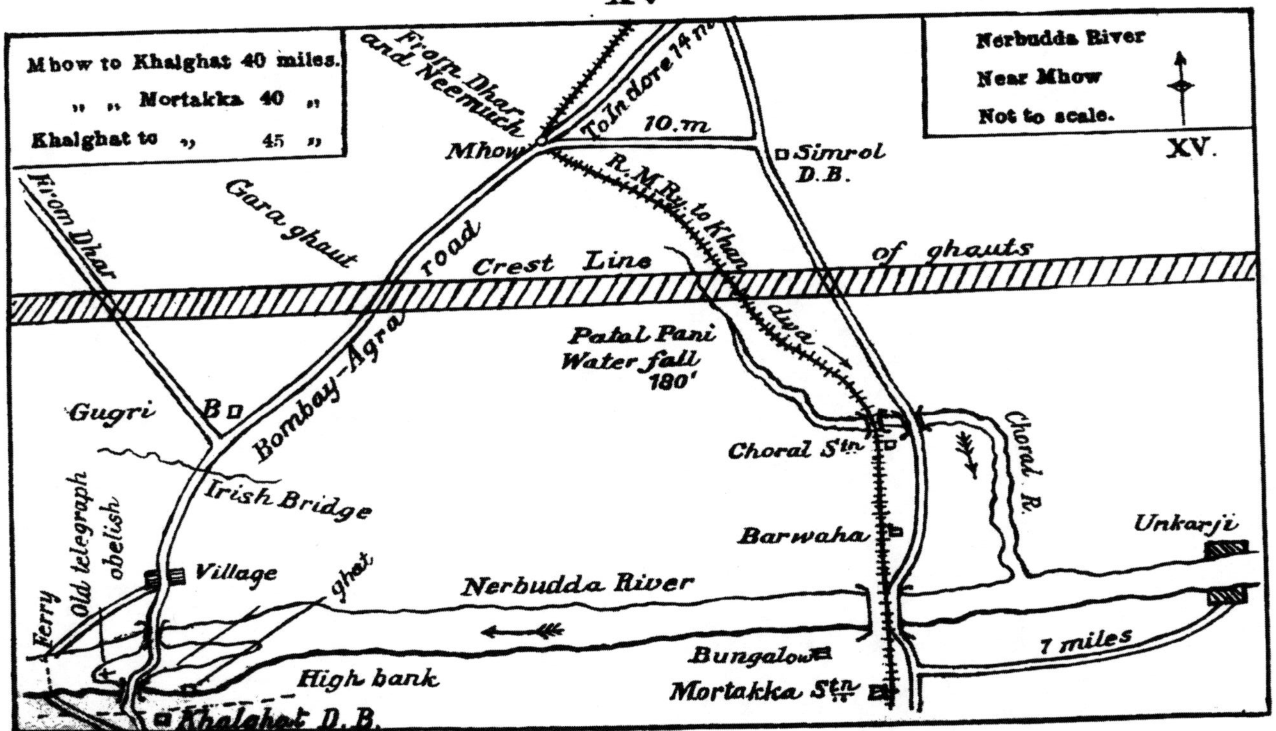
Mbow to Khalghat 40 miles.
" " Mortakka 40 "
Khalghat to " 45 "
Nerbudda River
Near Mhow
Not to scale.
XV.
From Dhar and Neemuch
To Indore 14 m
10.m
Mhow
Simrol D.B.
R.M.Ry. to Khandwa
From Dhar
Gara ghaut
Crest Line of ghauts
Bombay-Agra road
Patal Pani Water fall 180'
Gugri
B
Irish Bridge
Choral Stn
Choral R.
Barwaha
Unkarji
Village
Old telegraph obelisk
Ferry
ghat
Nerbudda River
7 miles
Bungalow
High bank
Mortakka Stn
Khalghat D.B.

"**Bhera Ghat or Marble Rocks**.—Thirteen miles, good driving road. There are two runs below and four or five above this ghat. And you can fish right up to Lumheta on both banks of the river."

"I found April, May and June the best months for fishing this river, it is also good after the rains in September. The fish will take nothing but gram, which should be freshly parched so that it may float well, and a small hole carefully drilled through each grain. These should be threaded on to mounted hooks passing the gut through the hole in the gram, and two grains should practically cover the hook. Gram is nearly always taken by the fish when it is allowed to float down a run as fast as possible by letting out line after casting. It is hardly ever taken when drawn up. Fish from 1 to 8 lbs. each."

The above notes should be taken in conjunction with those in the "Anglers' Handbook," they do not add much to them, but they are up to date.

The Nerbudda near Mhow.—The river can be reached at two places from this cantonment. First to deal with the more accessible—Mortakka. Here is a station on the R. M. R. and the railway crosses the river by an immense many spanned bridge. A short way below the bridge on the left hand bank is a furnished bungalow, to get the use of which it is necessary to ask for permission from the Executive Engineer of the line whose headquarters are at Mhow. The best fishing is just below the bridge from either bank, and greatest merit of all can be carried on at any month in the year except when the Nerbudda is coloured by the monsoon rains. May and June however are extremely hot, though on the other hand they are very good months from an angling point of view. The fish to be caught are mahseer and olive carp, the latter running up to 1 lb., seldom larger, and being very numerous. One's fishing may always be improved by sending a man down a day or two in advance to ground-bait certain runs by throwing in handfuls of gram morning and evening. The best runs of all are two just below the bungalow, and here we caught most of our mahseer. Below the bridge from either bank is the place for olive carp, or you can fish out of one of the big Nerbudda boats. If fishing below the bridge, however, remember the extreme sanctity of the river, and whenever a train passes over watch for bones of deceased Aryans which occasionally descend with unpleasant velocity. Also cocoanuts and other small offerings. There are lots of enormous turtles in the Nerbudda here, and in an unhealthy season also a fair sprinkling of corpses, which have been brought to be burnt at the water's edge. Now as regards tackle. An 11 ft. or 12 ft. fly rod, and trout cast. Use small hooks, somewhere about 8 or 10 Limericks (Thomas' scale or according to plate given in "The Mighty Mahseer"). These can either be eyed, or mounted to gut, though in the former case more care will be required to work the gram on to the hook. Fifty yards of line should suffice, though no harm in having 75. Parched gram (or chenna) is the bait, and to prepare it for mounting an ordinary large headed needle may be used, or it is better to have a small triangular pointed instrument made up for the purpose. Remember to take a large quantity of grains so prepared, one's orderly or shikari can easily do them, for one loses an immense number, and the putting on of fresh grains is the one trial of gram fishing. It is better to have the hook on a separate looped snood, and always to remove this and work the gram down over the loop and eye of hook; trying to work it on over the barb enlarges the hole too much, though some men prefer doing it this way to save trouble. Put on two grains at a time, since this helps to hide the hook, and if one flicks off leaves you the other to continue with if the fish are taking freely. Sometimes though they are extraordinarily canny, and will rise all round the hook, taking the ground bait but severely leaving your lure alone. The way to start is to approach the run or pool you mean to fish and then standing well back, throw in a handful of gram. Almost immediately fish will begin to rise and feed, and then watching till you see a bigger gulp than usual cast your lure towards the spot and pay out line slowly. But at a tug be ready to strike quickly, as if the fish fail to hook themselves, immediately they feel the steel they will eject your lure with great rapidity. In my shikar diary I see the following notes:—T. and self, 4th November, 8-11 A.M.—Mahseer 5 and 2 lbs., and 18 olive carp weighing 11 lbs. 15th November, afternoon and early morning of 16th, T. and self.—Mahseer 8½, 4½, 5¼, 2¾, 1 lb. and also a lot of olive carp. 16th and 25th April.—29 olive carp weighing 15 lbs., biggest $1\frac{1}{2}$, 1 lb., etc. The biggest fish we got was an 11 pound mahseer, caught by T., a real beauty ; and for pure sport the playing of a Nerbudda mahseer of over 5 lbs., on a small trout rod with fine gut, takes a lot of beating. After this I was away from Mhow for a time, fishing in the Himalayas, but I quote from some notes of T.'s:—"18-5-07.—In the rapids below rest-house, 40 fish, largest 3 lbs., weight 20 lbs. 30-5-07.—40 fish, several between 2 and 3 lbs., lost a lovely fish of between 10 and 12 lbs. when he was within a yard of being netted owing to hook drawing from the gut. 2-6-07.—Good sport in the rough water. Got 51 fish, largest 4 lbs., several between 1 and 3 lbs., lost one of about 5 or 6 lbs., which after about 10 minutes play got behind a rock and cut the gut. 7-6-07.—Tried fishing from the right bank, had to wade a lot, stones very slippery, sat down twice in the water quicker than I intended. Wind very strong and water slightly coloured, got 20 fish, largest 5 lbs., and 3 of 3 lbs. 9-6-07.—Sport poor, water got more discoloured during time I was fishing, only got about 10 fish, largest 3 lbs."

I was told of a man who after the rains caught several mahseer up to 28 lbs. here on spoon, but none of us ever seemed able to emulate his example.

The second place to make for on the Nerbudda is Khalghat, 40 miles from Mhow, on the Grand Trunk Road to Bombay. The road is good in parts, in others fair to bad, it makes a nice motor run with the six miles down the ghats which are encountered about 20 miles out from Mhow. Here in the cold weather are two or three temporary bridges from island to island across the Nerbudda, while in and after the rains an enormous ferry boat has to be resorted to. On the opposite bank, on a bluff overlooking the river, is a small furnished dâk bungalow, where one can spend a couple of days fishing very pleasantly. The best spots are below the bungalow off a small ghat, and from here down to the rapid below the bridge. This rapid holds some good mahseer, and can be fished either from the left bank or from off an island where stands one of the old telegraph obelisks. Fish first of all from the ghat—no one objects to this—and then when this is played out wade in either above or below as far as possible, and casting handfuls of gram to right and left work down river getting out as long casts as possible to either side and down stream, letting current swing your lure across. A great many nice fish lie behind rocks in this run which varies from 1 to 3 ft. in depth as a rule. Among other notes I see as follows:—January 14th, 8-11 A.M.—Mahseer 4, 2, 1½ lbs. and lot of olive carp in lower rapid. On 4th February a 4 and ¾ lb. mahseer in lower rapid. On 26th, 27th April, G. M. and self caught over 50 fish, mahseer and olive carp in reach off ghat. Also one can fish in the rapid under right bank, just below first bridge, as a lot of small fish and occasionally one or two good ones lie here.

About 25 miles above Mortakka railway bridge lies a very little known spot on the Nerbudda, and one which I fully believe would well repay a few days' careful fishing. It is, I think, one of the most fascinating places that

I have ever seen; unfortunately I only visited it during my last fortnight at Mhow, and then only got the inside of a day there; since then never having had an opportunity to revisit it. The Nerbudda, a big river here, gathers itself together, and swirling past three islands that bar its path, plunges head foremost a descent of 40 ft. in two fine falls and one great rapid. Below for some half a mile it runs in a great gorge, rumoured to be over 80 ft. in depth, and then roaring out through another neck it continues in a second gorge. Owing to appalling roads and great difficulties in getting our carts here at all, M. and I only got some two hours' fishing. He caught a 5 pounder and myself a 2½ pounder in the upper rapid, and I hooked a whopper who broke me in lower rapid, and then our time was up! To get there. Sanawad station on the R. M. R., thence 20 miles to Ponasa, a large walled village. Track very indifferent, and about three streams to ford *en route*. Nice tank at Ponasa. Carts hard to get at Sanawad (*N.B.*—If got, remember they are very small.) From Ponasa road leads due north to Dhari, seven miles all through thick jungle, last half mile very bad. Dhari is a small village on the opposite side of the falls. This side there is a ruined temple near which one can camp. We could only fish from this bank, so did not touch the better water. They told us a boat was kept at Dhari and would come across to a hail. This would enable one to get at all the good water. The jungle all round is dense, and we noticed innumerable tracks of tiger, sambhur, hyæna, etc., and saw peafowl, pigeon and a huge mugger in the gorge. This is presumably in Ponasa block, so a permit to shoot would have to be got from Forest Officer at Khandwa. Tarkari, which is seven miles by road from Ponasa, is said to be only three miles by footpath from here, and we were told that good fishing was to be had in some rapids there. At Ponasa is a dâk bungalow. Should this description tempt any one to try the above place, I should be most grateful and interested if they would write me their experiences. The spot is absolutely wild and cannot be poached. I visited it in November, but should think March, April, May (hot) and October would all be better months. We only tried spoons. The best way to get out is to arrive by the evening train from Mhow, and then making your bed in a bullock cart—remembering their exceeding smallness however—go out by night. There are villages every two miles, and it is the custom for each village chowkidar to show you on to the next village. This however occasionally breeds delays.

Unkerji Mandhata.—Seven miles by an excellent metalled road from Mortakka station lie the sacred fanes of Unkerji. Apart from any idea of fishing, these are well worth a visit from a sight-seeing point of view.

There are innumerable temples and fakirs here on both banks, though mostly on a hill on opposite side. A large number of boats are continually ferrying pilgrims across. Throw in a handful of gram in mid stream, and it is enough to make any angler's mouth water to see the shoals of fish that rush for the bait from monsters of 20 and 30 lbs. down to small fry of 6 and 4 ounces. It would be as much as your life were worth to fish here, though, but about half a mile down there is no objection, and there is a nice rapid. D and I tried in December but with indifferent success, but I have since met men who told me they had good sport there.

The Choral River.—Soon after the small metre gauge railway, that branches from the G. I. P. at Khandwa, starts to puff its toilsome way up the ghats to Mhow, you come to Choral station. Thence rumbling across a bridge the climb commences in earnest. If you look from the left hand window, any day in the hot weather, you will see a great boulder strewn gorge far below you, shimmering in the heat and innocent of any signs of moisture. Just before you reach the summit a fleeting glimpse is vouchsafed of Patal Pani, a waterfall of some height, a tiny trickle that hurls itself into a great green pool far below.

This is the Choral river. Wait however till the first break in the rains, and a great change takes place. From being a dry bed of rocks, the Choral river becomes a delightful little mountain stream of some size and a favourite spawning ground for the Nerbudda mahseer. But like all the hill tributaries of the latter river, it is necessary to fish in it the first break in the rains, for though a certain number of fish do remain up longer, by the time the second break comes one seldom seems to have much sport. There are two places worth going to from Mhow. First Choral station reached either by rail, or 18 miles by an excellent road suitable for motor. Start fishing from, and off, the road bridge which is only a hundred yards from the station and fish down stream. There is a deep kund, or pool, higher up near Kalakund station, which holds some big fish, but they are almost impossible to catch. This pool used to be a favourite spot for Tommies' fishing picnics on Sundays, but I don't think the fish ever suffered much harm. Some way down below the bridge, my memory unfortunately fails me as to the exact distance, is a very good pool, with a fall above it, and a good rapid below. Here one was generally certain of a run. I have a few notes as follows in my shikar diary: July 15th.—Had 3 inches of rain first three days of week, so G. and self went to Choral; caught a few fish, 4, 2½ lbs., etc., all on gram. July 22nd.—G., B. and self went to Choral. Rained hard, river colored, G. got a 3 pounder and G. and B. both got broken by big fish. August 1st.—T. went Choral, river very low and clear, he caught a 4 pounder on gram. A native on live-bait got a 15 lb. mahseer.

The second place is from Barwaha station, about 1¼ miles. Work off rather towards Nerbudda, not towards hills. Here there is some A-1 water, and if tried at first break in rains, one would be almost sure of good sport. The junction with the Nerbudda, a short way further down, is useless, the Choral river being—or it used to be—simply a small muddy canal the last quarter mile. My only note concerning this portion of the river is:—As we had something like 15 inches of rain last week, and hearing that the Choral river had had a spate of about 36 ft., went to Barwaha and fished down.

Water glorious and conditions perfect, but very few fish about. Hooked a couple on spoon and one on natural bait.

The Kanar River.—Now this and the following river are both finer streams than the Choral river, but unfortunately are not very accessible. Like the latter they are best tried at the first break in the rains, though I fancy—in the Lohar river especially—some fish remain up all the year round. It is quite possible that the junctions of either or both these streams with the Nerbudda might be found excellent places. Also like all the ghat streams near Mhow, they start their course as rivers proper with waterfalls. And some of these latter are fine beyond compare, and were they more accessible would draw sightseers from all parts of India. The waterfall south of Telakheri is easily seen on the march to the Lohar river, and is about 200 ft. high; it is one of the tributaries of the latter stream, and is a magnificent sight after heavy rain, when the roar can be heard five miles away. But the two main branches of the Lohar river are the falls to visit, and if seen after the first burst of the monsoon words utterly fail to describe their beauties. The nearer one is 350 ft. and further 430 ft. high. Well to reach the Kanar river. Mhow to Simrol dâk bungalow is 10 miles along a pukka road. From here the difficulties of the march commence. There is no need to go actually to the dâk bungalow. Just before the 10th milestone the Mhow road strikes the Indore Choral road, near the 14th milestone. Cross this road and a rough cart

XVI

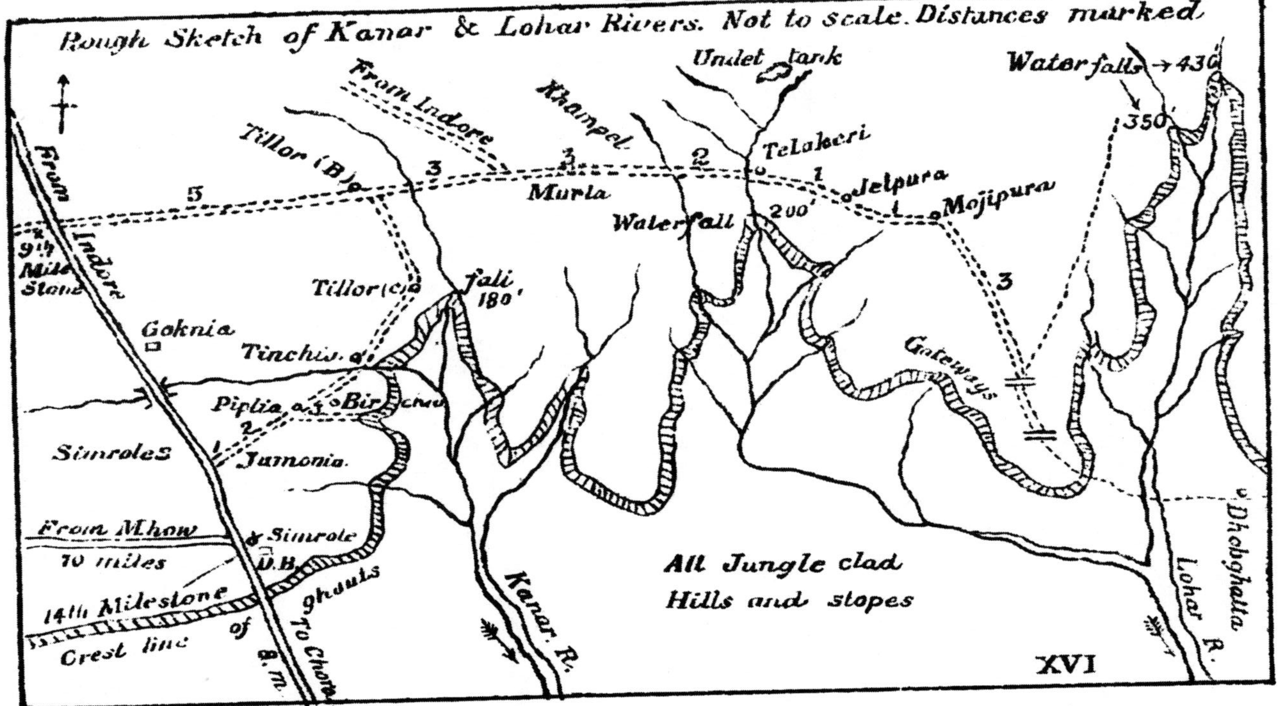

Rough Sketch of Kanar & Lohar Rivers. Not to scale. Distances marked
Undlet tank
Waterfalls → 430
350'
From Indore
Khampel
Tillor (B)
Telakeri
Jelpura
Mojipura
Murla
Waterfall
200'
9th Mile Stone
Tillor (c)
fall 180'
Goknia
Tinchis
Gateways
Piplia
Bir
Simroles
Jamonia
Dhobghatta
From Mhow
70 miles
Simrole
D.B.
14th Milestone
ghauts
Crest line of
To Chora
8. m.
All Jungle clad
Hills and slopes
Kanar. R.
Lohar R.
XVI

track will be found leading to the village of Jumnia one mile distant. Thence the track continues to Piplia two miles. From here there are two ways to the river. The north track leads 3½ miles to Tinchia, passing by a fine waterfall where one of the main streams leaves the tableland. Do not try and climb down here, we did with infinite difficulty, only to find our way barred by a sliding fall some 150 ft. deep, down which the water makes a further descent. This Tinchia route is longer and not so good as the following. Take southern track and proceed three miles to Birchia village. All these distances, etc., sound small, but the difficulty lies in the road being all through black cotton soil, and it must be remembered one does not make these trips till after the rains have commenced. From Birchia push forward along a spur that leads out like a pier towards the river. This is a nice place to pitch a camp. The climb down to the water is easy enough descending, but is a fair grind up. About a quarter mile down stream the second branch joins, and from the junction down is all A-1 water for some miles. I see by my notes we caught mahseer of 4, 2½ lbs. etc., both on spoon and gram, and have also a note of losing two considerably bigger ones as we were fishing very fine. This was the beginning of August. There is one particularly good pool, about half a mile if my memory serves me, below the junction, in which I moved fish after fish. It is a big pool with a good run into it and would be easily recognised. We took carts from Simrol to Birchia, but with a good deal of difficulty, we tried camels, but after heavy rain they were not a success.

The Lohar River.—This is quite one of the most delightful of Central Indian hill streams that I have seen, but its inaccessibility and the uncertainty of finding it clear make it a heart-breaking stream to visit. Proceed from Mhow 10 miles till the Indore-Choral road is met, and turn towards the former place. Pass Goknia village and a bridge over the head-waters of the Kanar river. After five miles, you come to the ninth milestone (from Indore). Up to here the road is all metalled and suitable for motors. Then one's troubles commence. Leave the main road and turning to the right along a cart track five miles brings one to the big village of Tillor, road fair up to here. Thence three miles to Murla, fording a tributary of the Kanar river, track indifferent. Three more miles to Khampel, passing a fair sized tank *en route*, road as before. Again two miles of bad road to Telakheri. Before reaching this village a big tributary of the Lohar river has to be forded, and under half a mile away lies a 200 ft. waterfall, which can be both seen and heard afar off after heavy rain. (Two or three miles north of this lies Undel where there is a fair sized tank.) One mile more leads to Jetpura, while a mile on lies Mojipura, road still bad. This is the last village, and three miles beyond one comes to a ruined gateway, part of what must in days gone by have been a very fine old fort. From here the track pushes out along a spur of the ghaut and no fault can be found with the scenery at any rate.

The whole road from Tillor is quite passable for carts in the dry season, but very heavy and bad after any rain. Beyond the first gateway come two small tanks on the right of the road and then a second gateway, near, or under, which a nice camp can be made. This is between 18 and 19 miles from where one leaves the main road, or 34 in all from Mhow. From this camp a regular old ghat road, now only fit for foot traffic however, leads down to the river about one mile distant, and crosses over to Dhobghetta village. Lots of small game about here—peafowl, quail, partridge, pigeon and some painted grouse, also thousands of doves. A short way down comes the junction of the two main branches, and the water below this is glorious, all rocky pools and rapids. One thing to remember is that after heavy rain, one's carts may be held up for hours outside Telakheri, or Tillor. On our way back we found the stream at latter place coming down in flood about 6 ft. deep and 20 ft. across. They soon run down at the fords, however, when rain ceases.

Fishing round Mhow.

The following few spots are mentioned, to help anyone who wishes to while away an hour or two with his rod, or who wants an excuse for an afternoon picnic.

Bircha Lake.—This is the water-supply of Mhow, and is a fine expanse of water. Seven miles by pukka road from cantonments, but road rather stony for motors or rubber-tyred vehicles. It is fairly full of all sorts of fish now, and as time goes on these should increase in size and multiply. There are one or two boats, to use which permission should be got from the Garrison Engineer, Mhow.

But though several men tried trolling while I was there no one had any success. That there are big fish who should take—like in the Oodeypore lakes—there is no doubt, as I picked up one day the head of a tengra which alone weighed 11 lbs. There are innumerable olive carp in the lake, who on some days will rise freely to gram. If float fishing the best place is off near bank about half way down the bund, fishing among the rough stones. Also at a break in the rains, if water is fairly clear, a trial might be given to the overflow stream at the far end of the bund, as I have seen quite nice fish moving here. A worm seems about the most useful all-round bait in Bircha. My notes show that fishing in August, September and October we caught the following species of fish:—Mahseer up to 2¼ lbs., mulley to 1½ lbs., murral (biggest 9 lbs., and another of 7 lbs.—O. Leucopunctatus—a very handsome fish caught off bank on a worm), olive carp, tengra, eels and turtles.

Curiously enough I have neither caught nor seen a rohu or labeo in this lake, though there should be some in it. Often there is a high wind and the lake is rough, which makes float fishing a bit difficult, but on those days the fish are generally biting freely.

The Chambal River.—Eighteen miles from Mhow along the Neemuch road, this river is spanned by a high bridge. If what geographers tell us is true, that the spring furthest from its mouth is the source of a river, then here we have the source of the Ganges. Crossing the bridge, walk up the left bank a short way till opposite the village of Ghat Billod. Here is a deep still pool in which you can try bottom fishing. That it does hold fair sized fish I know, it also holds more than one mugger. I have notes only of catching eels and Notopterous kapirat here, though I must say we never gave the place a fair trial. I should much like to get news concerning the Chambal in its lower reaches, as it flows through some fine gorges in the latter portion of its course, before joining the Jumna.

Sipra River.—Mhow to Indore 14 miles, thence continuing along the Grand Trunk road 15 miles brings one to a long causeway crossing this river. This is essentially a motor trip. Here a very pretty afternoon's sport can be put in using a small trout rod and fine tackle, with gram as bait. The fish are olive carp and run small, but bite freely and are numerous. About 200 yards down stream there is an anicut and some quite nice water. There must be some mahseer I should think, though we saw none the only occasion we fished.

Near Ujjain in the Sipra river fish are to be caught, also in the same river near Dewas. But sport most indifferent.

The same style of fishing could also be had in the Chota Kali Sind and the Kali Sind rivers 12 and 32 miles from Agar respectively.

Now a note in "The Anglers' Handbook" gives it that fishing is to be had near Maundsaur. Probably this comes under the "have beens," since, when I was in these parts in 1905 and 1906, I tried hard to discover any, but quite failed to do so. With this exception however, that there were two big still pools about one mile below the railway bridge, which held fish of various sorts. After the first break in the rains appeared to be the time to go for them, but the fishing was barely worth trying.

Near Mandal, a station half way between Chitorgarh and Ajmere, and about one mile from the line, is a big tank, wherein good sport may be had, both spinning off the bund for lansi, and also bottom fishing for other species.

In Mhow Cantonment gardens there is a small tank that holds a weird assortment of fish. A sporting assistant C. M. and myself fished one day with worm, to see what the tank did hold, putting back all the fish, and we got a most mixed bag, the pride of place belonging to a gold fish of over 1 lb. who fought most gamely.

Also a small tank in the fort used to hold quite a lot of mahseer, though what they lived on is beyond me. The tank is only a small pukka one fed by rain or pipe water, and who put the mahseer in is a mystery. The tank when the Ordnance had it was cleaned out about twice a year, the fish being carefully put into baths. I took the opportunity of one of these periods to mark four fish, with silver plate fastened through dorsal fin, but now that the Ordnance have handed over the fort I can get no particulars about these fish. It would be interesting to know if they are still there, the biggest was marked L. 18, was 14″ long, 11″ girth and weighed 2 lbs. By the way, there are a few such marked olive carp in

Bircha lake. Just as this book goes to press, a friend writing from Mhow, tells me that on his return to that station he finds this tank has been cleaned out, and all fish carefully transferred to Bircha. It is a great pity that no note was taken of the marked fish.

The two following are south of the Nerbudda, but may just be mentioned :—

Khandwa.—If you should be hung up here for any such reason as the trains missing connection, and want something to pass the time, drive out to the reservoir, which is 4 miles if I remember right, and below the dam you will find a small pond which used to be full of mahseer and olive carp, some of the former quite big. Possibly by now they have all been poached, but the pond was an old pumping station and very deep, so may be not. I caught six fish on gram in about an hour, the biggest mahseer 5 lbs., and was broken by a much bigger one. There are some duck and snipe to be got here in the season at the further end of reservoir.

The Tapti River.—One and a half miles from Chandi station, on G. I. P. A path leads through jungle to the river. There seem to be no runs or pools of any size here, but there appeared to be no lack of fish on the move when I visited the place in January. Lots of peafowl about and country very wild. I was told that a party of visitors from Bombay side came here every Christmas, and always caught a lot of fish. I repeat rumour for what it's worth.

NOTES ON FISHING IN BALUCHISTAN (DESCRIPTIVE PORTIONS FROM DISTRICT GAZETTEERS) IN THE RAKHNI, ANAMBAR, BEJI, NARI AND BOLAN RIVERS.

By Major A. Jacob, Political Agent at Sibi.

The Rakhni river rises in the hills north of Muhma. It has a perennial stream of good water running almost continuously through the length of the Rakhni valley. It runs generally speaking north and south along the eastern boundary of the Barkhan tahsil and receives the waters of a number of affluents from the west, of which the principal are the Chang, Churi and Baddhi. Up to its junction with the Chang, which drains the country south of the Rarkan plain, it is called Wandui. After traversing the Rakhni plain, it flows through the Chacha country south-westwards and near Mat is joined from the north-west by the Gujhi Nullah, which carries the drainage brought by the Malali and Karcha streams from the Daula hills. After passing Mat, the river runs south-west into the Kaha river in the Dera Ghazi Khan District. The bed of the stream is shingly down to a little below Mat, at which place it is very stony and impracticable. It varies in width from 50 to 150 yards and its banks throughout the valley to below Mat are low. This stream is full of fish between Mat and Rakhni and fish up to 16 lbs. have been caught in it. The easiest way of getting to this river is along the old Frontier road running from Dera Ghazi Khan to Peshin through

Loralai. The marches from Loralai (56 miles from Hurnai, N.-W. Ry.) are :—

Loralai	to	Wahar	...	20¼ miles.
Wahar	,,	Tor	...	15½ ,,
Tor	,,	Mekhtar	...	12 ,,
Mekhtar	,,	Sira Daka	...	12½ ,,
Sira Daka	,,	Kingri	...	22 ,,
Kingri	,,	Rankhan	...	15¾ ,,
Rankhan	,,	Rakhni	...	15¾ ,,

There are rest-houses at all the above places. From Dera Ghazi Khan to Rakhni the distances are :—

Dera Ghazi Khan	to	Sakhi Sarwar	...	27½ miles.
Sakhi Sarwar	,,	Rakhni	...	40 ,,

The height of Rakhni is 3,600 ft. One horse tum-tums are procurable at Harnai, Loralai and Dera Ghazi Khan and the road is a carriage road throughout.

The Anambar is the principal river in the Loralai District. It rises at Terai Momanrgai, in longitude 67° 46′ at the watershed between the Shahrig and the Bori tahsils, four miles to the east of Speraragha. Here it is a hill torrent and has no perennial supply of water. It flows in an easterly direction for about 32 miles up to its junction with the Dargai hill torrent, then turns south-east and about 48 miles below the junction it is joined by the Mara river from the north. This river rises in the hills between the Bori and the Zhob valleys, crosses the Damanghar range, and emerging through the Mara Tangi joins the Loralai river near Nawe Obo. At about two and a half miles further east the Loralai is joined by the Sehan and Watagan rivers from the north-east. Both these latter rivers have permanent water. Up to here the river is known as the Loralai, or Lorali, but after its junction with the Sehan it becomes the Anambar. The river then takes an abrupt turn to the south, and passes through the Zati Tangi, a gorge between the Kru and Gadabar ranges. Flowing through the Luni country, it is joined from the north-east by the Laki stream, and further south by the Narechi which has perennial water. A little below its junction with the Narechi river and about four miles from Chotiali, the river is crossed at Ghatipul by a masonry bridge and is thereafter known as the **Beji**. It then enters the Marri country retaining the name of Beji, is joined near Babar Kach by the Dada and Sangan streams from the north-west and through the Nari gorge debouches into the Sibi plain and is known as the **Nari**.

The best fishing in the Anambar is between Shadiani and Misri Kach. Shadiani is some 16 miles from Waha (20 miles from Loralai), a stage on the Peshin-Dera Ghazi Khan Frontier road. Fish weighing up to 13 lbs. have been caught in this part of the river. At Ghatipul there is a very large stagnant pool containing big fish which are very hard to catch, and when hooked are likely to break the line owing to the number of submerged logs, etc., in this pool. Below Ghatipul the Beji runs in a succession of rapids where good fishing with a fly-spoon is to be had. The fishing in the Beji is good right away down to its junction with the Nari and it has a great number of fine pools. Large bags of fish between 4 lbs. and 10 lbs. have been made at Pazha on the Beji in August, but the heat there is very great in that month. The Nari has a succession of excellent pools from Babar Kach (N.-W. Ry.) Railway Station to Nari

Station and there must be fish running up to 20 lbs. in this stream.

In the lower portions of the Nari river near the plains the fishes found are those of Hindustan and include many of the common sorts. The mahseer (Barbus mosal or tor) is plentiful throughout, and large fishes exceeding 12 lbs. in weight have been caught in the Anambar gap above the Duki plain. In the highland portions of the Nari drainage system the low country fishes give place to the mountain barbels of the genus Oreinus, which have not been satisfactorily classified and present a great individual variation. Loaches (Nemacheilus) are ubiquitous.

In the lower reaches of the Nari and especially in the neighbourhood of Babar Kach crocodiles (vernacular Sansar) are occasionally to be found.

The Bolan river rises near Kolpur, but the water only makes its first appearance at Sari-Bolan (36 miles from Quetta), and disappears again near Abigum where, however, a small flat or thal is first irrigated from its water. Near Bibi Nani, the Bolan is joined from the west by the Sarawan river, known locally as the Dardan, and also as the Kaur Bibi Nani, and from this point a perennial stream appears. After flowing through the Laleji plain past Kirta the river cuts its way through the Afghan Ponzak, and is joined at Kundalani from the west by the perennial waters of the Kumbela stream and emerges into the Dadhar plain near Pir Chauki. After passing through Dadhar, where the water is largely used for irrigation, the river is eventually dissipated into the great plain of Kachhi.

The depressions where water collects in pools are known as "dumb" and usually contain fish. Among them are Sur Dumb about one mile to the south of Kirta Kauntrani Dumb, one of the largest, between Touling and Kundalani; Kundalani Dumb close to the levy post; Tosha-na Dumb about a mile below Kundalani; and Drabbi Wala Dumb, about 3½ miles from Kundalani. A fish weighing 26 lbs. is said to have been caught in the Bolan river.

There are two ways of getting to this river, First, get out of the train at Nari Bank, a few miles out of Sibi, if they will stop the train for you and take a trolly from there to Rindli whence you can ride to Kundalani rest-house. Second, ride from Panir Railway Station to Kirta where there is a rest-house.

A 12 ft. to 14 ft. rod is sufficient for fishing in Baluchistan, with a line fine to medium and 80 yards to 100 yards in length. The volume of water in most of the streams is very small, and consequently there are in many places hardly any runlets. Wherever the latter exist good sport can be had with a fly-spoon ½″ to 1″. The fish in the pools are mostly bottom feeders and the best catches are to be made with dead bait or the entrails of fowls. Chilwa are plentiful in most of the streams and when used on Luscombe's Chilwa Tackle are very deadly. Fishermen visiting any of the streams in Baluchistan are advised to apply to the District Officer concerned for local men to act as guides and escort. For the Rakhni and Anambar rivers apply to the Political Agent,

Loralai, and for the Beji and Nari rivers to the Political Agent, Sibi. The Bolan River is within the jurisdiction of the Political Agent, Kalat, at Mustung.

THE FOLLOWING NOTES RELATE TO A TOUR UNDERTAKEN BETWEEN 21ST AUGUST AND 29TH SEPTEMBER 1895.

By Lieutenant-Colonel Cartwright and Major Roome Jacob's Horse.

Fort Sandeman to Kapip (bungalow) ...	8 miles.	...
Kashmir Villa (B.) ...	12 „	...
Toi Sir ...	24 „	Fair pools in upper end of Tangi leading to Palosin.
Palosin ...	12 „	Deep pools in lower end of Tangi. No way through by river. Road goes over hill. Caught 65 lbs. in 2 days. Nothing over 5 lbs. Broken twice.
Musa Khel (B.) ...	18 „	Good partridge shooting on left of road, about 6 miles.
Khod ...	11 „	Fishing, but the river was in flood. Plenty of partridges.
Khan Mahomed Kot (B.) ...	11 „	Fishing but river in flood.
Kingri (B.) and (P. O.)	18 „	Ditto Frontier road
Rankan (B.) ...	15 „	Ditto
Rakhni (B.) ...	17 „	Ditto
Chuk Pahar ...	8 „	Good water, 20 lbs., none over 2 lbs.
Chacha ...	8 „	Good water, 25 lbs., none over 4 lbs.
Baud Kach ...	6 „	Good water, 10 lbs., none over 2 lbs.
Mat ...	8 „	Good water, 12 lbs., none over 3 lbs.
Dingrah ...	14 „	Fair water, 7 lbs., lost one good fish.
Vitakri ...	12 „	Fair water, 15 lbs., one of 7 lbs.
Makmar-Keshom ...	20 „	Small pools no sport.
Kala Bhua ...	8 „	Small pools, 5 one pounders.
Sathwali ...	17 „	...
Mahmud ...	13 „	Deep pool, 24 lbs., one 5 lbs., one 4 lbs., one 3 lbs This is in Yagistan, and one is not supposed to go there.

Koondal	...	15 miles.	...
Bhor	...	17 ,,	...
Kolu	...	13 ,,	...
Zirran	...	20 ,,	...
Gumbaz (B.)	...	12 ,,	Anambar river. Deep pools below. Large fish, but hard to catch.
Ghatipul (B.)	...	7 ,,	Nice pools, 17 lbs., one 2½ pounder. Partridges.
China	...	15 ,,	Good water, 15 lbs., one 3 pounder. Partidges.
Wahar (B.)	...	17 ,,	Good water for 5 miles, and also in Anambar gap.
Loralai (B.)	...	14 ,,	...

Notes.—Toi Sir and Palosin are good ; Rakhni to Mat, good ; Mat to Vitakri, fair ; Mahmud, good ; Gumbaz to Wahar, good.

But they are all far apart from each other. R. and myself were doing a circular tour with rods, guns and dogs, and we did whatever came to hand by way of sport. We covered 390 miles in forty days. You have to have an escort, and carry your own supplies. You can get atta, etc , at Musa Khel, Khan Mahomed Kot, Kingri and Gumbaz. Otherwise you are dependent on what you can pick up in small villages.

Rakhni to Mat would be worth trying from Fort Munro, and Wahar to Gumbaz is handy to Loralai.

There is a good pool on the Beji river at Toong, about 12 miles from Babar Kach station on the Harnai Railway ; and also good water from Babar Kach to Nari Bank station (12 miles from Sibi) in Nara river and Beji river near Babar Kach. The spring is the best time ; it is now some years, however, since I visited these places.

There are also mahseer in the Bolan at Kundalani and South Kirta, and also at Kalat and in the river close to Fort Sandeman.

I have also killed mahseer in the Karezes at Panjgur, and in the Kej river, both in Mekran.

Usual lure fly-spoon and occasionally a frog or grasshopper when available.

The following notes were given me some time ago, they are sketchy, but are inserted so as to afford a clue as to where to look for fishing to new arrivals in Quetta or Karachi :—

Ziarat (the Hill station) is 40 miles from Quetta, a fair road, though rough in parts, and could be motored over. At Kalan, half way, small snow trout to be got. The Harnai river holds mahseer. From Quetta down Bolan Pass, 28 miles, road good, gradients easy, Mach half way fishing, also Bibi Nana (old station) better.

From Karachi, the Hub river holds mahseer. It is 17 miles, camels being the best way to get out. It is a fair sized river, consisting mostly of deep pools.

Notes on Fishing in the Rakhni, Nilaj and Manjhra Rivers, and round Fort Sandeman, *by Bt.-Col. W. Norman, 22nd Cavalry.*

The Rakhni.—This is one of the rivers in Baluchistan and takes its name from Rakhni, a small district and village on the Dera Ghazi Khan-Loralai route. The stream rises in the Bozdar hills some distance above Rakhni, but is very nearly absolutely dry from its source to a point about five miles below the point where the Loralai road crosses it. The Rakhni camping ground and old post are at the point where the road from Fort Monroe crosses the stream.

Starting then from the camping ground one has to ride some five miles down the valley to where the stream enters some low hills. Here the stream changes its character very suddenly, and instead of being a dry nullah bed becomes a series of small pools and rapids as far as the village of Chacha, some 15 miles from Rakhni. The next march is Mat, some ten miles on. Below Mat the stream passes through low mountains and eventually comes out near Harrand in the Dera Ghazi District, through the Kaha Pass. At Harrand it is known as the Kaha. From the Kaha Pass to the Indus the stream again becomes a dry water-course. The fishing from Rakhni to Mat is in a small way capital, fish running, usually from 4 to 6 lbs, but a few 10 and 12 pounders have been caught, and there was a report that in old days, when Rakhni was occupied by troops, a 20 lb. mahseer was caught below Mat. The fish take almost anything from spoon and natural bait to atta. Between Rakhni and Chacha, there is also capital shooting in the cold weather—sand-grouse, duck, houbara, quail, snipe, chikor, black and grey partridge. There are also a number of small crocodile in the stream, but how they came there is a mystery, for the stream has no connection with the Indus, into which it flows, except during the sudden floods when the rainfall in the hills tears down through the passes.

One march beyond Rakhni, *en route* to Loralai, is Rankan, here there is a small stream not worth fishing. The next march is Kingri where another stream is crossed. This is better and gives fish up to two and three pounds. The

Kingri stream flows on to Khan Mahomed Kot, an outpost held from Loralai. At Khan Mahomed Kot the stream is joined by the Rod, and the combined streams enter a very difficult gorge about two miles below the post. Whether there is any fishing or not in this gorge I cannot say, but there are some lovely pools, waterfalls and rapids. Unfortunately whenever I tried this river it was badly discoloured after rain, but given favourable water I feel sure there must be some good fish here.

The Nilag and Manjhra.

These are both rather inaccessible for the ordinary fisherman, but since the fishing is capital I give a short account. The Nilag enters the plains near Sibi and the Manjhra, a tributary of the former, can be reached, though with difficulty, from Rakhni on the Dera Ghazi Khan-Loralai route. Possibly the latter can also be reached from Loralai cantonments, but of this I have no information. The marches from Sibi are—

Nilag, 14 miles, no village. At eight miles enter the hills. Camp on Nilag river.

Kaura Duff, 14 miles, no village. At eight miles the Kaura stream joins in and the road proceeds up the latter. There is a bannia's hut here.

Boza Kach, 12 miles, no village. At about three miles there is a very fair gorge.

Mahmud, eight miles, a stiff march, walled village in Murree country. There is an alternative road to Trichibun which is preferable.

Trimmin Suthanwali, 12 miles, no village. At one mile reach the Manjhra river.

Trimmin Mahmar, 15 miles, no village.

Neghoz, eight miles, no village.

Vitakri, 14 miles, walled village and old site of cantonment abandoned soon after Afghan War, 1880.

Haji Kot, 22 miles, large Khetran village.

Bhoori Tangi, 15 miles, no village.

Rakhni, 15 miles.

It will be seen from the above that supplies are necessarily a difficulty. The road by no manner of means follows the course of the various streams but often leaves them for some miles. But when one does strike a stream it is worth while fixing up the rod and tackle. From one pool on the Manjhra I took out a 15 pounder, besides others, the second largest being 6 lbs. In a pool near Neghoz I took on a very small fly-spoon 19 fish, one after another some of which were 3 to 4 lbs.

The marches given above were not arranged for a fishing trip, and I had little time to spare to follow the actual course of the streams, but from the look of the Manjhra and the scrappy fishing I was able to obtain, I feel confident that it would be well worth while to march down the Manjhra. The 15 pounder taken could not have been the largest fish in the river. One great point about these rivers are, that so far as I know, they are never fished in and never netted, they are virgin water for the angler. I believe that I am perhaps the only one who has thrown a line into them.

Fishing round Fort Sandeman.

In the immediate vicinity of Fort Sandeman is the Zhob river. Fishing commences at Viala some 7 miles out from cantonments and extends down to Kajuri Kach where the Zhob joins the Gomal. It is unnecessary to mention the marches and rest-houses, as those quartered at Fort Sandeman will be well acquainted with them. Fish are caught up to 4 lbs., but generally do not run up to more than 2 or 3 lbs. Viala is a charming little place to picnic at from Fort Sandeman, and what is more, affords a very suitable place for breeding and preserving fish, for here there is a small tributary, only about a mile long, where it would be the simplest matter in the world to make breeding tanks. A little money for initial outlay and a small monthly subscription by the residents to appoint a chowkidar over the tanks would suffice. The gain in improvement of fishing would be immense.

The Gomal rises in Afghanistan and enters British territory at Dobandi, some four miles above the Gulkach Post. It enters the Gomal Pass in the Waziri hills, about four miles below the post and passing the Toi Khula Post takes in the Zhob at Kajuri Kach. Thence it proceeds on through the pass till it enters the plains of the Derajat at Murtaza, about two marches from Kajuri Kach. The best fishing is from Dobandi to Toi Khula and here the largest taken by me was a ten pounder just below Dobandi.

The Kundar joins the Gomal at Dobandi. There is nothing big to be taken here, but on one occasion I half filled a kerosene tin, which my servant carried for bath water, with small fish of about 1 to 1½ lbs. They simply came one after another at a small ½ inch fly-spoon. The river runs past to the Zhob Levy posts of Gustoi, Hosain Nika and Chechoba.

The Sir-i-Toi is a very curious little stream. It is reached *viâ* Naia Oba and Ambara, along the road which leads to Gustoi *viâ* Chukan. Though the actual bed of the nala is many miles in extent the part containing water is only about four miles long and in that portion known as the Ambara Tangi. In this ridiculous little patch of water there are several mahseer of a splendid bronze colour running up to 3 lbs., they give good sport with light tackle.

The Musa Khel Toi is reached from Musa Khel Bazar where it practically rises. It flows on down through a long gorge to Drug. Here there is some capital fishing and the story goes that a mahseer of about 15 lbs. was taken, but this must have been an exceptional article, usually 2 to 3 lbs. are size caught.

To anyone camping in Baluchistan I can recommend a dish of imitation white bait, by capturing the small fry with which the streams abound. The plan is to take a degchi, cut a hole about three inches in diameter in a jharan and tie the jharan over the mouth of the degchi, then make some atta into a cone and place it inside, with the tip of the cone in the centre of the hole in the jharan. Place this trap in shallow water, stand back a little and before long the fry will tumble inside the degchi. This little game is not without its interest and the dish obtained is first class.

NOTES ON THE ZHOB RIVER.

By Capt. W. H. Lane, 94th Russell's Infantry.

When the follower of the gentle art has to protect his person with an armed posse of 6 to 12 men, in the humble opinion of the writer it is preferable to meditate on past and future glories than to wet a line under such adverse conditions. Such conditions rule at Fort Sandeman in the Zhob valley. The Zhob river contains mahseer, smaller ones in its upper reaches, and below its junction with the Gomal reports affirm that the fish run to a considerable weight. Once, and only once, was an expedition attempted in the Zhob, though other anglers went out more frequently, and returned with some good creels. The result of this excursion is given below :—

27*th June* 1908.—10*th mile from Fort Sandeman to Brunj.* Basket 3 carp of unknown species, 28 mahseer, 2 eels. Total weight—8½ lbs.

Fished with worm. There were three good pools in the stretch. The fish took freely. The catch included 2 mahseer of 1 lb. each. I lost one cast on a fish.

28*th June* 1908.—*Same water.* Basket 23 mahseer, scaling 15 lbs.

Fished with dough kneaded up with cotton wool instead of worm. In the early morning the fish were taking well, 1 of 1½ lbs., several of 1 lb.

Notes on Angling in Burma.

By Major J. H. Whitehead, 93rd Burma Infantry.

Burma is well provided with fishable streams. The Irrawaddy roughly bisects the country from north to south, into it flow many tributaries of considerable size and they again have numerous feeders.

The Irrawaddy itself has proved a good mahseer river from the north end of the upper defile to the administrative frontier. It is probable that all tributaries flowing over rocky or shingly beds hold mahseer. Many of them have been tried with success and many yet remain virgin water. The next big river eastwards of the Irrawaddy, the Salwin, has been a disappointment to fishermen and its tributaries no less so. The somewhat inaccessible Shan States, which they drain, have however not been properly explored by anglers, and it may be hoped that fine fishing will eventually be had there. In the Irrawaddy mahseer have been taken up to 91 lbs., and there is good reason to hope that the Indian record of 104 lbs. may yet be beaten by some lucky angler in "Far Cathay." The big fish are usually caught by trolling from a "dug-out" with large spoons, No. 10 and upwards; this is the dullest class of angling, but has to be resorted to in certain parts of the river. There are many spots where casting is practicable and superior to trolling, and again quiet backwaters and eddies among rocks abound, where excellent sport with smaller fish may be had with fly spoon or Devon minnow. In the larger tributaries of the Irrawaddy spoon and fly-spoon are the favourite baits, though in certain streams in the Chin Hills these are generally discarded for atta, paste, Indian-corn, etc. Though the spoon has up to now proved a sufficiently attractive lure, the season of 1909 has shown that the mahseer are beginning to be shy of it, and it is probable that real and artificial fish will have to be increasingly used.

When a river is first tried no one could wish for a better bait than the spoon. A fisherman a year or two since had the good fortune to visit a tract of unadministered territory lying between Northern Burma and Assam. Through this territory flows a tributary of the Irrawaddy and its affluents. They are full of mahseer and practically untried by anglers.

A half day in one of these tributaries, from 12-30 till evening, produced a bag of 16 mahseer weighing ¼ lb. short of 100 lbs.; this was in the month of April and the bait used was a No. 7 hog-backed spoon mounted on a "Killin" wire trace with a one ounce anti-kink lead. Another few hours in the same stream, between 3-30 P.M. and dark, gave six fish, including a 46 pounder and a 20 pounder; the bag on that occasion would have been much larger, had not the big fellow fought like a demon in very strong, broken water, using up an hour and forty minutes of the limited daylight available.

In some of the smaller streams of Upper Burma the worm has been found extraordinarily successful, and small black crickets, mole-crickets, locusts and grasshoppers have taken their toll of fish.

A fisherman three years ago had five days in a stream some 15 to 20 yards wide on the Chinese frontier ; he fished with worm only and averaged 30 mahseer a day; they were small but gave the best of sport on a light 10 ft. 6 in. trout rod. The best fish taken by this style of fishing was a 10 pounder, and it may be imagined that, with the tackle used, landing it was a lengthy operation.

Fly-fishers in Burma have had on the whole but poor sport, though there are one or two small lakes and streams where any lake trout fly is readily taken. Dark coloured flies are most favoured

In spite of the many good mahseer that have been had in Burma, the extent of fishing is so considerable, and there is so much water yet untried, that it still provides fishing grounds, where the high hopes of anglers are not likely to be falsified by the event.

Tank angling may be had in certain localities. A 29 lb. labeo was some years ago caught in a small pond erstwhile the bathing place of Thibaw's queen. Smaller ones are still being caught there.

Notes on Fishing in the Chin Hills, Burma.

By Capt. W. H. Lane, 94th Russell's Infy.

In *The Angler's Handbook for India* Dr. R. Brookers in his notes on fishing in Burma has quoted a short paragraph on the possibilities of sport with rod and line in this locality. That well-known angler Colonel H. D. Keary furnishes in the same volume some very useful hints and experiences which came to his lot in the district. The present writer spent over three years in the Chin Hills and their vicinity, and during this residence the advantages afforded by the numerous streams that drain this extensive basin were put to the test at every available opportunity. The angler who is desirous of spending his holiday in the pursuit of his favourite pastime had better give the Chin Hills a wide berth, for his movements owing to local conditions will be very much restricted, but as Colonel Keary very aptly sums up the situation:—'If one has the bad luck to have to live in the Chin Hills, the sport obtainable is a pleasant break in the otherwise monotony of life there.'

The traveller to these distant tracts will disembark from the Irrawaddy steamer at Kalewa, the junction of the Myittha river with the Chindwin. Hence the various places wherein mahseer fishing is practicable will be touched upon *seriatim* :—

Myittha River.—Between Kalewa and Kalemyo, at the rapids, about seven miles above the former township, the Myittha bursts through a barrier of low hills. In this reach which extends for about five miles the current swirls between rocks and round boulders. The bed of the Myittha is much contracted in breadth, and the mean depth must be considerable. Though the writer never actually wetted a line in this stretch, there can be little doubt that mahseer, and large ones to boot, should be found in its dark pools. Perseverance would probably receive its own reward—at any rate this particular reach is worthy of more than a casual trial.

Kalemyo.—This small military police out-post may be termed the secondary supply base for the Chin Hills. The Myittha here, except during the rains, attains only a very moderate depth and the current is too sluggish, and the bottom too muddy for mahseer. Six miles south, however, along the Panmanchoung road a small stream is encountered. In the hot weather it shrinks to a mere rivulet, but in November its volume is not inconsiderable. The following extracts from a fishing diary will show what sport is obtainable :—

Sindon Choung, 1st November 1901.—Five mahseer scaling 12 lbs. ; weights 1 lb., $1\frac{1}{4}$ lbs., $1\frac{1}{2}$ lbs., $1\frac{3}{4}$ lbs., $6\frac{1}{2}$ lbs.; caught with 14 ft. rod and No. 5 narrow hogged spoon ; had several more runs. I also caught 5 large chilwa.

1*st November* 1902.—Five mahseer, weight unknown but estimated at 4 lbs.

Panmanchoung.—Eighteen miles from Kalemyo. There is an inspection bungalow here, and a small stream flows close at hand containing mahseer.

22*nd October* 1901.—Four small mahseer caught with fly-spoon, fishing only for an hour or two ; the fish were not taking freely.

Myo Choung.—A small stream on the Panmanchoung-Falam road.

21*st October* 1901.—Two small mahseer, fished with trout flies ; there was too much water, and wading was a labour. Returning to Kalemyo another stream on the Kalemyo-Fort White road is passed.

Sun Num or *No.* 2 *Stockade Stream*, 9 to 11 miles from Kalemyo.

1*st May* 1901.—Six mahseer 3¾ lbs., caught with fly-spoon.

2*nd May* 1901.—Six mahseer 3 lbs. 10 oz., 3 caught in the morning, and 3 in the afternoon with fly-spoon.

3*rd May* 1901.—Eight mahseer 2¼ lbs., caught in the morning with fly-spoon, 10 mahseer about 3¼ lbs, caught in the evening with fly, mostly on Lee's favourite.

2*nd November* 1901.—Ten mahseer 2¼ lbs., caught with fly; stream was full; fish were not rising freely; they mostly took "the butcher" and "march brown." I think working up stream with worm would have secured the bigger ones. The next piece of water to be considered is the Manipur river.

The Manipur River rises in the Manipur Lake and flows due south through the heart of Chinland till it reaches the vicinity of Falam, whence it bears eastwards and joins the Myit-tha below Sihaung village in the Kalè valley. Throughout its course till it debouches from the hills, the Manipur river holds excellent mahseer. The new-comer, should he be at all an experienced angler, will, inwardly at any rate, disbelieve the statement of the older resident that fishing with a spoon bait is futile. After hours and perhaps days of toil, he will assuredly arrive at the melancholy conclusion that spinning is a method which does not appeal to the Nankathè mahseer. An occasional fish may be creeled thus, but such a case will prove, and has proved, the exception and not the rule.

Bottom fishing with dough flavoured with "ballachoung" is undoubtedly the most effective bait. An easy chair and a book add to the comfort of a *seance* of this description.

The northernmost out-post of Chinland is Tiddim, and while stationed there the Manipur river was visited on several occasions. The following notes speak for themselves.

Bel Tung, below Tiddim :—

19th January 1901.—Two mahseer 7¼ lbs., one of 3½ lbs., the other of 3¾ lbs.

2nd February 1901.—Two mahseer 20 lbs. 10 oz., weight 2 lbs. 2 oz. and 18½ lbs.

3rd April 1901.—B. 1 mahseer 7 lbs. in evening ; D. and self *nil*.

4th April 1901.—Self 3 mahseer, 4, 13½ and 4 lbs., total lbs., all caught in morning, 21½ ; D. *nil ;* B. in evening 2 of 17 lbs. and 9 lbs.

5th April 1901.—D. and self *nil ;* B. 1 mahseer of 22¼ lbs. weighed 2½ hours after capture.

Below Myobingee :—

22nd March 1901.—Self 1 mahseer 17½ lbs. caught in evening ; B. 3 mahseer, 14, 11, 7 lbs. in morning. A tremendous thunderstorm raged the night before. B. got off early, and had 2 fish when I arrived.

24th March 1901.—Self 1 mahseer 2 lbs caught in same pool in the evening ; B. fishing from opposite bank beached one mahseer of 13 lbs. in the morning.

25th March 1901.—Self *nil ;* B. 2 mahseer of 22 lbs. and 17 lbs. caught in the morning.

The road from Tiddim *viâ* Fort White to Falam, the head-quarters of the Chin Hills territory, strikes the Manipur river again at the mouth of the Lomban stream. From this place it follows the left bank down for 2½ miles and crosses the river by a suspension bridge. During the rains of 1901 a chance arose of ascertaining the capabilities of the Lomban stream. On arrival at the junction the tributary was found to be perfectly clear, but the main channel was, of course, a mud-laden turbid torrent. It so happened that where the two currents met the height of the Nankatti was such as to form a small back-water and of considerable depth. At first sight the spot looked to hold some fair sized fish, but the writer had reckoned only on securing smaller fry and was armed with an 11 ft. trout fly rod. With tackle suitable to the occasion a good basket should have been recorded.

20*th June* 1901.—Four mahseer 13 lbs., weights 2 lbs., 2½ lbs., 2½ lbs., 4 lbs. ; lost several hooks in fish ; also hooked a large one ; it got out into the heavy current, ran out all the line and eventually broke me. These were all caught with worm.

2*nd July* 1901.—Four mahseer 6¾ lbs., weights 3¾ lbs., 1¼ lbs., 1 lb., ¾ lb., all caught worm. I also tried with live bait but touched nothing.

In the middle of autumn this locality again furnished excellent sport. The Manipur river was still too muddy and too full for angling purposes in the ordinary backwater. Moderate sized fish were only expected, so a 14 ft. trout fly rod and a trout landing net formed the equipment Very foolishly the writer set out unattended. The following incidents are recorded.

16*th October* 1901.—One mahseer 15 lbs. The trudge from the suspension bridge to the Lomban stream proved very hot, I baited the triangle with dough and threw it into the edge of the clear and muddy water. Placing the rod on a forked stick I went down to the edge to bathe my face. In the middle of this operation the reel screeched and unfortunately the stake fell over, and the rod began dancing towards the river. I seized it, but the delay had allowed the fish to get out into the main current. He took a hundred yards of line out before he pulled up. With great difficulty and not without considerable danger, by dint of clambering over slippery boulders, I got down to him. All efforts to get him into the landing net were ineffectual. He was far too big for that; in desperation I tried to drag him out by the trace, but his weight wrenched the hook out of his mouth, and he dropped back into the water at my feet and was never seen again! I went back to the pool, and in the evening hooked another fish, played him for about 20 minutes and eventually dragged him up a shelving spit of sand, dropped the rod and pounced on him, weight 15 lbs.

This incident had furnished a useful lesson. Two days later the same pool was fished and an orderly was in attendance.

18*th October* 1901.—One mahseer 16½ lbs. Fished with 14 ft. fly rod and baited with dough, got a fish on early, played him for about ten minutes, when the hookhold gave and he got off. In the evening caught the one of 16½ lbs. Just above the suspension bridge there was an excellent pool and below it there was a gigantic whirlpool, which held good fish. The following incident was experienced in the upper pool :—

17th November 1901.—Two mahseer 36½ lbs. The bait was the usual lump of dough seasoned with ballachoung. I had two rods picketed out, a 17½ ft. salmon and the 14 ft. trout fly rod mentioned above. I got a mahseer of 13½ lbs. on the smaller rod which took me nearly a quarter of an hour to land. About 12-45 P M., a big beast got on to the smaller rod. He dashed straight out into the current, and then raced down stream. Nothing could stop him. Eventually he took out 175 yards of line and forced me to follow down the bank for 60 yards, before he pulled up in the pool below the bridge. I got down to him with the utmost difficulty, but after a truly exciting 25 minutes, safely landed him from the whirlpool.

This, on paper, does not convey to the reader the magnitude of the task. Standing on the centre of the bridge and looking downstream the spectator cannot fail to be impressed with the force of the current as it dashes over the rocks and forms the mighty vortex of waters below. It is a veritable cataract. Crawling under the bridge was also no mean feat. A slip must have ended in certain death, and it is more than probable that the body of the luckless victim would never have again come to the surface.

19th November 1901.—*Pool above suspension bridge.*—One mahseer 12 lbs., caught with usual bait on 17½ ft. rod.

21st November 1901.—*Same pool.*—One mahseer 23½ lbs., caught on 17½ ft. rod. This fish also tried to leave the pool and go below the bridge. I checked it after it had run out 60 yards of line and forced it to swim up stream by having stones thrown into the current below it.

Date unrecorded—Pool below bridge.—One mahseer 12 lbs.

During March and April 1902 the present writer was detailed to accompany the Assistant Political Officer on a lengthy tour through the western and northern portions of the Falam Sub-division. Several opportunities were afforded of angling for mahseer. The following baskets have been recorded :—

Lai Varr.—This is a small stream easily fordable almost anywhere during the hot months. At this season the bed is choked up with a dense mass of weeds. But in places it runs into still deep pools, where all the fish seem to congregate.

March 1902.—Twelve mahseer, 13 lbs., caught with entrails of chicken strung on to a No. 1 Limerick hook and with 11 ft. fly rod; light tackle. Several fish over 1½ lbs., none under ½ lb.

March 1902.—Fourteen mahseer, 9 lbs., caught in the same pool as creel recorded above, but with worm.

March 1902.—Ten mahseer, 6½ lbs., caught with worm in a pool just below camp.

March 1902.—Five mahseer, weight 2½ lbs., Went about 1½ miles further down before I came to another good pool, caught with worm.

For some distance the boundary between Chinland and the Lushai Hills is defined by the Tyao river. Even in the hot weather this forms a fair-sized stream, but when the rains have just cleared, its volume must be considerable and it should furnish good fish

The sport to be enjoyed during March and April is, however, not to be despised as the following notes will show :—

Tyao River :—

March 1902.—Forty mahseer scaling 34 lbs. Had a long march down to the river and at first could not find a decent pool but came across a good one about 200 yards above junction of a small stream with the Tyao. The pool is very deep; lost several better ones than those creeled; caught on 11 ft. fly rod and worm. Nine over 2 lbs. and under 3 lbs; 14 between 1 and 2 lbs.; 17 between ½ lb. and 1 lb.

As may be judged from the results the fun was fast and furious. Seldom has the writer enjoyed a better day's sport with rod and line. The basket would have been heavier had the supply of worms not failed towards evening.

Tyao River, March 1902.—Four mahseer 5 lbs. S. and self were fishing in the pool at the place where the path on the march from Reet Lake to Kwayin leaves the Tyao River. S. could not get his worm out far enough so asked me to have a cast. I did so, and at once hooked a 2½ pounder, evidently the patriarch of the pool.

Tyao River, March 1902.—S. and self went down from Reet Lake to the Tyao, and first fished in one pool about one mile below the bridge. Then we went down to another pool two miles further. The latter looked as if it had been specially stocked for our benefit, and the fish were ravenous.

Self 60 mahseer weighing 30 lbs.; S. 70 fish scaling 38 lbs. Several were over 2 lbs. and many over 1 lb.

Of the 130 fully 100 must have been caught in the lower pool. The pool was very deep but its lateral and longitudinal dimensions were small—say about the size of a tennis court. What better sport could any angler want on a single-handed trout rod?

On the return journey the Manipur river was reached below a place called Kopwell and three mahseer of 11½ lbs were captured with dough. A terrific thunderstorm was encountered and the Namkettri at once became coloured a dirty brick red. Angling with paste was therefore at a complete discount. Live baiting was thereupon essayed. On three occasions the rod was left out all night, as during the daytime all efforts in this direction proved unsuccessful. The rod was securely fastened so that nothing could move it. A certain amount of excitement was always afforded on visiting the rod in the morning. On the 1st occasion, *April 15th*, 1902, it was found that about 60 yards of line had been run out and on reeling up a fish made itself felt. It was quickly hauled ashore and turned the scale at 11½ lbs.—a mahseer.

On the second occasion the 200 yards of line had been run out to the knot. It was discovered that the victim had got into the rapids at the foot of the pool and broken the hook. It must have been a large one. On *April 20th* 1902, the bait had once more been taken and only a few yards of line were left on the drum. The line had got jammed round a boulder, which necessitated the Gurkha orderly having to swim out and release it. The fish was still on, and after a good fight was brought to the net—a fresh water shark of 22 lbs.! On several subsequent occasions similar tactics were attempted, and the writer even went to the extent of having his bed put right alongside the rod. It was a curious coincidence, but under such conditions never once was a fish touched. Before closing these notes one fact is worthy of mention. Wherever feasible every small stream was either netted or poisoned by the local inhabitants. Whether a remedy has now been found to lessen this evil cannot be positively stated. In the interests of angling in general in these tracts it is to be hoped that such is the case. If these poaching habits could be eradicated, the streams would yield phenomenal sport. Such as it is, the fishing to be enjoyed in these inhospitable regions is assuredly a perfect Godsend. Without it life would hardly be endurable."

The following are a few notes which I have been able to glean concerning the introduction of trout (Fario) into Kulu, an experiment which cannot but be of interest to all anglers in Northern India:—

"Some few years ago, Sir Louis Dane, now Lieutenant-Governor of the Punjab, was Resident of Kashmir, and being much interested in Pisiculture and the acclimatisation of trout, he persuaded the Kashmir Government to try the experiment of introducing trout into the waters of that valley. The amazing success of that scheme suggested to Sir Louis the idea of trying a similar experiment in the valley of Kulu, in which part of the Kangra district he always took the greatest interest since he was Assistant Commissioner there in the early days of his service. This idea finally took shape last year (1908) during which Sir Louis Dane caused to be sent down to Kulu a batch of 30,000 trout ova, which under the able superintendence of Mr. Howell, the Assistant Commissioner, assisted by General Osborn, an old fisherman and naturalist, were distributed, some in hatching boxes in various suitable streams near Naggar, Kulu, and a certain proportion of the ova kept for hatching out at the Naggar trout breeding ponds, situated in a most excellent site where the Naggar Trout Hatchery now stands. During the month of February 1909, the above-mentioned batch of 30,000 eyed trout ova were purchased from the Kashmir Government Trout Fishery, which is under the charge of Mr. Mitchell. This batch of ova was sent down in charge of the Kulu Hatchery Keeper, who had been sent to Kashmir to learn their methods, and an expert from the Kashmir Hatchery who had been lent by Mr. Mitchell. The ova arrived safe and sound in Naggar, Kulu, and in the same month, namely February, distributed in hatching boxes, as follows, in certain tributaries of of the Beas close to Naggar:—

No. 1. In the Saran Stream, 9,000.
No. 2. In the Hurripur Stream, 6,000.
No. 3. In the Naih Behal Stream, 2,000.
No. 4. In the Chakki Stream, 3,000.
No. 5. In the Hatchery trout pond, 10,000.

The ova thus placed in all the above streams was inspected daily, and all hatched out well, with no more casualties than might be expected, and in due course the fry liberated themselves through holes in the boxes left for the purpose, are now in their respective streams, and are doing well. The ova hatched out in the Naggar trout ponds are also doing well; should all proceed satisfactorily, it is proposed to keep as many trout in the ponds as may be required for breeding purposes, and to distribute those not required for breeding among other streams in the Kulu Valley, which are not yet stocked. This experiment is being carried out by Mr. Howell, Assistant Commissioner, Kulu, and General Osborn, now resident in the valley."

It is most sincerely to be hoped that this scheme will prosper, and there is no reason to anticipate failure. And in time to come, there can be no doubt that the angler in this country may rise up and call himself lucky, for not only will the Mighty Mahseer be his prey, but also the speckled favourite of his boyhood will be with him, running far bigger than at home, and to be caught amidst ideal surroundings.

Tanks.

This section is but meagre, for the Punjab and the North is a land of rivers, and tanks suitable to fish in are but few and far between.

Delhi, Roshanara Tank.—Generally this tank, which stands in gardens of its own, is leased by a party of sportsmen in Delhi each year, who preserve it and have the weeds kept down. In that case permission should be asked to fish it. The year that I visited it however no one had leased the tank, and it was very overgrown with weeds. I saw some enormous rohu rising, and there were 2 or 3 cutlah about.

There are some machans built out, off which one can fish. There is an island in the centre with some big trees on it, latter being generally crowded with waterfowl. This is perhaps the best place to fish from, if there is a boat to take you across. About half the tank is entirely surrounded with high reeds.

Also near the Ajmere Gate, Delhi, is the larger Shahji-ki-Talao, but this often runs nearly dry, and the accounts of it from an angling point of view are not promising.

At Allahabad is the Macpherson Tank, a large sheet of water, which belongs to the Grass Farms, and in which fair bottom fishing is to be had. The Farms I believe rent it out to a syndicate of Allahabad sportsmen, but anyone visiting the station could soon glean all particulars.

Gorakhpur.—I am told of excellent tank fishing to be had here. Most of the tanks in and round the station hold rohu and other fish. The tank near Gurkha Depôt used to fish well, and I knew one man who caught a 23 and a 26 lb. rohu here some few years ago.

Hissar.—On the Rewari-Ferozepore line. There used to be two tanks here, one on each side of the canal. In 1907 however when I visited the place, the one on the right bank was practically dry, and the fishing a thing of the past. The one on the left bank still holds fish, rohu and kalabanse. The best spots to fish are down near the temple and especially under some shady peepul trees under the walls of the temple. There are generally two or three Dhobis at work on the side nearest the road, and these men will always point out the best places, and are free too with all sorts of other advice.

In the Police Lines, Hissar, is also a small tank made years ago by a very well-known angler, Mr. H. S. Dunsford; it was stocked with rohu and kalabanse who were thriving well in 1907. To fish in this tank permission should be asked from the D. S. P., Hissar.

At Hissar is a well found, fully furnished dâk bungalow.

A correspondent kindly told me of the following, but the information is not very recent:—

At Dhana (5 miles from Hansi on the Rohtak road) there used to be a large tank with very big rohu. Hansi is on the railway line. Also there was a tank at foot of dâk bungalow compound, Hansi, but the fish were very canny here.

Karnal.—In the railway tank here I am told of rohu up to 20 lbs. This tank lies but 100 yards from the station. Also there is another tank on Government farm lands, holding rohu of equal size. If fishing in the former tank, the best place is from the side next the line, just in front of a pumping tower. In the Depôt (or farm) tank, the best place is off a small pier, just in front of a tumbled down thatched hut.

Mr. H. S. Dunsford very kindly sends me the following:—

"Notes of a few days' fishing in Kaithal Tank, Karnal District, by two rods, whom we will call A. and B.

10*th August* 1905.—A—one rohu 10¾ lbs.; B—one rohu 11¾ lbs., one white carp 1 lb.

11*th August.*—A—one rohu 8 lbs.; B—two rohu, 4 and 5 lbs.

12*th August.*—A—three rohu, 6¾, 1, 4 lbs. and 4 kalabanse 1½, 2, 2½, and 2 lbs. (B did not fish).

13*th August.*—A—four rohu, 10½, 8, 10¾, 7¾ lbs. and one kalabanse 1¾ lbs.; B—5 rohu, 9¾, 6¼, 7, 10¾, 7½ lbs.

14*th August.*—A—four rohu, 9, 12½, 10½, 9¾ lbs. and one kalabanse 2 lbs.; B—one rohu, 9¾ lbs.

The fishing was for about 2½ hours in the morning and same in the evening. B was only able to fish occasionally. The tank had not been previously ground-baited. The advantages of ground-baiting are shown in the improvement in the takes after the first three days, when the tank was baited after fishing. A was a lady who had only fished once or twice before. With more experience, and consequently fewer fish lost, her bag would have been considerably larger."

Unfortunately this tank has fallen off terribly; for the last two years the Surusti stream that ran into it has failed, and the tank has been nearly dry, so that most of the fish have died. Without two or three years' good rain, I fear the tank will not recover itself.

Kaithal is 39 miles by pukka road from Karnal, and there is a dâk bungalow there.

Since inserting the above, I have been told that this year (1909) some canal water has run into this tank, and now there are a fair number of mulleys therein, running up to 5 lbs., to be caught on live bait.

At Hoshiarpur.—Sixty-eight miles by good road from Amritsar, or 26 miles from Katarpur on Grand Trunk Road, I am told there is a tank, stocked with fish by a native, who is always ready to allow Sahibs to fish.

At Sangrur.—Got at by rail from Ludhiana. A sporting Sergeant informed me that he had had excellent tank fishing for rohu and other fish. The tanks are private, and a permit is required from Jhind Raja. There is a State Guest House here to occupy which permission can be obtained.

At Patiala City.—Here there are one or two tanks holding fish, the one behind the hospital being the best, so I was told.

Marching through Amritsar I tried to find out *re* Batala tanks that are mentioned in Angler's Handbook, but all the information I could get was negative, and amounted to the fact that there were no fish left in the tanks. But possibly this is not true. Two miles out along the Jullundur road, two tanks are passed on the left in which fish were rising as we marched by. These probably are stocked by the overflow of a small canal which runs near by.

At Kamoke also a stage on Grand Trunk Road, I heard rumours of a good tank here, but the khabar came too late to verify it.

Mr. Philip Kitchen most kindly sends me the following excellent khabar, which should be of great use to anyone down in those parts:—

"I am sending you the names of a few tanks, in which during the rains some excellent fishing is to be had. They are all strictly private, and the use of nets is prohibited, but permission for a rod can be readily obtained from the Managers of the different collieries in which the tanks are situated."

Place.	How got at.	On whose authority.	Sport.
(*a*) Rani Band ...	E. I. Railway to Katras Station.	Raja of Katras ...	Rohi, Cutlah, Mirga and Notopterus kapirat.
(*b*) Bunnoo Band ...	E. I. Railway to Katras Station.	Free to rod fishing ...	Rohi, Cutlah and Mirga.
(*c*) Dhurmo Band ...	E. I. Railway to Katras Station.	Do. ...	Rohi and Cutlah.
(*d*) Nai Band ...	E I. Railway to Katras Station.	Do. ...	Rohu, Mirga and Cutlah.

The above four tanks are all close to Katras Railway Station and hold fish up to 25 lbs. in weight. Rani Band is a *very* large tank and holds fish up to 80 lbs. in weight.

Place.	How got at.	On whose authority.	Sport.	REMARKS.
(*a*) Jogta (Two tanks)	E. I. Railway. Tanks close to the Railway Station.	Manager, Jogta Colliery, *Sejua P. O.*	Rohi, Mirga, Wallagu attu.	Fish bite freely.
(*b*) Sejua (Two tanks)	E. I. Railway. Tanks close to the Railway Station.	Manager, Sejua Colliery, *Sejua P. O.*	Rohi Mirgil, Cutla, Wallagu Attu.	Very large fish. Canny.
(*c*) Loyabad (Old quarry.)	E. I. Railway. Tanks close to Bansjora Railway Station.	Manager, Loyabad Colliery, *Bansjora P. O.*	Rohi, Labeo, Mirgil, Wallagu attu.	Very large fish, but hard to catch owing to depth of water.
(*d*) Katras (Two tanks)	E. I. Railway. Tanks about 2 miles from Katras Railway Stations.	Raja of Katras, *Katras P. O.*	Rohi, Mirga, Labeo and Wallagu attu.	Fish are regular monsters and bite freely.
(*e*) Tetulmurrie (One tank.)	E. I. Railway. Tanks close to Tetulmurrie Railway Station.	Manager, Tetulmurrie Colliery, *Sejua P. O.*	Rohi and Mirga ...	Fish rather small.

N. B.—All the above-mentioned tanks lie close to one another, and can be readily approached from any of the Railway Stations already named.

Baroda possesses a large tank, the Ajwa Lake, built in 1892, for the water-supply of the city. It is 18 miles out by road, and must by now hold fair sized fish.

Calcutta.—Concerning the Fishing Club here, this is another instance I fear where the word "Ichabod" must be used. The last Secretary, I believe, made strenuous efforts to keep it going, but lack of funds, the usual cry, was responsible for its demise. There are however many fine tanks in Calcutta, which hold fish, and anyone resident or visiting there, could I fancy soon glean some information on the point.

Dinapore.—There is a nullah here that runs into the Ganges, where good sport may sometimes be had trolling for mulleys, with a spoon. It is also full of rohu and other fish, and late in the season it is netted out. But as during the monsoon it becomes annually restocked, the keen angler at Dinapore can or used to be able to always manage to get some sport therein.

Bareilly.—About 4 miles distant down the Badaun road is a large deep tank filled by the overflow of the Ramgunga river. The railway passes right across the middle on a big bridge, the building of which was responsible for considerable deepening of the original tank. It lies about ¾ mile from the main road, and can be driven up to along a kutcha track. It holds enormous quantities of fish—rohu, mirga, mulley, murral, tengra, cutlah and mohi. In old days there used to be a Fishing Club at Bareilly, the small subscriptions being used both to keep the tank more or less private, and also to buy stout wire netting and stakes. These last were driven in across the entrance and exit to the tank, so that when once thoroughly stocked from the Ramgunga, the fish could not get back again. If this Club is no longer in existence, as is probably the case, it would be well worth resuscitating it, should there be a few keen anglers in Bareilly, as the sport to be had used to be A-1 and it gave one a most pleasant outing on a monsoon afternoon.

I am told of quite good tank fishing near Multan. Some 5 to 10 miles out by road, along the line between Muzaffarabad and Sher Shah stations are two very deep tanks. They are fed by springs, and, owing to their depth and rocky nature of the bottom, are not netted by contractors as are all the other tanks within reach of Multan. The fish probably come into the tanks in times of flood, when the Chenab, some 5 miles distant, overflows its banks. The fish are rohu, with a few tengra The best bag I heard of was 3 rods, 32 fish averaging over 2 lbs., largest fish a rohu of 2½ lbs. The best bait seems to be worms, and for ground-bait my informant told me they used kullee, soaked in water for one might, and then mixed with cow-dung and asafœtida.

Fishing Diary.

Date.	River.	Place.	Actual spot in stream.	Fish.	Weight, lbs.	Bait used.	Remarks.

Fishing Diary.

Date.	River.	Place.	Actual spot in stream.	Fish.	Weight, lbs.	Bait used.	REMARKS.

Fishing Diary.

Date.	River.	Place.	Actual spot in stream.	Fish.	Weight, lbs.	Bait used.	REMARKS.

Fishing Diary.

Date.	River.	Place.	Actual spot in stream.	Fish.	Weight, lbs.	Bait used.	REMARKS.

Fishing Diary.

Date.	River.	Place.	Actual spot in stream.	Fish.	Weight, lbs.	Bait used.	REMARKS.

Fishing Diary.

Date.	River.	Place.	Actual spot in stream.	Fish.	Weight, lbs.	Bait used.	REMARKS.

Fishing Diary.

Date.	River.	Place	Actual spot in stream.	Fish.	Weight, lbs.	Bait used.	REMARKS.

Fishing Diary.

Date.	River.	Place.	Actual spot in stream.	Fish.	Weight, lbs.	Bait used.	REMARKS.

NOTES.

INDEX.

Note.—R. stands for river, S.=stream, N.=nullah, L.=lake, T.=tank.